Ruby Best Practices

Ruby Best Practices

Gregory Brown
foreword by Yukihiro "Matz" Matsumoto

O'REILLY®

Beijing · Cambridge · Farnham · Köln · Sebastopol · Taipei · Tokyo

Ruby Best Practices
by Gregory Brown

Copyright © 2009 Gregory Brown. All rights reserved.
Printed in the United States of America.

Published by O'Reilly Media, Inc., 1005 Gravenstein Highway North, Sebastopol, CA 95472.

O'Reilly books may be purchased for educational, business, or sales promotional use. Online editions are also available for most titles (*http://my.safaribooksonline.com*). For more information, contact our corporate/institutional sales department: 800-998-9938 or *corporate@oreilly.com*.

Editor: Mike Loukides	**Indexer:** Ellen Troutman Zaig
Production Editor: Sarah Schneider	**Cover Designer:** Karen Montgomery
Copyeditor: Nancy Kotary	**Interior Designer:** David Futato
Proofreader: Sada Preisch	**Illustrator:** Robert Romano

Printing History:

June 2009:	First Edition.

ISBN: 978-0-596-52300-8

[M]

1244219908

Table of Contents

Foreword

In 1993, when Ruby was born, Ruby had nothing. No user base except for me and a few close friends. No tradition. No idioms except for a few inherited from Perl, though I regretted most of them afterward.

But the language forms the community. The community nourishes the culture. In the last decade, users increased—hundreds of thousands of programmers fell in love with Ruby. They put great effort into the language and its community. Projects were born. Idioms tailored for Ruby were invented and introduced. Ruby was influenced by Lisp and other functional programming languages. Ruby formed relationships between technologies and methodologies such as test-driven development and duck typing.

This book introduces a map of best practices of the language as of 2009. I've known Greg Brown for years, and he is an experienced Ruby developer who has contributed a lot of projects to the language, such as Ruport and Prawn. I am glad he compiled his knowledge into this book.

His insights will help you become a better Ruby programmer.

—Yukihiro "Matz" Matsumoto
June 2009, Japan

Preface

Some programming languages excel at turning coders into clockwork oranges. By enforcing rigid rules about how software must be structured and implemented, it is possible to prevent a developer from doing anything dangerous. However, this comes at a high cost, stifling the essential creativity and passion that separates the masterful coder from the mediocre. Thankfully, Ruby is about as far from this bleak reality as you can possibly imagine.

As a language, Ruby is designed to allow developers to express themselves freely. It is meant to operate at the programmer's level, shifting the focus away from the machine and toward the problem at hand. However, Ruby is highly malleable, and is nothing more than putty in the hands of the developer. With a rigid mindset that tends to overcomplicate things, you will produce complex Ruby code. With a light and unencumbered outlook, you will produce simple and beautiful programs. In this book, you'll be able to clearly see the difference between the two, and find a clear path laid out for you if you choose to seek the latter.

A dynamic, expressive, and open language does not fit well into strict patterns of proper and improper use. However, this is not to say that experienced Rubyists don't agree on general strategies for attacking problems. In fact, there is a great degree of commonality in the way that professional Ruby developers approach a wide range of challenges. My goal in this book has been to curate a collection of these techniques and practices while preserving their original context. Much of the code discussed in this book is either directly pulled from or inspired by popular open source Ruby projects, which is an ideal way to keep in touch with the practical world while still studying what it means to write better code.

If you were looking for a book of recipes to follow, or code to copy and paste, you've come to the wrong place. This book is much more about how to go about solving problems in Ruby than it is about the exact solution you should use. Whenever someone asks the question "What is the right way to do this in Ruby?", the answer is always "It depends." If you read this book, you'll learn how to go with the flow and come up with good solutions even as everything keeps changing around you. At this point, Ruby stops being scary and starts being beautiful, which is where all the fun begins.

Audience

This book isn't really written with the Ruby beginner in mind, and certainly won't be very useful to someone brand new to programming. Instead, I assume a decent technical grasp of the Ruby language and at least some practical experience in developing software with it. However, you needn't be some guru in order to benefit from this book. The most important thing is that you actually care about improving the way you write Ruby code.

As long as you have at least an intermediate level of experience, reading through the book should be enjoyable. You'll want to have your favorite reference book handy to look things up as needed. Either *The Ruby Programming Language (http://oreilly.com/catalog/9780596516178/)* by David Flanagan and Yukihiro Matsumoto (O'Reilly) or *Programming Ruby*, Third Edition, by Dave Thomas (Pragmatic Bookshelf) should do the trick.

It is also important to note that this is a Ruby 1.9 book. It makes no attempt to provide notes on the differences between Ruby 1.8 and 1.9 except for in a brief appendix designed specifically for that purpose. Although many of the code samples will likely work with little or no modifications for earlier versions of Ruby, Ruby 1.9 is the way forward, and I have chosen to focus on it exclusively in this book. Although the book may still be useful to those maintaining legacy code, it is admittedly geared more toward the forward-looking crowd.

About This Book

This book is designed to be read by chapter, but the chapters are not in any particular order. The book is split into two parts, with eight chapters forming its core and three appendixes included as supplementary material. Despite the fact that you can read these topics in any order that you'd like, it is recommended that you read the entire book. Lots of the topics play off of each other, and reading through them all will give you a solid base in some powerful Ruby techniques and practices.

Each of the core chapters starts off with a case study that is meant to serve as an introduction to the topic it covers. Every case study is based on code from real Ruby projects, and is meant to provide a practical experience in code reading and exploration. The best way to work through these examples is to imagine that you are working through a foreign codebase with a fellow developer, discussing the interesting bits as you come across them. In this way, you'll be able to highlight the exciting parts without getting bogged down on every last detail. You are not expected to understand every line of code in the case studies in this book, but instead should just treat them as useful exercises that prepare you for studying the underlying topics.

Once you've worked your way through the case study, the remainder of each core chapter fills in details on specific subtopics related to the overall theme. These tend to mix real code in with some abstract examples, preferring the former but falling back to the latter when necessary to keep things easy to understand. Some code samples will be easy to run as they are listed; others might only be used for illustration purposes. This should be easy enough to figure out as you go along based on the context. I wholeheartedly recommend running examples when they're relevant and stopping frequently to conduct your own explorations as you read this book. The sections are kept somewhat independent of one another to make it easy for you to take as many breaks as you need, and each wraps up with some basic reminders to refresh your memory of what you just read.

Although the core chapters are the essential part of this book, the appendixes should not be overlooked. You'll notice that they're slightly different in form and content from the main discussion, but maintain the overall feel of the book. You'll get the most out of them if you read them after you've completed the main part of the book, as they tend to assume that you're already familiar with the rest of the content.

That's pretty much all there is to it. The key things to remember are that you aren't going to get much out of this book by skimming for content on a first read, and that you should keep your brain engaged while you work your way through the content. If you read this entire book without writing any code in the process, you'll probably rob yourself of the full experience. So pop open your favorite editor, start with the topic from the chapter listing that interests you most, and get hacking!

Conventions Used in This Book

The following typographical conventions are used in this book:

Italic
> Indicates new terms, URLs, email addresses, filenames, and file extensions.

`Constant width`
> Used for program listings, as well as within paragraphs to refer to program elements such as variable or function names, databases, data types, environment variables, statements, and keywords.

`Constant width bold`
> Shows commands or other text that should be typed literally by the user.

`Constant width italic`
> Shows text that should be replaced with user-supplied values or by values determined by context.

Using Code Examples

This book is here to help you get your job done. In general, you may use the code in this book in your programs and documentation. You do not need to contact us for permission unless you're reproducing a significant portion of the code. For example, writing a program that uses several chunks of code from this book does not require permission. Selling or distributing a CD-ROM of examples from O'Reilly books does require permission. Answering a question by citing this book and quoting example code does not require permission. Incorporating a significant amount of example code from this book into your product's documentation does require permission.

We appreciate, but do not require, attribution. An attribution usually includes the title, author, publisher, and ISBN. For example: "*Ruby Best Practices* by Gregory Brown. Copyright 2009 Gregory Brown, 978-0-596-52300-8."

If you feel your use of code examples falls outside fair use or the permission given here, feel free to contact us at *permissions@oreilly.com*.

Safari® Books Online

Safari When you see a Safari® Books Online icon on the cover of your favorite technology book, that means the book is available online through the O'Reilly Network Safari Bookshelf.

Safari offers a solution that's better than e-books. It's a virtual library that lets you easily search thousands of top tech books, cut and paste code samples, download chapters, and find quick answers when you need the most accurate, current information. Try it for free at *http://my.safaribooksonline.com*.

How to Contact Us

Please address comments and questions concerning this book to the publisher:

O'Reilly Media, Inc.
1005 Gravenstein Highway North
Sebastopol, CA 95472
800-998-9938 (in the United States or Canada)
707-829-0515 (international or local)
707-829-0104 (fax)

O'Reilly has a web page for this book, where we list errata, examples, and any additional information. You can access this page at:

http://oreilly.com/catalog/9780596523008/

Gregory maintains a community-based page for this book at:

http://rubybestpractices.com

To comment or ask technical questions about this book, send email to:

bookquestions@oreilly.com

For more information about our books, conferences, Resource Centers, and the O'Reilly Network, see our website at:

http://www.oreilly.com

Acknowledgments

Over the course of writing *Ruby Best Practices*, I was thoroughly supported by my friends, family, and fellow hackers. I want to thank each and every one of the folks who've helped out with this book, because it would not exist without them.

This book did not have a typical technical review process, but instead was supported by an excellent advisory board whose members participated in group discussion and the occasional review as each chapter was released. These folks not only helped catch technical errors, but helped me sketch out the overall vision for how the book should come together as well. Participants included James Britt, Francis Hwang, Hart Larew, Chris Lee, Jeremy McAnally, and Aaron Patterson.

Rounding out the group was the best pair of guiding mentors I could hope for, Brad Ediger and James Edward Gray II. Both have published Ruby books, and have worked with me extensively on a number of Ruby projects. James and Brad were both instrumental in producing this book, and to my career as a software developer in general. I have learned a ton from each of them, and thanks to their help with *RBP*, I can now pass their knowledge on to you.

Much of the source code in this book comes from the open source Ruby community. Although I talk about my own projects (Prawn and Ruport) a lot, most of the code I show is actually from other contributors or at least originated from good ideas that came up in mailing list discussions, feature requests, and so on. In addition to these two projects, I also have benefited from studying a whole slew of other gems, including but not limited to: activesupport, builder, camping, faker, flexmock, gibberish, haml, highline, lazy, nokogiri, pdf-writer, and rspec. Great thanks go out to all of the developers of these projects, whom I've tried to acknowledge directly wherever I can throughout the text.

Of course, without Yukihiro Matsumoto (Matz), we wouldn't have Ruby in the first place. After writing this book, I am more impressed than ever by the language he has designed. If I'm lucky, this book will help show people just how beautiful Ruby can be.

Producing the technical content for this work was daunting, but only part of the overall picture. My editor, Mike Loukides, and the entire O'Reilly production team have made publishing this book a very comfortable experience. After overcoming major fears about the hurdles of working with a mainstream publisher, I've found the folks at O'Reilly to be helpful, accommodating, and supportive. It is especially nice that this book will become an open community resource less than a year after it prints. This measure is one I hope to see other technical book publishers adopt, and one I'm very thankful that O'Reilly was open to.

Finally, I need to thank the folks who've helped me keep my sanity while working on this huge project. My future wife, Jia Wu, has been amazingly supportive of me, and helped make sure that I occasionally ate and slept while working on this book. On the weekends, we'd usually escape for an bit and spend time with my close friends and family. Though they didn't have anything to do with the project itself, without Pete, Paul, Mom, Dad, and Vinny, I doubt you'd be reading this book right now. Thanks to all of you, even if you'll never need to read this book.

So many people helped out in countless different ways, that I'm sure I've missed someone important while compiling this list. To make sure these folks get their well-deserved credit, please keep an eye on the acknowledgments page at *http://rubybestpractices .com* and let me know if there is someone who needs to be added to the list. But for now, if I've failed to list you here, thank you and please know that I've not forgotten what you've done to help me.

## CHAPTER 1

Driving Code Through Tests

If you've done some Ruby—even a little bit—you have probably heard of *test-driven development* (TDD). Many advocates present this software practice as the "secret key" to programming success. However, it's still a lot of work to convince people that writing tests that are often longer than their implementation code can actually lower the total time spent on a project and increase overall efficiency.

In my work, I've found most of the claims about the benefits of TDD to be true. My code is better because I write tests that document the expected behaviors of my software while verifying that my code is meeting its requirements. By writing automated tests, I can be sure that once I narrow down the source of a bug and fix it, it'll never resurface without me knowing right away. Because my tests are automated, I can hand my code off to others and mechanically assert my expectations, which does more for me than a handwritten specification ever could do.

However, the important thing to take home from this is that automated testing is really no different than what we did before we discovered it. If you've ever tried to narrow down a bug with a print statement based on a conditional, you've already written a primitive form of automated testing:

```
if foo != "blah"
  puts "I expected 'blah' but foo contains #{foo}"
end
```

If you've ever written an example to verify that a bug exists in an earlier version of code, but not in a later one, you've written something not at all far from the sorts of things you'll write through TDD. The only difference is that one-off examples do not adequately account for the problems that can arise during integration with other modules. This problem can become huge, and is one that unit testing frameworks handle quite well.

Even if you already know a bit about testing and have been using it in your work, you might still feel like it doesn't come naturally. You write tests because you see the long-term benefits, but you usually write your code first. It takes you a while to write your tests, because it seems like the code you wrote is difficult to pin down behavior-wise.

In the end, testing becomes a necessary evil. You appreciate the safety net, but except for when you fall, you'd rather just focus on keeping your balance and moving forward.

Masterful Rubyists will tell you otherwise, and for good reason. Testing may be hard, but it truly does make your job of writing software easier. This chapter will show you how to integrate automated testing into your workflow, without forcing you to relearn the troubleshooting skills you've already acquired. By making use of the best practices discussed here, you'll be able to more easily see the merits of TDD in your own work.

A Quick Note on Testing Frameworks

Ruby provides a unit testing framework in its standard library called *minitest/unit*. This library provides a user-level compatibility layer with the popular *test/unit* library, which has been fairly standard in the Ruby community for some time now. There are significant differences between the *minitest/unit* and *test/unit* implementations, but as we won't be building low-level extensions in this chapter, you can assume that the code here will work in both *minitest/unit* and *test/unit* without modification.

For what it's worth, I don't have a very strong preference when it comes to testing frameworks. I am using the `Test::Unit` API here because it is part of standard Ruby, and because it is fundamentally easy to hack on and extend. Many of the existing alternative testing frameworks are built on top of `Test::Unit`, and you will almost certainly need to have a working knowledge of it as a Ruby developer. However, if you've been working with a noncompatible framework such as RSpec (*http://rspec.info*), there's nothing wrong with that. The ideas here should be mostly portable to your framework of choice.

And now we can move on. Before digging into the nuts and bolts of writing tests, we'll examine what it means for code to be easily testable, by looking at some real examples.

Designing for Testability

Describing testing with the phrase "Red, Green, Refactor" makes it seem fairly straightforward. Most people interpret this as the process of writing some failing tests, getting those tests to pass, and then cleaning up the code without causing the tests to fail again. This general assumption is exactly correct, but a common misconception is how much work needs to be done between each phase of this cycle.

For example, if we try to solve our whole problem all in one big chunk, add tests to verify that it works, then clean up our code, we end up with implementations that are very difficult to test, and even more challenging to refactor. The following example illustrates just how bad this problem can get if you're not careful. It's from some payroll management code I wrote in a hurry a couple of years ago:

```ruby
def time_data_for_week(week_data,start,employee_id)

  data = Hash.new { |h,k| h[k] = Hash.new }

  %w[M T W TH F S].zip((0..6).to_a).each do |day,offset|

    date = (start + offset.days).beginning_of_day

    data[day][:lunch_hours] = LunchTime.find(:all, conditions:
      ["employee_id = ? and day between ? and ?",
        employee_id, date, date + 1.day - 1.second] ).inject(0) { |s,r|
          s + r.duration
        }

    times = [[:sick_hours    , "Sick"    ],
             [:personal_hours, "Personal"],
             [:vacation_hours, "Vacation"],
             [:other_hours,    "Other"   ]]
    times.each do |a,b|
      data[day][a] = OtherTime.find(:all, conditions:
        ["employee_id = ? and category = '#{b}' and date between ? and ?",
          employee_id, date, date + 1.day - 1.second] ).inject(0) { |s,r|
            s + r.hours
          }
    end

    d = week_data.find { |d,_| d == date }
    next unless d

    d = d[-1]
    data[day].merge!(
      regular_hours: d.inject(0) { |s,e|
        s + (e.end_time ? (e.end_time - e.start_time) / 3600 : 0)
      } - data[day][:lunch_hours],
      start_time: d.map { |e| e.start_time }.sort[0],
        end_time: d.map { |e| e.end_time }.compact.sort[-1]
    )
  end

  sums = Hash.new(0)

  data.each do |k,v|
    [:regular_hours, :lunch_hours, :sick_hours,
     :personal_hours, :vacation_hours, :other_hours].each { |h|
       sums[h] += v[h].to_f }
  end

  Table(:day,:start_time,:end_time,:regular_hours,:lunch_hours,
        :sick_hours,:personal_hours,:vacation_hours, :other_hours) do |t|
    %w[M T W TH F S].each { |d| t << {day: d}.merge(data[d]) }
    t << []
    t << { day: "<b>Totals</b>" }.merge(sums)
  end
end
```

When you looked at the preceding example, did you have an easy time understanding it? If you didn't, you don't need to worry, because I can hardly remember what this code does, and I'm the one who wrote it. Though it is certainly possible to produce better code than this without employing TDD, it's actually quite difficult to produce something this ugly if you are writing your tests first. This is especially true if you manage to keep your iterations nice and tight. The very nature of test-driven development lends itself to breaking your code up into smaller, simpler chunks that are easy to work with. It's safe to say that we don't see any of those attributes here.

Now that we've seen an example of what not to do, we can investigate the true benefits of TDD in the setting of a real project. What follows is the process that I went through while developing a simple feature for the Prawn PDF generation library. But first, a small diversion is necessary.

A Test::Unit Trick to Know About

Usually, test cases written with *minitest/unit* or *test/unit* look like this:

```
class MyThingieTest < Test::Unit::TestCase
  def test_must_be_empty
    #...
  end

  def test_must_be_awesome
    #...
  end
end
```

But in all the examples you'll see in this chapter, we'll be writing our tests like this:

```
class MyThingieTest < Test::Unit::TestCase
  must "be empty" do
    #...
  end

  must "be awesome" do
    #...
  end
end
```

If you've used `Test::Unit` before, you might be a bit confused by the use of the `must()` method here. This is actually a custom addition largely based on the `test()` method in the *activesupport* gem. All this code does is automatically generate test methods for you, improving the clarity of our examples a bit. You don't really need to worry about how this works, but for the curious, the implementation can be found at *http://github.com/sandal/rbp/tree/master/testing/test_unit_extensions.rb*.

We also discuss this in Chapter 3, *Mastering the Dynamic Toolkit*, as an example of how to make custom extensions to preexisting objects. So although you only need to understand how `must()` is used here, you'll get a chance to see how it is built later on.

The code we're about to look at was originally part of Prawn's early support for inline styling, which allows users to make use of bold and italic typefaces within a single string of text. In practice, these strings look very similar to the most basic HTML markup:

```
"This is a string with <b>bold, <i>bold italic</i></b> and <i>italic</i> text"
```

Although the details of how Prawn actually converts these strings into stylized text that can be properly rendered within a PDF document are somewhat gory, the process of breaking up the string and parsing out the style tags is quite straightforward. We'll focus on this aspect of things, stepping through the design and development process until we end up with a simple function that behaves as follows:

```
>> StyleParser.process("Some <b>bold</b> and <i>italic</i> text")
=> ["Some ", "<b>", "bold", "</b>", " and ", "<i>", "italic", "</i>", " text"]
```

This example demonstrates the final product, but the initial pass at things wasn't so polished. I started by considering the possibility of passing all the strings rendered in Prawn through style processing, so the initial case I thought of was actually to allow the method to return the string itself when it did not detect any style data. My early example looked something like this:

```
class TestInlineStyleParsing < Test::Unit::TestCase
  must "simply return the string if styles are not found" do
    @pdf = Prawn::Document.new
    assert_equal "Hello World", @pdf.parse_inline_styles("Hello World")
  end
end
```

My initial functionality looked something like this:

```
class Prawn::Document
  def parse_inline_styles(text)
    text
  end
end
```

This caused my example to run without failure, and is quite possibly the most boring code imaginable. However, working in small steps like this helps keep things simple and also allows you to sanity-check that things are working as expected. Seeing that this was the case, I was able to move forward with another set of examples. The modified test case ended up looking like this:

```
class TestInlineStyleParsing < Test::Unit::TestCase
  must "simply return the string if styles are not found" do
    @pdf = Prawn::Document.new
    assert_equal "Hello World", @pdf.parse_inline_styles("Hello World")
  end

  must "parse italic tags" do
    @pdf = Prawn::Document.new
    assert_equal ["Hello ", "<i>", "Fine", "</i>", " World"],
                 @pdf.parse_inline_styles("Hello <i>Fine</i> World")
  end
```

```
    must "parse bold tags" do
      @pdf = Prawn::Document.new
      assert_equal ["Some very ", "<b>", "bold text", "</b>"],
        @pdf.parse_inline_styles("Some very <b>bold text</b>")
    end

  end
```

Despite the fact that I'm writing a book titled *Ruby Best Practices*, I freely admit that I write some dumb code sometimes. For evidence, we can look at the first bit of code that made this example work:

```
def parse_inline_styles(text)
  require "strscan"

  sc = StringScanner.new(text)
  output = []
  last_pos = 0

  loop do
    if sc.scan_until(/<\/?[ib]>/)
      pre = sc.pre_match[last_pos..-1]
      output << pre unless pre.empty?
      output << sc.matched
      last_pos = sc.pos
    else
      output << sc.rest if sc.rest?
      break output
    end
  end

  output.length == 1 ? output.first : output
end
```

That's way longer than it needs to be. Luckily, a useful aspect of using automated behavior verification is that it is helpful during refactoring. I had planned to send this code out to the *ruby-talk* mailing list so that I could learn the elegant solution that I knew must exist but couldn't quite muster in my first pass. Before I could do that though, I needed to add another example to clarify the intended behavior:

```
    must "parse mixed italic and bold tags" do
      @pdf = Prawn::Document.new
      assert_equal ["Hello ", "<i>", "Fine ", "<b>", "World", "</b>", "</i>"],
        @pdf.parse_inline_styles("Hello <i>Fine <b>World</b></i>")
    end
```

Some folks might make the claim that a good test suite makes it easier to communicate with customers, but I've never been too sure about that. What I do know is that tests are downright awesome for describing a problem to your fellow developers. Within minutes of posting my examples to *ruby-talk*, I had a much better implementation in hand:[*]

---

[*] Thanks to Robert Dober, *ruby-talk* post #309593.

```
def parse_inline_styles(text)
  segments = text.split( %r{(</?.*?>)} ).reject {|x| x.empty? }
  segments.size == 1 ? segments.first : segments
end
```

Running the examples showed that this code accomplished what my earlier code did, as there were no failures. However, your code is only as correct as the examples you choose, and as it turns out, this code gave me more than I bargained for. It parsed out anything within angle braces, meaning it'd pull out the tags in the following string:

```
"Hello <indigo>Charlie</indigo>"
```

Though this might be useful in some situations, I really wanted to parse out only the two specific tags I planned to handle, so I added an example to cover this:

```
must "not split out other tags than <i>, <b>, </i>, </b>" do
  @pdf = Prawn::Document.new
  assert_equal ["Hello <indigo>Ch", "</b>", "arl", "</b>", "ie</indigo>"],
    @pdf.parse_inline_styles("Hello <indigo>Ch</b>arl</b>ie</indigo>")
end
```

This new example resulted in a failure, as expected. The required change was simple, and caused everything to pass again:

```
def parse_inline_styles(text)
  segments = text.split( %r{(</?[ib]>)} ).delete_if{|x| x.empty? }
  segments.size == 1 ? segments.first : segments
end
```

I originally planned to pass through this function every string that Prawn attempted to render, and this influenced the way the initial interface was specified. However, later I realized that it would be better to check to see whether a string had any style tags in it before attempting to parse it. Because the process of rendering the text is handled in two very different ways depending on whether there are inline styles present, I needed to handle only the case when there were tags to be extracted in my parser:

```
def parse_inline_styles(text)
  text.split( %r{(</?[ib]>)} ).delete_if{|x| x.empty? }
end
```

This cleanup caused one of my examples to fail, because it broke the old default behavior:

```
1) Failure:
test_simply_return_the_string_if_styles_are_not_found(TestInlineStyleParsing) [...]:
<"Hello World"> expected but was
<["Hello World"]>.
```

As this example was no longer relevant, I simply removed it and was back under the green light. But I still needed a related feature, which was the ability to test whether a string needed to be parsed. I considered making this a private method on `Prawn::Document`, but it led to some ugly code:

```
must "be able to check whether a string needs to be parsed" do
  @pdf = Prawn::Document.new
  assert ! @pdf.send(:style_tag?, "Hello World")
  assert @pdf.send(:style_tag?, "Hello <i>Fine</i> World")
end
```

Most of the time when I need to use send() to call a private method in one of my tests, I try to rethink my interface. Sometimes it's a necessary evil, but most of the time it just means that things are looking to be refactored. When I first added Document#parse_inline_styles, it didn't concern me much to add a single utility method for this purpose. However, once I found out that I needed an additional helper method, I began to rethink the problem. I realized things would look better if I wrapped the code up in a module.

I updated my examples to reflect this change, and cleaned them up a bit by adding a setup method, which gets run before each individual test:

```
class TestInlineStyleParsing < Test::Unit::TestCase

  def setup
    @parser = Prawn::Document::Text::StyleParser
  end

  must "parse italic tags" do
    assert_equal ["Hello ", "<i>", "Fine", "</i>", " World"],
      @parser.process("Hello <i>Fine</i> World")
  end

  must "parse bold tags" do
    assert_equal ["Some very ", "<b>", "bold text", "</b>"],
      @parser.process("Some very <b>bold text</b>")
  end

  must "parse mixed italic and bold tags" do
    assert_equal ["Hello ", "<i>", "Fine ", "<b>", "World", "</b>", "</i>"],
      @parser.process("Hello <i>Fine <b>World</b></i>")
  end

  must "not split out other tags than <i>, <b>, </i>, </b>" do
    assert_equal ["Hello <indigo>Ch", "</b>", "arl", "</b>", "ie</indigo>"],
      @parser.process("Hello <indigo>Ch</b>arl</b>ie</indigo>")
  end

  must "be able to check whether a string needs to be parsed" do
    assert @parser.style_tag?("Hello <i>Fine</i> World")
    assert !@parser.style_tag?("Hello World")
  end

end
```

Because these features didn't really rely on anything within Prawn::Document, it made me happy to give them a home of their own, ready to be expanded later as needed. I

created the module and dropped in the trivial check that made up the `style_tag?`
feature:

```ruby
module StyleParser
  extend self

  def process(text)
    text.split( %r{(</?[ib]>)} ).delete_if{|x| x.empty? }
  end

  def style_tag?(text)
    !!(text =~ %r{(</?[ib]>)})
  end
end
```

With the tests passing, I snuck in one more bit of cleanup under the green light, just to
make things a little more DRY:[†]

```ruby
module StyleParser
  extend self

  TAG_PATTERN = %r{(</?[ib]>)}

  def process(text)
    text.split(TAG_PATTERN).delete_if{|x| x.empty? }
  end

  def style_tag?(text)
    !!(text =~ TAG_PATTERN)
  end
end
```

With these two simple features in hand, I was then ready to work on implementing the
inline styling support in Prawn, which I can assure you was far less pleasant to hack
together.[‡] Even though this example was quite simple, it captures the entire process of
evolving a feature by using progressively tweaked examples from start to finish. Although the end result is an automated safety net that verifies that my methods behave
as I've specified them, you can see that the process of problem discovery, refactoring,
and iterative design are the true fruits of test-driven development. This is what justifies
spending time writing tests that are often longer than your implementation. The resulting examples are mostly a helpful side effect; the power of this technique is in what
insight you gain through writing them in the first place.

Now that we've seen the process in action, we'll take a step back and go over some
testing fundamentals. Although this stuff may be familiar to folks who are already ac-
customed to TDD, it doesn't hurt to brush up on the essentials, as they form a foundation for the more advanced stuff that we'll tackle a little later.

[†] Don't Repeat Yourself.

[‡] In fact, it wasn't until several months later that an acceptable inline styling tool saw the light of day, thanks
to the efforts of Jamis Buck.

Testing Fundamentals

A few good habits go a long way when it comes to TDD. We'll now take a look at some key techniques that help make writing solid and maintainable tests much easier.

Well-Focused Examples

A common beginner habit in testing is to create a single example that covers all of the edge cases for a given method. An example of this might be something along these lines:

```ruby
class VolumeTest < Test::Unit::TestCase
  must "compute volume based on length, width, and height" do
    # defaults to l=w=h=1
    assert_equal 1, volume

    #when given 1 arg, set l=x, set w,h = 1
    x = 6
    assert_equal x, volume(x)

    # when given 2 args, set l=x, w=y and h=1
    y = 2
    assert_equal x*y, volume(x,y)

    # when given 3 args, set l=x, w=y and h=z
    z = 7
    assert_equal x*y*z, volume(x,y,z)

    # when given a hash, use :length, :width, :height
    assert_equal x*y*z, volume(length: x, width: y, height: z)
  end
end
```

Though it is relatively easy to type things out this way, there are some limitations that are worth noting. One of the most obvious issues with this approach is that it isn't very organized. Compare the previous example to the next, and you'll see how much easier it is to read things when they are cleanly separated out:

```ruby
class VolumeTest < Test::Unit::TestCase

  must "return 1 by default if no arguments are given" do
    # defaults to l=w=h=1
    assert_equal 1, volume
  end

  must "set l=x, set w,h = 1 when given 1 numeric argument" do
    x = 6
    assert_equal x, volume(x)
  end

  must "set l=x, w=y, and h=1 when given 2 arguments" do
    x, y = 6, 2
    assert_equal x*y, volume(x,y)
  end
```

```
must "set l=x, w=y, and h=z when given 3 arguments" do
  x,y,z = 6, 2, 7
  assert_equal x*y*z, volume(x,y,z)
end

must "use :length, :width, and :height when given a hash argument" do
  x,y,z = 6, 2, 7
  assert_equal x*y*z, volume(length: x, width: y, height: z)
end

end
```

However, the improved clarity is actually one of the lesser reasons why this code is better. In the former example, your failure report will include only the first assertion that was violated; the code that follows it will not even be executed. When you get the report back, you'll get a message that shows you the numeric expected/actual values, but it will be titled something like, "a volume function should compute volume based on length width and height," which is not very instructive for determining which case caused the problem.

In the latter approach, every single example will run, testing all of the cases simultaneously. This means that if a change you make to your code affects three out of the four cases, your tests will report back three out of four cases rather than just the first failed assertion in the example. They'll have more useful names, too, each uniquely pointing back to the individual must() call that failed.

Although the code shown here is unlikely to have side effects, there is an additional benefit to splitting up examples: each one runs in its own clean-slate environment. This means you can use setup and teardown methods to manage pre- and postprocessing, but the code will run largely independent of your other examples. The benefit here is that you'll avoid the problem of accidentally depending on some side effect or state that is left hanging around as a result of another method call. Because of this, your tests will be more isolated and less likely to run into false positives or strange errors.

Testing Exceptions

Code is not merely specified by the way it acts under favorable conditions. Although it'd be great if we could assume conservative input and liberal output constraints, this just doesn't seem to be practical in most cases. This means that our code will often need to raise appropriate exceptions when it isn't able to handle the request it has been given, or if it detects misuse that deserves further attention. Luckily, Test::Unit makes it easy for us to specify both when code should raise a certain error, and when we expect it to run without error. We'll take a look at a trivial little lockbox object that provides rudimentary access control to get a feel for how this looks. See if you can understand the tests just by reading through them:

```ruby
class LockBoxTest < Test::Unit::TestCase

  def setup
    @lock_box = LockBox.new( password: "secret",
                             content: "My Secret Message" )
  end

  must "raise an error when an invalid password is used" do
    assert_raises(LockBox::InvalidPassword) do
      @lock_box.unlock("kitten")
    end
  end

  must "Not raise error when a valid password is used" do
    assert_nothing_raised do
      @lock_box.unlock("secret")
    end
  end

  must "prevent access to content by default" do
    assert_raises(LockBox::UnauthorizedAccess) do
      @lock_box.content
    end
  end

  must "allow access to content when box is properly unlocked" do
    assert_nothing_raised do
      @lock_box.unlock("secret")
      @lock_box.content
    end
  end

end
```

As you can see, these tests read pretty clearly. Testing your exceptions is as easy as using the assert_raises() and assert_nothing_raised() methods with the relevant error class names. We can take a quick look at the implementation of LockBox to see what the code that satisfies these tests looks like:

```ruby
class LockBox

  UnauthorizedAccess = Class.new(StandardError)
  InvalidPassword    = Class.new(StandardError)

  def initialize(options)
    @locked   = true
    @password = options[:password]
    @content  = options[:content]
  end

  def unlock(pass)
    @password == pass ? @locked = false : raise(InvalidPassword)
  end
```

```
      def content
        @locked ? raise(UnauthorizedAccess) : @content
      end
    end
```

Nothing too fancy is going on here—just a few conditional arguments and a pair of custom exceptions.§ But if we failed to test the cases that generated the exceptions, we wouldn't have full test coverage. Generally speaking, any time your methods might intentionally raise an error, you'll want to set up test cases that cover both the condition where this error is raised as well as the case where it is not. This will help make sure that your error can actually be raised, while ensuring that it isn't raised unconditionally. Testing this way will help you catch trivial mistakes up front, which is always a good thing.

Run the Whole Suite at Once

Though the examples we have worked with so far might fit well in a single file, you'll eventually want to split up your tests across several files. However, that doesn't mean that you should run them only in isolation!

A key feature of automated testing is that it gives you a comprehensive sense of how your software is running as a system, not just on a component-by-component basis. To keep aware of any problems that might occur during refactoring or wiring in new features, it is beneficial to run your entire suite of examples on every change. Luckily, using Ruby's standard project automation tool, this is trivial. Here is a sample `Rakefile` that uses some of the most common conventions:

```
require "rake/testtask"

task :default => [:test]

Rake::TestTask.new do |test|
  test.libs << "test"
  test.test_files = Dir[ "test/test_*.rb" ]
  test.verbose = true
end
```

This code makes it so `rake test` will run every Ruby file in the *test/* folder of your project that starts with *test_* and ends with the *.rb* extension. A typical directory layout that works with this sort of command looks like this:

```
test/
  test_foo.rb
  test_bar.rb
```

§ The syntax used for creating errors here is just a shortcut for `class MyCustomError < StandardError; end.`

You can tweak which files get run by changing the glob pattern passed to `Dir`. These work pretty much the same as they do on the command line, so you can just put one together that suits your file layout.

Now, if you've got some expensive resources you're writing tests against, such as file I/O, database interaction, or some network operation, you may be a bit nervous about the idea of running all your tests on every change you make. This may be due to performance concerns or due to the fact that you simply can't afford to do frequent *live* tests of your external resources. However, in most cases, this problem can be worked around, and actually leads to better tests.

The solution I'm alluding to is *mock objects*, and how they can be used to avoid dependencies on external resources. We'll go over several advanced concepts in the following section, but mocks are as good a place to start as any, so we'll work with them first. Before we do that though, let's review some of the key guidelines that outline testing fundamentals:

- Keep your test cases atomic. If you are testing a function with multiple interfaces, write multiple examples. Also, write an example for each edge case you want to test.
- Don't just check function input and output, also use `assert_raises()` and `assert_nothing_raised()` to test that exceptions are being thrown under the right conditions, and not unexpectedly.
- Use a rake task to automate running your test suite, and run all of your examples on every change to ensure that integration issues are caught as soon as they are introduced. Running tests individually may save time by catching problems early, but before moving from feature to feature, it is crucial to run the whole suite.

Advanced Testing Techniques

The most basic testing techniques will get you far, but when things get complicated, you need to break out the big guns. What follows are a few tricks to try out when you run into a roadblock.

Using Mocks and Stubs

In a perfect world, all the resources that we needed would be self-contained in our application, and all interactions would take place in constant time. In our real work, life is nothing like this. We've got to deal with user input, database interaction, web service calls, file I/O, and countless other moving parts that live outside of our application. Testing these things can be painful.

Sure, we could set up a development database that gets blown out and reloaded every time our tests run—that's what Rails does. We could read and write from temporary files, clearing out our leftovers after each example runs. For things like web services, we could build a fake service that acts the way we expect our live service to act and run it on a staging server. The question here is not whether it is possible to do this, but whether it is necessary.

Sometimes, you really do need to deal with real-world data. This is especially true when you want to tune and optimize performance or test resource-dependent interactions. However, in most cases, our code is mainly interested only in the behavior of the things we interact with, not what they really are. This is where either a mock or a stub could come in handy.

There are additional benefits to removing dependencies on external code and resources as well. By removing these extra layers, you are capable of isolating your examples so that they test only the code in question. This purposefully eliminates a lot of interdependencies within your tests and helps make sure that you find and fix problems in the right places, instead of everywhere their influence is felt.

Let's start with a trivial example, to help you get your head around the concepts of mocks and stubs, and form a working definition of what they are.

What follows is some basic code that asks a user a yes or no question, waits for input, and then returns `true` or `false` based on the answer. A basic implementation might look like this:

```ruby
class Questioner

  def ask(question)
    puts question
    response = gets.chomp
    case(response)
    when /^y(es)?$/i
      true
    when /^no?$/i
      false
    else
      puts "I don't understand."
      ask question
    end
  end

end
```

Go ahead and toy around with this a bit by executing something similar to this little chunk of code, to get a sense for how it works:

```ruby
q = Questioner.new
puts q.ask("Are you happy?") ? "Good I'm Glad" : "That's Too Bad"
```

Interacting with this code by just running a simple script in the console is enough to show that it pretty much works as expected. However, how do we test it? Is it enough to break down the code so that it's a bit more testable, allowing us to write tests for everything but the actual user interaction?

```
class Questioner

  def ask(question)
    puts question
    response = yes_or_no(gets.chomp)
    response.nil? ? ask(question) : response
  end

  def yes_or_no(response)
    case(response)
    when /^y(es)?$/i
      true
    when /^no?$/i
      false
    end
  end

end
```

Now most of the work is being done in **yes_or_no**, which is easily testable:

```
class QuestionerTest < Test::Unit::TestCase

  def setup
    @questioner = Questioner.new
  end

  %w[y Y  YeS YES yes].each do |yes|
    must "return true when yes_or_no parses #{yes}" do
      assert @questioner.yes_or_no(yes), "#{yes.inspect} expected to parse as true"
    end
  end

  %w[n N no nO].each do |no|
    must "return false when yes_or_no parses #{no}" do
      assert ! @questioner.yes_or_no(no), "#{no.inspect} expected to parse as false"
    end
  end

  %w[Note Yesterday xyzaty].each do |mu|
    must "return nil because #{mu} is not a variant of 'yes' or 'no'" do
      assert_nil @questioner.yes_or_no(mu), "#{mu.inspect} expected to parse as nil"
    end
  end

end
```

These examples will all pass, and most of your code will be tested, except for the trivial
ask() method. However, what if we wanted to build code that relies on the results of
the **ask()** method?

```
class Questioner

  def inquire_about_happiness
    ask("Are you happy?") ? "Good I'm Glad" : "That's Too Bad"
  end
```

```
    def ask(question)
      puts question
      response = yes_or_no(gets.chomp)
      response.nil? ? ask(question) : response
    end

    def yes_or_no(response)
      case(response)
      when /^y(es)?$/i
        true
      when /^no?$/i
        false
      end
    end
  end
```

If we want to write tests that depend on the return value of `ask()`, we'll need to do something to prevent the need for direct user input. A relatively simple way to test `inquire_about_happiness()` is to replace the `ask()` method with a stub that returns our expected values for each scenario:

```
class HappinessTest < Test::Unit::TestCase
  def setup
    @questioner = Questioner.new
  end

  must "respond 'Good I'm Glad' when inquire_about_happiness gets 'yes'" do
    def @questioner.ask(question); true; end
    assert_equal "Good I'm Glad", @questioner.inquire_about_happiness
  end

  must "respond 'That's Too Bad' when inquire_about_happiness gets 'no'" do
    def @questioner.ask(question); false; end
    assert_equal "That's Too Bad", @questioner.inquire_about_happiness
  end
end
```

If we wanted to be a bit more formal about things, we could use a third-party tool to make our stubbing more explicit and easier to work with. There are lots of options for this, but one I especially like is the *flexmock* gem by Jim Weirich. We'll look at this tool in much greater detail when we discuss formal mocking, but for now, let's just look at how it can be used to clean up our stubbing example:

```
require "flexmock/test_unit"

class HappinessTest < Test::Unit::TestCase
  def setup
    @questioner = Questioner.new
  end

  must "respond 'Good I'm Glad' when inquire_about_happiness gets 'yes'" do
    stubbed = flexmock(@questioner, :ask => true)
    assert_equal "Good I'm Glad", stubbed.inquire_about_happiness
  end
```

```
  must "respond 'That's Too Bad' when inquire_about_happiness gets 'no'" do
    stubbed = flexmock(@questioner, :ask => false)
    assert_equal "That's Too Bad", stubbed.inquire_about_happiness
  end
end
```

The example code accomplishes the same task as our manual stubbing, but does so in an arguably more pleasant and organized way. Though it might be overkill to pull in a third-party package just to stub out a method or two, you can see how this interface would be preferable if you needed to write tests that were a little more complicated, or at least more involved.

No matter how we implement them, stubs do allow us to improve our test coverage a bit more here. Still, let's pause for a moment and ask ourselves a question: did we really finish our job? Looking at the code, we find that our naive implementation sans tests looks like this:

```
class Questioner

  def inquire_about_happiness
    ask("Are you happy?") ? "Good I'm Glad" : "That's Too Bad"
  end

  def ask(question)
    puts question
    response = gets.chomp
    case(response)
    when /^y(es)?$/i
      true
    when /^no?$/i
      false
    else
      puts "I don't understand."
      ask question
    end
  end

end
```

Our test-driven results turn out like this:

```
class Questioner

  def inquire_about_happiness
    ask("Are you happy?") ? "Good I'm Glad" : "That's Too Bad"
  end

  def ask(question)
    puts question
    response = yes_or_no(gets.chomp)
    response.nil? ? ask(question) : response
  end
```

```
def yes_or_no(response)
  case(response)
  when /^y(es)?$/i
    true
  when /^no?$/i
    false
  end
end

end
```

Though we've successfully split out our yes_or_no parser for testing, we still don't have any automated checks for how our code will display a question to the user and how it will respond based on that code. Presently, the only safety net we have for our I/O code is our limited testing in our terminals, which can hardly be called robust. Although it is of course better to have some coverage than no coverage at all, we can do better here.

Ruby ships with a StringIO class, which essentially is an IO object that is implemented to work against a string rather than the typical file handles. Although I hesitate to call this a mock object, it comes close in practice. We'll take a quick look at how you might use it to test I/O code, which is a nice stepping stone that can lead us into real mock territory.

But before we can test with StringIO, we need to make it so that our Questioner class allows us to swap out the input and output sources for our own custom objects:

```
class Questioner

  def initialize(in=STDIN,out=STDOUT)
    @input  = in
    @output = out
  end

  def ask(question)
    @output.puts question
    response = @input.gets.chomp
    case(response)
    when /^y(es)?$/i
      true
    when /^no?$/i
      false
    else
      @output.puts "I don't understand."
      ask question
    end
  end

end
```

By default, nothing will change and I/O will still go to STDIN and STDOUT. However, this opens the door for replacing these I/O objects with a pair of StringIO objects, allowing us to totally rethink our tests:

```ruby
class QuestionerTest < Test::Unit::TestCase

  def setup
    @input   = StringIO.new
    @output  = StringIO.new
    @questioner = Questioner.new(@input,@output)
    @question   = "Are you happy?"
  end

  ["y", "Y", "YeS", "YES", "yes"].each do |y|
    must "return false when parsing #{y}" do
      provide_input(y)
      assert @questioner.ask(@question), "Expected '#{y}' to be true"
      expect_output "#{@question}\n"
    end
  end

  ["n", "N", "no", "nO"].each do |no|
    must "return false when parsing #{no}" do
      provide_input(no)
      assert !@questioner.ask(@question)
      expect_output "#{@question}\n"
    end
  end

  [["y", true],["n", false]].each do |input,state|
    must "continue to ask for input until given #{input}" do
      provide_input "Note\nYesterday\nxyzaty\n#{input}"
      assert_equal state, @questioner.ask(@question)
      expect_output "#{@question}\nI don't understand.\n"*3 + "#{@question}\n"
    end
  end

  def provide_input(string)
    @input << string
    @input.rewind
  end

  def expect_output(string)
    assert_equal string, @output.string
  end

end
```

Without too much more effort, we were able to specify and test the full behavior of this trivial little program. We are able to test both the logic, and the actual I/O operations, to verify that they work as we expect them to. In this particular case, we were pretty lucky that Ruby ships with a library that acts like an I/O object and makes our testing easier. We won't always be so lucky. What's more, we don't really need most of what StringIO has to offer here. A lighter (albeit more abstract) approach would be to use a formal mocking framework to do the job. Let's take a look at how this problem might be solved in flexmock, to make things a bit clearer:

```
require "flexmock/test_unit"

class QuestionerTest < Test::Unit::TestCase

  def setup
    @input   = flexmock("input")
    @output  = flexmock("output")
    @questioner = Questioner.new(@input,@output)
    @question   = "Are you happy?"
  end

  ["y", "Y", "YeS", "YES", "yes"].each do |y|
    must "return false when parsing #{y}" do
      expect_output @question
      provide_input(y)
      assert @questioner.ask(@question), "Expected '#{y}' to be true"
    end
  end

  ["n", "N", "no", "nO"].each do |no|
    must "return false when parsing #{no}" do
      expect_output @question
      provide_input(no)
      assert !@questioner.ask(@question)
    end
  end

  [["y", true], ["n", false]].each do |input, state|
    must "continue to ask for input until given #{input}" do
      %w[Yesterday North kittens].each do |i|
        expect_output @question
        provide_input(i)
        expect_output("I don't understand.")
      end

      expect_output @question
      provide_input(input)

      assert_equal state, @questioner.ask(@question)
    end
  end

  def provide_input(string)
    @input.should_receive(:gets => string).once
  end

  def expect_output(string)
    @output.should_receive(:puts).with(string).once
  end

end
```

The interesting thing about this example is that `flexmock()` returns a completely generic object, yet this accomplishes the same results as using `StringIO`, which is finely tuned for emulating a real `IO` object. The end result is that the latter example tends to focus on the interactions between your code and the resource, and that the former example is more directly bound to what an I/O object actually is. It can be beneficial to avoid such tight distinctions, especially when working in Ruby, where what an object actually is tends to be less important than what it can do.

To generalize: mock objects essentially break interactions down into the messages that an object should receive, the arguments that accompany the messages, the return values of the methods, whether a block is yielded, and whether any errors should be raised. If this sounds like a lot, don't worry too much. The beauty of a mock object is that you need to specify only those things that are necessary to handle in your code.

Flexmock (like many of the other Ruby mocking options) is quite robust, and to go over it extensively here would take more than just a single section of a chapter. However, through this simple example, you can see that there are ways to avoid actively hitting your external resources while still being able to test your interactions with them.

Of course, using a mock object comes with its own cost, like anything else. In this example, if we changed the internal code to use `print()` instead of `puts()`, we would need to modify our mock object, but we would not need to modify our `StringIO`-based solution. Although a mock object completely eliminates the need to worry about the internal state of your dependencies, it creates a tighter coupling to their interfaces. This means that some care should be taken when deciding just how much you want to mock out in any given test suite.

Learning how to build decent mock objects without going overboard takes some practice, but is not too hard once you get the hang of it. It ultimately forms one of the *hard* aspects of testing, and once that bridge is crossed, only a few more remain.

Testing Complex Output

Dealing with programs that need to generate complex output can be a pain. Verifying that things actually work as you expect them to is important, but simply comparing raw output values in an automated test leads to examples that are nearly impossible to follow. However, we often resort to just dumping our expected data into our tests and comparing it to what we're actually generating. This sort of test is useful for detecting when a problem arises, but finding the source of it, even with decent diff utilities, can be a real pain.

Imagine we've got a basic blog that needs to output RSS, which is really just a specialized XML format. The following example is a simplified version of what I use to generate the feeds in my blog. James Gray actually wrote the code for it, using XML Builder, another great gem from Jim Weirich:

```
require "builder"
require "ostruct"

class Blog < OpenStruct
```

```ruby
def entries
  @entries ||= []
end

def to_rss
  xml = Builder::XmlMarkup.new
  xml.instruct!
  xml.rss version: "2.0" do
    xml.channel do
      xml.title       title
      xml.link        "http://#{domain}/"
      xml.description description
      xml.language    "en-us"

      @entries.each do |entry|
        xml.item do
          xml.title       entry.title
          xml.description entry.description
          xml.author      author
          xml.pubDate     entry.published_date
          xml.link        entry.url
          xml.guid        entry.url
        end
      end
    end
  end
end

end
```

We need to test that the output of this **to_rss** method is what we expect it to be. The lazy approach would look like this:

```ruby
require "time"

class BlogTest < Test::Unit::TestCase

FEED = <<-EOS
<?xml version="1.0" encoding="UTF-8"?><rss version="2.0"
><channel><title>Awesome</title><link>http://majesticseacreature.com/</link>
<description>Totally awesome</description><language>en-us</language><item>
<title>First Post</title><description>Nothing interesting</description>
<author>Gregory Brown</author><pubDate>2008-08-08 00:00:00 -0400</pubDate>
<link>http://majesticseacreature.com/awesome.html</link>
<guid>http://majesticseacreature.com/awesome.html</guid></item></channel></rss>
EOS

  def setup
    @blog = Blog.new
    @blog.title       = "Awesome"
    @blog.domain      = "majesticseacreature.com"
    @blog.description = "Totally awesome"
    @blog.author      = "Gregory Brown"
```

```
      entry = OpenStruct.new
      entry.title            = "First Post"
      entry.description      = "Nothing interesting"
      entry.published_date   = Time.parse("08/08/2008")
      entry.url              = "http://majesticseacreature.com/awesome.html"

      @blog.entries << entry
    end


    must "have a totally awesome RSS feed" do
      assert_equal FEED.delete("\n"), @blog.to_rss
    end

  end
```

You could make this slightly less ugly by storing your output in a file, but it's not much better:

```
  class BlogTest < Test::Unit::TestCase

    def setup
      @blog = Blog.new
      @blog.title       = "Awesome"
      @blog.domain      = "majesticseacreature.com"
      @blog.description = "Totally awesome"
      @blog.author      = "Gregory Brown"

      entry = OpenStruct.new
      entry.title            = "First Post"
      entry.description      = "Nothing interesting"
      entry.published_date   = Time.parse("08/08/2008")
      entry.url              = "http://majesticseacreature.com/awesome.html"

      @blog.entries << entry
    end

    must "have a totally awesome RSS feed" do
      assert_equal File.read("expected.rss"), @blog.to_rss
    end

  end
```

In the end, the issue boils down to the fact that you're definitely not focusing on the important parts of the problem if you have to check the output character by character. An RSS feed with some extra whitespace in it would be no less valid than the file shown here, yet it would cause an annoying failure in your tests.

Unless it really isn't worth your time, the best way to deal with complex output is to parse it into a workable dataset before doing your comparisons. There are a few RSS feed parsers out there that would make quick work of a file like this. However, in the interest of generality, we could use a generic XML parser without much more effort.

There are a few solid choices for XML parsing in Ruby, and even support for it in the standard library. However, the library that I find most pleasant to work with is the *nokogiri* gem, written by Aaron Patterson. Here's what part of the tests look like after they've been reworked to use Nokogiri:

```ruby
require "time"
require "nokogiri"

class BlogTest < Test::Unit::TestCase

  def setup
    @blog = Blog.new
    @blog.title       = "Awesome"
    @blog.domain      = "majesticseacreature.com"
    @blog.description = "Totally awesome"
    @blog.author      = "Gregory Brown"

    entry = OpenStruct.new
    entry.title          = "First Post"
    entry.description    = "Nothing interesting"
    entry.published_date = Time.parse("08/08/2008")
    entry.url            = "http://majesticseacreature.com/awesome.html"

    @blog.entries << entry
    @feed = Nokogiri::XML(@blog.to_rss)
  end

  must "be RSS v 2.0" do
    assert_equal "2.0", @feed.at("rss")["version"]
  end

  must "have a title of Awesome" do
    assert_equal "Awesome", text_at("rss", "title")
  end

  must "have a description of Totally Awesome" do
    assert_equal "Totally awesome", text_at("rss", "description")
  end

  must "have an author of Gregory Brown" do
    assert_equal "Gregory Brown", text_at("rss", "author")
  end

  must "have an entry with the title: First Post" do
    assert_equal "First Post", text_at("item", "title")
  end

  def text_at(*args)
    args.inject(@feed) { |s,r| s.send(:at, r) }.inner_text
  end

end
```

This is a huge improvement! Now, our tests actually look like they're verifying the things we're interested in, rather than simply checking our output against some amorphous code blob that we can't easily inspect and verify.

Of course, this approach to testing complex data requires you to trust whatever you are using to parse your output, but as long as you can do that, the ability of whatever library you use to parse your output is from the very start an indication that you are producing meaningful results.

Not every file format you will encounter will have parsers available for it, of course. Some of the formats you need to produce may even be fully custom-made. However, providing that it isn't impossible to build one, a parser will come in handy for making your tests more flexible and expressive. Consider this possibility before turning to direct file comparison as a last resort only.

We're about to wrap up with a mixed bag of tips and tricks for keeping your test suite maintainable, but before we do that, let's go over some of the highlights of the advanced testing techniques discussed in this section:

- Mocks and stubs can be used to remove external dependencies from tests while still verifying proper behavior and interaction.
- Stubs are used when we want to replace some functionality with canned results to make testing other code easier.
- Mocks are used to create objects that can act in place of an external resource for the purpose of testing. Mock objects are set up with expected responses, which are then verified when the tests are run. This means that if you have something like `my_obj.should_receive(:foo).once` and `foo` is never called on `my_obj`, this will result in a test failure. This is the primary difference between mocks and stubs.
- When testing complex output, it is best to find a tool that parses the output format you are generating, and write your tests against its results.
- When you can't find a tool for parsing your output format, you might consider building one that parses only the values you are interested in, in addition to necessary basic validation of the document's structure.
- If it isn't possible to parse your generated data without great effort, consider storing your expected output in its own file and loading it into your tests as needed, using a diff utility to compare expected and actual output.
- For most XML formats, Nokogiri does a great job of parsing the document and making it easily searchable.

Keeping Things Organized

Just like other code, test suites tend to grow in both size and complexity throughout the lifecycle of a project. The following techniques help keep things tidy and well factored, allowing your tests to continue to serve as a road map to your project.

Embedding Tests in Library Files

If you are working on a very small program or library, and you want to be able to run your tests while in development, but then require the code as part of another program later, there is a simple idiom that is useful for embedding your tests:

```
class Foo
  ...
end

if __FILE__ == $PROGRAM_NAME
  require "test/unit"

  class TestFoo < Test::Unit::TestCase
    #...
  end
end
```

Simply wrapping your tests in this `if` statement will allow running `ruby foo.rb` to execute your tests, while `require "foo"` will still work as expected without running the tests. This can be useful for sharing small programs with others, or for writing some tests while developing a small prototype of a larger application. However, once you start to produce more than a few test cases, be sure to break things back out into their normal directory structure. Giant files can be a bit unwieldy to deal with, and it is a bit awkward (even though it is possible) to treat your *lib/* directory as if it were also your test suite.

Test Helpers

When you begin to chain together a large amount of test cases, you might find that you are repeating some information across them. Some of the most common things in this regard are `require` statements and basic helper functions.

A good solution to keep things clean is to create a *test/test_helpers.rb* file and then do all of your global configuration there. In your individual tests, you can require this file by expanding the direct path to it, using the following idiom:

```
require File.dirname(__FILE__) + '/test_helpers'
```

This allows your test files to be run individually from any directory, not just the top-level directory. Here is a sample *test_helpers.rb* from the Prawn project to give you a sense of what kinds of things might go into the file:

```
require "rubygems"
require "test/unit"

$LOAD_PATH << File.join(File.dirname(__FILE__), '..', 'lib')
require "prawn"
gem 'pdf-reader', ">=0.7.3"
require "pdf/reader"
```

```
def create_pdf
  @pdf = Prawn::Document.new(  left_margin: 0,  right_margin: 0,
                             top_margin: 0, bottom_margin: 0 )
end

def observer(klass)
  @output = @pdf.render
  obs = klass.new
  PDF::Reader.string(@output,obs)
  obs
end

def parse_pdf_object(obj)
  PDF::Reader::Parser.new(
      PDF::Reader::Buffer.new(StringIO.new(obj)), nil).parse_token
end

puts "Prawn tests: Running on Ruby Version: #{RUBY_VERSION}"
```

Here you can see that load path adjustments, project-specific dependencies, and some basic helper functions are being loaded. The helper functions are obviously Prawn-specific, but as you can see, they provide wrappers around common operations that need to be done in a number of our tests, which result in something like this in practice:

```
class PolygonTest < Test::Unit::TestCase

  must "draw each line passed to polygon()" do
    @pdf = Prawn::Document.new
    @pdf.polygon([100,500],[100,400],[200,400])

    line_drawing = observer(LineDrawingObserver)
    assert_equal [[100,500],[100,400],[200,400],[100,500]],
                   line_drawing.points
  end

end
```

It's completely up to you how far you wish to take this sort of thing. As a rule of thumb, if you find yourself using a feature in more than a few places, consider adding it to *test_helpers.rb*. If you want a little more of a clean approach, you can wrap your helpers in a module, but depending on what you're doing, just defining them at the top level might be fine as well.

Your helper file essentially allows you to centralize the support features for your test suite. When used effectively, this approach can greatly simplify your tests and reduce duplicated code that can lead to problems.

Custom Assertions

In addition to building helper functions to support your examples, you can actually build custom assertions to augment the vocabulary of your tests.

Porting an example from RSpec's documentation, it is easy to see how simple it is to add a custom assertion to your tests. We want to transform a basic statement that looks like this:

```
assert bob.current_zone.eql?(Zone.new("4"))
```

into something a bit more friendly, such as:

```
assert_in_zone("4", bob)
```

To do this in `Test::Unit`, we'll make use of the low-level function `assert_block()`. Here's how you would define `assert_in_zone` and its complement, `assert_not_in_zone`:

```
def assert_in_zone(expected, person)
  assert_block("Expected #{person.inspect} to be in Zone #{expected}") do
    person.current_zone.eql?(Zone.new(expected))
  end
end

def assert_not_in_zone(expected_zone, person)
  assert_block("Expected #{person.inspect} not to be in Zone #{expected}") do
    !person.current_zone.eql?(Zone.new(expected))
  end
end
```

With these definitions in place, you can use the assertions as we specified earlier. When the statement is true, the assertion will pass; when it is false, the assertion will fail and display the custom message. All of the assertions in `Test::Unit` can be built upon `assert_block`, which indicates how powerful it can be for creating your own higher-level assertions.

We're winding to a close with the discussion of testing practices, but here's the recap of things you can do to keep your testing code neat and well formed:

- If you're working with a tiny program, don't bother with the formal directory structure—just use the simple idiom that allows your script to be both loaded as a library and run as an executable.

- If your application is bigger, eliminate duplication by centralizing your boilerplate and support code in a *test/test_helpers.rb* file that is required by all of your tests.

- If your code seems to be doing a lot of complicated stuff and `Test::Unit`'s built-in assertions aren't doing the trick, build your own via the simple `assert_block` function.

Conclusions

Testing is a big topic—one that can easily span across several books. Each respective testing framework available in Ruby can be an equally huge topic, and one that is worth studying in its own right. Nevertheless, the goal of this chapter was to teach the principles behind test-driven development, rather than the exact technical applications you might encounter. It is important to remember that testing is meant to make your code better and more maintainable, not to lead you into confusion or make you feel like you're stuck doing busywork instead of doing real coding.

Also remember that if your solution seems difficult to test, it may be a sign that your design is not flexible enough to easily be refactored or interacted with. By writing the tests before the code, and cleaning up after every small feature spike, it becomes easier and easier to avoid the common pitfalls of overly complex code.

Of course, there are cases in which things really just are difficult to test. You'll know when you run into these things, as they often include dependence on a complex or difficult-to-pin-down external resource, or have some other special thing about them that just makes testing *hard*. In these cases, don't let testing dogma get in your way: it doesn't make sense to freeze in place simply because you can't think of a good testing strategy. But by the same token, don't let these things steal your focus away from the parts of your application that you actually can test. Try to remember that partial coverage is usually much better than no coverage at all.

The good thing is that for the most part, Ruby is a language that truly makes testing enjoyable, as long as you learn how to do it properly. The topics covered in this chapter will hopefully put you well on your way, but the best way to get into the swing of things is simply to get out there and start writing some tests. The rest will come together naturally.

## CHAPTER 2

Designing Beautiful APIs

As developers, we experience the difference between good and bad programmatic interfaces every single day. Some modules we work with seem to speak right to us, clearly expressing their role in our project in a loud, confident voice. Others mumble nonsense and occasionally freak out on us in ways we'd never expect. In many ways, our code is only as good as its application programming interface (API). Good APIs provide exactly what we need, in the way we need it. Bad APIs confuse us and make us jump through hoops to get things working, pushing us one step closer to the dreaded "Big Rewrite." Ruby provides the tools to build beautifully clear interfaces, but these same tools can produce chaos and disarray when placed in misguided hands.

In this chapter, we'll take a look at the infrastructure Ruby provides to help you design solid interfaces. We'll examine both the technical details and the motivation behind the various different approaches, allowing you to see both the how and why that's involved in designing "Rubyish" APIs. We'll begin by looking through a practical example of API design from a real project, and then move on to more specific tips and tricks. Along the way, you'll gain both conceptual and technical understanding of how to design suitable APIs for your Ruby projects.

Designing for Convenience: Ruport's Table( ) feature

In Ruby Reports (Ruport), virtually all of our users will need to work with tabular data at some point. This data can come from any number of sources, ranging from a simple CSV file to a complex data analysis procedure that produces tables as its output. Providing a simple, clear API that works well for all of these cases is a bit of a challenge. Although the ultimate goal of each of the different tasks that we can imagine is fundamentally the same, the means for accomplishing them are quite different.

Our first instinct was to reflect this in the API, resulting in several different constructors for the different ways of building tables:

```
table1 = Ruport::Data::Table.new(
   :column_names => %w[first_name last_name],
   :data         => [["Gregory","Brown"],["Deborah","Orlando"]] )
```

```
table2 = Ruport::Data::Table.load("people.csv")

csv = "first_name,last_name\nGregory,Brown\nDeborah\nOrlando\n"
table3 = Ruport::Data::Table.parse(csv)
```

Although it is clear enough what is going on here, it is necessary to remember the names and signatures of several different methods. We were convinced we could do better, and eventually came up with this:

```
table1 = Table(%w[first_name last_name],
    :data => [["Gregory","Brown"],["Deborah","Orlando"]])

table2 = Table("people.csv")

csv = "first_name,last_name\nGregory,Brown\nDeborah,Orlando\n"
table3 = Table(:string => csv)
```

Though the difference here is somewhat subtle, there is definitely something more natural about the way this code reads. Rather than feeling like we're initializing a class, it feels more as if we're converting our data into a `Table` object. This is similar to the way a number of Ruby's built-in methods work, including `Integer()`, `Array()`, and friends.

Introducing the `Table()` method was a big win, as it simplified things for the most common cases in Ruport. However, rather than trashing the old interface, we instead opted to wrap it. This approach gives curmudgeons who dislike magic an alternative avenue while providing some additional benefits. The most obvious one is that the `Table()` method itself is fairly simple code:

```
def Table(*args,&block)
  table = case args[0]
  when Array
    opts = args[1] || {}
    Ruport::Data::Table.new({:column_names => args[0]}.merge(opts),&block)
  when /\.csv$/i
    Ruport::Data::Table.load(*args,&block)
  when Hash
    if file = args[0].delete(:file)
      Ruport::Data::Table.load(file,args[0],&block)
    elsif string = args[0].delete(:string)
      Ruport::Data::Table.parse(string,args[0],&block)
    else
      Ruport::Data::Table.new(args[0],&block)
    end
  else
      Ruport::Data::Table.new(:data => [], :column_names => args,&block)
  end

  return table
end
```

Though it may be a little bit busy with so much going on, the entire purpose of this method is simply to recognize the kind of table loading you are doing, then delegate to the appropriate constructor method. We do this by treating the arguments passed to the method as an array. We also capture any block passed to the method so that we can pass it down into the constructors, but we'll get back to that later. For now, let's simply focus on the array of arguments passed in.

We can walk through the examples already shown to get a sense of what's going on. In our first example, we called the method with an array of column names, and a hash of options:

```
table1 = Table(%w[first_name last_name],
   :data => [["Gregory","Brown"],["Deborah","Orlando"]])
```

In this case, `args` contains two elements: an array of column names and a hash of options. The structure looks like this:

```
[ %w[first_name last_name],
   { :data => [["Gregory","Brown"],["Deborah","Orlando"]] } ]
```

Our case statement matches `args[0]` as an `Array`, and pulls the `Hash` out from `args[1]`. After processing, our final call is equivalent to this:

```
Ruport::Data::Table.new(
   :column_names => %w[first_name last_name],
   :data         => [["Gregory","Brown"],["Deborah","Orlando"]] )
```

As you can see, this is exactly equivalent to the very first call shown in this chapter. If we left out the data parameter in our `Hash`, we'd see the following translation:

```
headings = %w[first_name last_name]
Ruport::Data::Table.new(:column_names => headings) == Table(headings) #=> true
```

Working with our second example is even easier. We're passing a CSV filename like so:

```
table2 = Table("people.csv")
```

In this situation, `args` is a single element array with `args[0]` as `"people.csv"`. Our case statement immediately matches this and then uses the array splat operator (*) to pass the arguments directly to `Ruport::Data::Table.load()`. In this case, our `Table()` method is just being lazy, ultimately just acting identically to `Ruport::Data::Table.load()` as long as your file ends in *.csv*.

What if your file has a nonstandard extension or no extension at all? Both you and `Table()` need to do a bit more work. The most simple form would look like this:

```
Table(:file => "people.txt")
```

In this case, `args` is a single element array containing a `Hash`. However, we know this is not ambiguous, because our third example was also of this form:

```
csv = "first_name,last_name\nGregory,Brown\nDeborah,Orlando\n"
table3 = Table(:string => csv)
```

Also, although it has not been shown yet, `Table()` also provides a compatible interface with `Ruport::Data::Table.new()`. This means that the following code is also valid:

```
table4 = Table( :column_names => %w[first_name last_name],
                :data         => [["Gregory","Brown"],["Deborah","Orlando"]] )
```

These three different cases are distinguished fairly easily, as you can see here:

```
if file = args[0].delete(:file)
  Ruport::Data::Table.load(file,args[0],&block)
elsif string = args[0].delete(:string)
  Ruport::Data::Table.parse(string,args[0],&block)
else
  Ruport::Data::Table.new(args[0],&block)
end
```

This code attempts to be polite by removing the `:file` or `:string` option from the `options` hash before delegating to the relevant constructor. This is a good practice when forwarding options hashes downstream, so as to avoid providing the underlying methods with options that it may not handle properly.

Putting this all together, we find that it is possible to be extremely flexible with Ruby interfaces. In fact, the following examples show even more advanced behavior that is possible with `Table()`:

```
# removes records that don't have a first name of Gregory
table = Table("foo.csv") do |t,r|
  t.filter { |r| r.first_name == "Gregory" }
  t << r
end

# doubles the first column's values
table = Table("a","b","c") do |t|
  t.transform { |r| r["a"] *= 2 }
  t << [1,2,3]
  t << [4,5,6]
end
```

Both examples build up a table within a block, but there is a key difference between the two. The first example is an iterator, walking over the rows of a CSV file as they are read in and parsed. The second example starts with an empty table and no data source to feed from, and allows users to build up a table from whatever sources they wish. The power here is that we can allow our blocks to act differently based on the expected number of arguments. This is only the tip of the iceberg when it comes to the kinds of things you can do with blocks, and in just a little bit, we'll look at some fresh examples to really get a sense of one of Ruby's most powerful API building tools.

For now, let's take a step back and look at some kinds of argument processing that Ruby can do. The methods that Ruport's `Table()` method delegates to are a little too domain-specific to show this stuff off usefully, so instead we'll use a few more basic examples to demonstrate the various different kinds of interfaces you can provide for methods in Ruby.

Ruby's Secret Power: Flexible Argument Processing

When you think of a method, how do you envision its parameters? Depending on whom you ask, you might get a lot of different answers. Some folks might think of something vaguely mathematical, such as $f(x,y,z)$, where each argument is necessary, and the order in which they are provided is significant. Others might think of methods as manipulating configuration data, where keyword-like parameters seem natural, e.g., `create_person( first_name: "Joe", last_name: "Frasier")`. You might also contemplate mixing the two together, or dreaming up something else entirely.

Ruby provides a great deal of flexibility in how it handles method arguments, which might lead to some confusion. However, this is also a key part of building beautiful APIs in Ruby. The following examples give just a small taste of the kind of diversity you can expect in Ruby:

```ruby
# Standard ordinal arguments
def distance(x1,y1,x2,y2)
  Math.hypot(x2 - x1, y2 - y1)
end

# Ordinal arguments, with an optional argument
def load_file(name,mode="rb")
  File.open(name,mode)
end

# Pseudo-keyword arguments
def story(options)
  "#{options[:person]} went to town, riding on a #{options[:animal]}"
end

# Treating arguments as an Array
def distance2(*points)
  distance(*points.flatten)
end
```

Invoking these methods shows how they look in action:

```ruby
>> distance(3,3,4,5)
=> 2.23606797749979

>> load_file "foo.jpg"
=> #<File:foo.jpg>
>> load_file "foo.jpg", "r"
=> #<File:foo.jpg>
>> load_file "foo.jpg", "kitten"
ArgumentError: illegal access mode kitten ...

>> story(animal: "Tiger", person: "Yankee Doodle")
=> "Yankee Doodle went to town, riding on a Tiger"
>> story(person: "Yankee Doodle", animal: "Tiger")
=> "Yankee Doodle went to town, riding on a Tiger"
```

```
>> distance2 [3,3], [4,5]
=> 2.23606797749979
```

Each approach shown here has its merits, and how to choose the right one depends mainly on what your method needs to do. Let's look at each of these trivial methods one by one to get a sense of their pros and cons.

Standard Ordinal Arguments

```
def distance(x1,y1,x2,y2)
  Math.hypot(x2 - x1, y2 - y1)
end

>> distance(3,3,4,5)
=> 2.23606797749979
```

Ordinal argument processing is the most simple, but also the most restrictive way to pass arguments into your methods in Ruby. In this case, it may be all we need. All four arguments are necessary to do the calculation, and there is a logical way to order them. In situations like these, the no-frills approach is frequently good enough.

Ordinal Arguments with Optional Parameters

```
def load_file(name,mode="rb")
  File.open(name,mode)
end

>> load_file "foo.jpg"
=> #<File:foo.jpg>
>> load_file "foo.jpg", "r"
=> #<File:foo.jpg>
>> load_file "foo.jpg", "kitten"
ArgumentError: illegal access mode kitten ...
```

The ability to set default values makes ordinal arguments a bit more pleasant to work with in some cases. The example code provides a trivial wrapper on `File.open()` that causes it to default to reading a binary file. For this default use, the method appears to accept a single argument, keeping the call clean and straightforward. However, a second argument can be provided if needed, due to this more flexible way of defining the interface.

However, what happens when we have more than one optional argument, such as in the following example code?

```
def load_file2(name="foo.jpg",mode="rb")
  File.open(name,mode)
end
```

For the obvious cases, this works as we might expect:

```
>> load_file2
=> #<File:foo.jpg>
```

```
>> load_file2 "bar.jpg"
=> #<File:bar.jpg>

>> load_file2 "bar.jpg", "r"
=> #<File:bar.jpg>

>> load_file2 "bar.jpg", "kitten"
ArgumentError: invalid access mode kitten ...
```

However, the trouble arises when we want to use the default value for the first argument and override the second one. Sadly enough, we simply cannot do it using this approach. We'd need to supply both values, like this:

```
>> load_file2 "foo.jpg", "r"
=> #<File:foo.jpg>
```

For this reason, it's relatively rare to find a good use for multiple optional parameters in the ordinal format. When you do find yourself needing this sort of thing, there are most likely better options available, anyway.

Pseudo-Keyword Arguments

```
def story(options)
  "#{options[:person]} went to town, riding on a #{options[:animal]}"
end

>> story(animal: "Tiger", person: "Yankee Doodle")
=> "Yankee Doodle went to town, riding on a Tiger"
>> story(person: "Yankee Doodle", animal: "Tiger")
=> "Yankee Doodle went to town, riding on a Tiger"
```

Although Ruby doesn't have support for real keyword arguments, it does a pretty good job of imitating them. If we peek behind the curtain though, we find that we're really dealing with something much more basic:

```
>> argument_hash = { :animal => "Tiger", :person => "Yankee Doodle" }
>> story(argument_hash)
=> "Yankee Doodle went to town, riding on a Tiger"
```

Seen in this form, all the magic disappears. The method is really only processing a single argument in the form of a basic Hash of key/value pairs.

Utilizing some syntactic sugar, we can rearrange things a bit:

```
>> argument_hash = { animal: "Tiger", person: "Yankee Doodle" }
>> story(argument_hash)
=> "Yankee Doodle went to town, riding on a Tiger"
```

If our hash happens to be the last (or the only) argument to the method, we can leave off the brackets when passing a Hash literal. This gets us full circle back to the original:

```
>> story(animal: "Tiger", person: "Yankee Doodle")
=> "Yankee Doodle went to town, riding on a Tiger"
```

With a basic understanding of the underlying mechanics, you can begin to see the benefits of this style of API. Perhaps the most significant is that the order in which you specify the arguments doesn't matter at all, as you've seen in the example code. If we combine that feature with a basic idiom for setting default values passed in the hash, we come up with something pretty interesting:

```ruby
def story2(options={})
  options = { person: "Yankee Doodle", animal: "Tiger" }.merge(options)
  "#{options[:person]} went to town, riding on a #{options[:animal]}"
end
```

```ruby
>> story2
=> "Yankee Doodle went to town, riding on a Tiger"
>> story2(person: "Joe Frasier")
=> "Joe Frasier went to town, riding on a Tiger"
>> story2(animal: "Kitteh")
=> "Yankee Doodle went to town, riding on a Kitteh"
>> story2(animal: "Kitteh", person: "Joe Frasier")
=> "Joe Frasier went to town, riding on a Kitteh"
```

As you can see here, it is possible to handle multiple default values fairly elegantly. This avoids the problems we encountered when attempting to do something similar via simple default values for ordinal arguments. Though this example is a bit contrived, it's worth mentioning that if one or more of your arguments are really mandatory, it's worth it to break them out, like so:

```ruby
def write_story_to_file(file,options={})
  File.open(file,"w") { |f| f << story2(options) }
end
```

which enables fun stuff like:

```ruby
>> write_story_to_file "output.txt"
>> write_story_to_file "output.txt", animal: "Kitteh"
>> write_story_to_file "output.txt", person: "Joe Frasier"
>> write_story_to_file "output.txt", animal: "Slug", person: "Joe Frasier"
```

Though you could write code to ensure that certain options are present in a hash, generally it is most natural to just let Ruby do the hard work for you by placing your mandatory arguments before your options hash in your method definition.

Treating Arguments As an Array

```ruby
def distance2(*points)
  distance(*points.flatten)
end
```

```ruby
>> distance2 [3,3], [4,5]
=> 2.23606797749979
```

A powerful feature involves treating the passed arguments as an array. In the case of a distance method, we might want to provide the arguments in one of several different ways, depending on our situation. The previous example shows the primary use of this approach, which is to allow the data to be passed as two points. However, if you play around, you'll find that a lot of other possibilities exist, some more sane than others. Here are a few to give you a sense of what's going on here:

```
>> distance2 [3],[3],[4],[5]
=> 2.23606797749979
>> distance2 3,3,4,5
=> 2.23606797749979
>> distance2 [3,3,4],5
=> 2.23606797749979
```

It should be clear at this point that Ruby is treating the arguments as one big array, flattening it down to eliminate any nesting, and then passing the four values as arguments to the original `distance()` method. With this in mind, the following issues shouldn't be too surprising:

```
>> distance2 [3,3,4]
ArgumentError: wrong number of arguments (3 for 4) ...

>> distance2 [3,3,4],5,6
ArgumentError: wrong number of arguments (5 for 4) ...
```

Still, our error messages are a bit obscure, and the fact that we're wrapping another method might make things seem a bit tricky. Considering this issue, we can try to make something a little more solid using the same general approach:

```
def distance3(*points)
  case(points.length)
  when 2
    x1,y1,x2,y2 = points.flatten
  when 4
    x1,y1,x2,y2 = points
  else
     raise ArgumentError,
        "Points may be specified as [x1,y1], [x2,y2] or x1,y1,x2,y2"
  end
  Math.hypot(x2 - x1, y2 - y1)
end
```

In this case, our method behaves much more strictly:

```
>> distance3 [3,3,4]
ArgumentError: Points may be specified as [x1,y1], [x2,y2] or x1,y1,x2,y2 ...

>> distance3 3,3,3,4,5
ArgumentError: Points may be specified as [x1,y1], [x2,y2] or x1,y1,x2,y2 ...

>> distance3 [3,3,3,4]
ArgumentError: Points may be specified as [x1,y1], [x2,y2] or x1,y1,x2,y2 ...

>> distance3 [3,3],[3,4]
=> 1.0

>> distance3 3,3,3,4
=> 1.0
```

Though this may be a more robust way to write the method, it is more complicated. Playing fast and loose might not be a bad thing if you can expect your users to provide sane input. The following version is the compromise I might use in production code:

```
def distance4(*points)
  x1,y1,x2,y2 = points.flatten
  raise ArgumentError unless [x1,y1,x2,y2].all? { |e| Numeric === e }
  Math.hypot(x2 - x1, y2 - y1)
end
```

This code checks the first four arguments after flattening any nesting to make sure that they are Numeric values, and then assigns them to the variables x1, y1, x2, and y2. Though it does not cover all edge cases, it does some sanity checks and makes sure that you've provided all the necessary data in a form that is usable by the method. In many cases, this will be good enough.

Although we've covered only some of the most basic argument forms here, these techniques form the basis for building solid Ruby APIs. The following short list of guidelines will help you in designing your methods:

- Try to keep the number of ordinal arguments in your methods to a minimum.
- If your method has multiple parameters with default values, consider using pseudo-keyword arguments via an options hash.
- Use the array splat operator (*) when you want to slurp up your arguments and pass them to another method.
- The *args idiom is also useful for supporting multiple simultaneous argument processing styles, as in Table(), but can lead to complicated code.
- Don't use *args when a normal combination of mandatory ordinal arguments and an options hash will do.
- If some parameters are mandatory, avoid putting them in an options hash, and instead write a signature like foo(mandatory1, mandatory2, options={}), unless there is a good reason not to.

Although having a decent understanding of how argument processing works in Ruby will take you far, there are many situations that need a little more firepower. Ruby's ability to utilize code blocks in association with method calls is often the answer. We'll now dive into the various ways that working with blocks can simplify your interface as well as the internals of your methods.

Ruby's Other Secret Power: Code Blocks

In Ruby, code blocks are everywhere. If you've ever used Enumerable, you've worked with blocks. But what are they? Are they simply iterators, working to abstract away our need for the for loop? They certainly do a good job of that:

```
>> ["Blocks","are","really","neat"].map { |e| e.upcase }
=> ["BLOCKS", "ARE", "REALLY", "NEAT"]
```

But other blocks don't really iterate over things—they just do helpful things for us. For example, they allow us to write something like:

```
File.open("foo.txt","w") { |f| f << "This is sexy" }
```

instead of forcing us to write this:

```
file = File.open("foo.txt","w")
file << "This is tedious"
file.close
```

So blocks are useful for iteration, and also useful for injecting some code between preprocessing and postprocessing operations in methods. But is that all they're good for? Sticking with Ruby built-ins, we find that isn't the case. Blocks can also shift our scope temporarily, giving us easier access to places we want to be:

```
"This is a string".instance_eval do
  "O hai, can has reverse? #{reverse}. kthxbye"
end

#=> "O hai, can has reverse? gnirts a si sihT. kthxbye"
```

But blocks aren't necessarily limited to code that gets run right away and then disappears. They can also form templates for what to do down the line, springing to action when ready:

```
>> foo = Hash.new { |h,k| h[k] = [] }
=> {}
>> foo[:bar]
=> []
>> foo[:bar] << 1 << 2 << 3
=> [1, 2, 3]
>> foo[:baz]
=> []
```

So even if we label all methods that accept a block as iterators, we know the story runs deeper than that. With this in mind, we can leverage some basic techniques to utilize any of the approaches shown here, as well as some more advanced tricks. By doing things in a way that is consistent with Ruby itself, we can make life easier for our users. Rather than piling on new concepts, we can allow them to reuse their previous knowledge. Let's take a look at a few examples of how to do that now.

Working with Enumerable

The most common use of blocks in Ruby might be the most trivial. The following class implements a basic sorted list, and then mixes in the Enumerable module. The block magic happens in each():

```
class SortedList

  include Enumerable
```

```
def initialize
  @data = []
end

def <<(element)
  (@data << element).sort!
end

def each
  @data.each { |e| yield(e) }
end

end
```

Our each() method simply walks over each element in our @data array and passes it through the block provided to the method by calling yield. The resulting iterator works exactly the same as Array#each and Hash#each and all the Ruby built-ins, and indeed simply wraps Array#each in this case:

```
>> a = SortedList.new
=> #<SortedList:0x5f0e74 @data=[]>
>> a << 4
=> [4]
>> a << 5
=> [4, 5]
>> a << 1
=> [1, 4, 5]
>> a << 7
=> [1, 4, 5, 7]
>> a << 3
=> [1, 3, 4, 5, 7]

>> x = 0
=> 0
>> a.each { |e| x += e }
=> [1, 3, 4, 5, 7]
>> x
=> 20
```

This shouldn't be surprising. What is really the interesting bit is that by including the module Enumerable, we gain access to most of the other features we're used to working with when processing Ruby's built-in collections. Here are just a few examples:

```
>> a.map { |e| "Element #{e}" }
=> ["Element 1", "Element 3", "Element 4", "Element 5", "Element 7"]
>> a.inject(0) { |s,e| s + e }
=> 20
>> a.to_a
=> [1, 3, 4, 5, 7]
>> a.select { |e| e > 3 }
=> [4, 5, 7]
```

In a lot of cases, the features provided by Enumerable will be more than enough for traversing your data. However, it's often useful to add other features that build on top of the `Enumerable` methods. We can show this by adding a simple reporting method to `SortedList`:

```
class SortedList
  def report(head)
    header = "#{head}\n#{'-'*head.length}"
    body = map{|e| yield(e)}.join("\n") + "\n"
    footer = "This report was generated at #{Time.now}\n"

    [header, body, footer].join("\n")
  end
end
```

which, when run, produces output like this:

```
>> puts a.report("So many fish") { |e| "#{e} fish" }
So many fish
------------
1 fish
3 fish
4 fish
5 fish
7 fish

This report was generated at 2008-07-22 22:47:20 -0400
```

Building custom iterators is really that simple. This provides a great deal of flexibility, given that the code block can execute arbitrary expressions and do manipulations of its own as it walks across the elements. But as mentioned before, blocks can be used for more than just iteration.

Using Blocks to Abstract Pre- and Postprocessing

We looked at the block form of `File.open()` as an example of how blocks can provide an elegant way to avoid repeating tedious setup and teardown steps. However, files are surely not the only resources that need to be properly managed. Network I/O via sockets is another place where this technique can come in handy.

On the client side, we'd like to be able to create a method that allows us to send a message to a server, return its response, then cleanly close the connection. The first thing that comes to mind is something simple like this:

```
require "socket"

class Client

  def initialize(ip="127.0.0.1",port=3333)
    @ip, @port = ip, port
  end

  def send_message(msg)
    socket = TCPSocket.new(@ip,@port)
    socket.puts(msg)
```

```
      response = socket.gets
    ensure
      socket.close
    end

  end
```

This is reasonably straightforward, but what happens when we want to add another method that waits to receive a message back from the server?

```
require "socket"

class Client

  def initialize(ip="127.0.0.1",port=3333)
    @ip, @port = ip, port
  end

  def send_message(msg)
    socket = TCPSocket.new(@ip,@port)
    socket.puts(msg)
    response = socket.gets
  ensure
    socket.close
  end

  def receive_message
    socket = TCPSocket.new(@ip,@port)
    response = socket.gets
  ensure
    socket.close
  end

end
```

This is starting to look messy, as we have repeated most of the code between send_message and receive_message. Ordinarily, we'd break off the shared code into a private method that the two could share, but the trouble here is that the difference between these two methods is in the middle, not in a single extractable chunk. This is where blocks come to the rescue:

```
require "socket"

class Client
  def initialize(ip="127.0.0.1",port=3333)
    @ip, @port = ip, port
  end

  def send_message(msg)
    connection do |socket|
      socket.puts(msg)
      socket.gets
    end
  end
```

```ruby
def receive_message
  connection { |socket| socket.gets }
end

private

def connection
  socket = TCPSocket.new(@ip,@port)
  yield(socket)
ensure
  socket.close
end

end
```

As you can see, the resulting code is a lot cleaner. As long as we use our `connection()` method with a block, we won't need to worry about opening and closing the `TCPSocket`—it'll handle that for us. This means we've captured that logic in one place, and can reuse it however we'd like.

To make things a bit more interesting, let's take a look at a simple server with which this code can interact, which gives us a chance to look at yet another way that blocks can be useful in interface design.

Blocks As Dynamic Callbacks

There is a lot of power in being able to pass around code blocks just like they were any other object. This allows for the capability of creating and storing dynamic callbacks, which can later be looked up and executed as needed.

In order to play with our `Client` code from the previous example, we're going to create a trivial `TCPServer` that attempts to match incoming messages against patterns to determine how it should respond. Rather than hardcoding behaviors into the server itself or relying on inheritance to handle responses, we will instead allow responses to be defined through ordinary method calls accompanied by a block. Our goal is to get an interface that looks like this:

```ruby
server = Server.new

server.handle(/hello/i) { "Hello from server at #{Time.now}" }
server.handle(/goodbye/i) { "Goodbye from server at #{Time.now}" }
server.handle(/name is (\w+)/) { |m| "Nice to meet you #{m[1]}!" }

server.run
```

The first two examples are fairly simple, matching a single word and then responding with a generic message and timestamp. The third example is a bit more interesting, repeating the client's name back in the response message. This will be accomplished by querying a simple `MatchData` object, which is yielded to the block.

Though making this work might seem like black magic to the uninitiated, a look at its implementation reveals that it is actually a fairly pedestrian task:

```ruby
class Server

  def initialize(port=3333)
    @server   = TCPServer.new('127.0.0.1',port)
    @handlers = {}
  end

  def handle(pattern, &block)
    @handlers[pattern] = block
  end

  def run
    while session = @server.accept
      msg = session.gets
      match = nil

      @handlers.each do |pattern,block|
        if match = msg.match(pattern)
          break session.puts(block.call(match))
        end
      end

      unless match
        session.puts "Server received unknown message: #{msg}"
      end
    end
  end

end
```

The `handle()` method slurps up the provided block using the `&block` syntax, and stores it in a hash keyed by the given pattern. When `Server#run` is called, an endless loop is started that waits for and handles client connections. Each time a message is received, the hash of handlers is iterated over. If a pattern is found that matches the message, the associated block is called, providing the match data object so that the callback can respond accordingly.

If you'd like to try this out, use the following code to spin up a server:

```ruby
server = Server.new

server.handle(/hello/i) { "Hello from server at #{Time.now}" }
server.handle(/goodbye/i) { "Goodbye from server at #{Time.now}" }
server.handle(/name is (\w+)/) { |m| "Nice to meet you #{m[1]}!" }

server.run
```

Once you have that running and listening for connections, execute the following client code:

```ruby
client = Client.new
```

```
["Hello", "My name is Greg", "Goodbye"].each do |msg|
  response = client.send_message(msg)
  puts response
end
```

You will get back something like this:

```
Hello from server at Wed Jul 23 16:15:37 -0400 2008
Nice to meet you Greg!
Goodbye from server at Wed Jul 23 16:15:37 -0400 2008
```

It would be easy to extend both the client and server to do more interesting things that build on this very simple foundation. Feel free to take a few minutes to play around with that,* and then we'll look at one more block trick that's fairly common in Ruby.

Blocks for Interface Simplification

Does it feel like the word "server" is written too many times in this code?

```
server = Server.new

server.handle(/hello/i) { "Hello from server at #{Time.now}" }
server.handle(/goodbye/i) { "Goodbye from server at #{Time.now}" }
server.handle(/name is (\w+)/) { |m| "Nice to meet you #{m[1]}!" }

server.run
```

When you see code like this, it might be a sign that you could do better. Although there are merits to this somewhat standard approach, we can cheat a little bit with blocks (of course) and make things prettier. It would be nice to be able to write this instead:

```
Server.run do
  handle(/hello/i) { "Hello from server at #{Time.now}" }
  handle(/goodbye/i) { "Goodbye from server at #{Time.now}" }
  handle(/name is (\w+)/) { |m| "Nice to meet you #{m[1]}!" }
end
```

As you may recall from an earlier example, it is possible to execute a block within the scope of an instantiated object in Ruby. Using this knowledge, we can implement this handy shortcut interface as a simple class method:

```
class Server

  # other methods same as before

  def self.run(port=3333,&block)
    server = Server.new(port)
    server.instance_eval(&block)
    server.run
  end

end
```

---

* Of course, you might want to look at GServer in the standard library for a real generic server implementation.

This is all you need to get the new interface running, and rounds off our quick exploration of the different ways that you can use blocks to improve your API design while simplifying your method implementations.

Keep the following things in mind when using blocks as part of your interface:

- If you create a collection class that you need to traverse, build on top of `Enumerable` rather than reinventing the wheel.
- If you have shared code that differs only in the middle, create a helper method that yields a block in between the pre/postprocessing code to avoid duplication of effort.
- If you use the `&block` syntax, you can capture the code block provided to a method inside a variable. You can then store this and use it later, which is very useful for creating dynamic callbacks.
- Using a combination of `&block` and `instance_eval`, you can execute blocks within the context of arbitrary objects, which opens up a lot of doors for highly customized interfaces.
- The return value of `yield` (and `block.call`) is the same as the return value of the provided block.

Between clever use of code blocks and powerful argument processing, Ruby makes designing beautiful interfaces a joy. However, it takes a little more than this to really complete the picture. Before we wrap things up, let's take a quick look at some common conventions for naming your methods as well as what to do when things go wrong.

Avoiding Surprises

Though Ruby is a language that embraces the TIMTOWTDI[†] concept, it is also one that seeks the "Ruby Way" of doing things. In this section are a number of miscellaneous tips to help you move your API in that direction.

Use attr_reader, attr_writer, and attr_accessor

In Ruby, there is no direct external access to the internal state of objects. This means that it is necessary for you to provide public accessors for your internal objects.

Technically, the following code does that just fine:

```ruby
class Message

  def initialize(m)
    @message = m
  end
```

[†] "There Is More Than One Way To Do It."

```
    def get_message
      @message
    end

    def set_message(m)
      @message = m
    end

  end

>> m = Message.new('foo')
=> #<Message:0x603bf0 @message="foo">
>> m.get_message
=> "foo"
>> m.set_message('bar')
=> "bar"
>> m.get_message
=> "bar"
```

However, this approach is almost never seen in code written by practicing Rubyists. Instead, you'll see the preceding code example implemented like this:

```
class Message

  attr_accessor :message

  def initialize(m)
    @message = m
  end

end

>> m = Message.new('foo')
=> #<Message:0x5f3c50 @message="foo">
>> m.message
=> "foo"
>> m.message = "bar"
=> "bar"
>> m.message
=> "bar"
```

Aside from requiring less typing overall, this code is very clear and expressive, because it doesn't include the unnecessary get and set verbs. However, you might wonder how to do data verification/protection with this approach.

If you need to add some special logic on write, you can still use attr_reader to provide the reading side of things and then use a custom method to handle the writing:

```
class Message
  attr_reader :message

  def message=(m)
    @message = m.dup
  end
end
```

On the other hand, if you need to do some handling on read but can afford to use the default writer, `attr_writer` is what you want:

```ruby
class Message
  attr_writer :message

  def message
    @message.encode!("UTF-8")
  end
end
```

Of course, if you need both custom readers and writers, there is no need for the `attr_*` helpers. However, in this case, remember that unless there is a good reason to name things otherwise, use the methods `something()` and `something=()` instead of `get_something()` and `set_something()`.

Understand What method? and method! Mean

In Ruby, question marks and exclamation points are allowed at the end of method names. Although there is no doubt that Matz wants us to be able to express ourselves freely, these special characters have conventional baggage that comes along with them, and it is useful to honor these conventions when developing your own interfaces.

Question marks

The purpose of the question mark is pretty straightforward. It allows us to query our object about things and make use of the response in conditionals. In essence, it allows things like this:

```ruby
unless some_string.empty?
  puts some_string.reverse
end
```

In practice, the exact way that this sort of method is implemented varies, but the return value is always some sort of logical boolean. If you write a method that looks like `foo.is_dumb?` that returns `:no`, most Rubyists will disagree with you. If the condition described by the method is not satisfied, be sure that it returns either `false` or `nil`.

Purists might say that when you use this convention, the result should return boolean objects, meaning `true` and `false` only. In this case, a hack for converting Ruby objects to their boolean values is often used:

```ruby
>> !!(:blah)
=> true
>> !!(false)
=> false
>> !!(nil)
=> false
>> !!(123)
=> true
```

This hack is somewhat controversial, but will negate the negation of the boolean status of your object, giving you back a boolean. So one might write a method like this:

```
def person?
  !! @person
end
```

However, there is something to be said for the other side of this argument. Sometimes it is useful to return the actual object, as in the following case:

```
if user = foo.person?
  user.say_hello
end
```

This is ultimately a matter of personal taste, but people on both sides of the fence agree that the use of a question mark in a Ruby method should return some logically boolean value that can be used meaningfully in conditional statements. If that is not the purpose you had in mind, consider avoiding the question mark in your method names.

Exclamation points

Most people tend to conceptually grasp the question mark convention fairly quickly, but the use of exclamation points is sometimes a little less intuitive. However, the convention itself is not that complicated and can be quite useful.

A common misconception is that we use the exclamation point when we want to let people know we are modifying the receiving object. This is probably due to the fact that, in many cases, this is what the exclamation point (also known as a bang) is warning us of. Here are just a few examples from Ruby's built-in classes:

```
>> a = "foo"
=> "foo"
>> a.delete!("f")
=> "oo"
>> a
=> "oo"

>> a = [1,2,3]
=> [1, 2, 3]
>> a.map! { |e| e + 1 }
=> [2, 3, 4]
>> a
=> [2, 3, 4]

>> a = { foo: "bar" }
=> {:foo=>"bar"}
>> a.merge!(baz: "foobar")
=> {:foo=>"bar", :baz=>"foobar"}
>> a
=> {:foo=>"bar", :baz=>"foobar"}
```

However, what about Hash#update?

```
>> a = { foo: "bar" }
=> {:foo=>"bar"}
>> a.update(baz: "foobar")
=> {:foo=>"bar", :baz=>"foobar"}
>> a
=> {:foo=>"bar", :baz=>"foobar"}
```

This does the same thing as Hash#merge!, but no bang is present. I can think of tons of other examples where this is true. String#replace doesn't have a bang, and neither does Array#push or Array#pop. If the convention was really to slap an exclamation point at the end of every method that changed something about its receiver, we'd have more exclamation points in Ruby's method list than a teenager could use in an IM session.

Truthfully, the purpose of this convention is to mark a method as special. It doesn't necessarily mean that it will be destructive or dangerous, but it means that it will require more attention than its alternative. This is why it doesn't make much sense to have some method foo!() without a corresponding foo() method that does something similar. So essentially, if you have only one way of doing something destructive, write this:

```
class Message
  def destroy
    #...
  end
end
```

instead of this:

```
class Message
  def destroy!
    #...
  end
end
```

Following this idea that an exclamation point doesn't necessarily mean that a method is doing a *destructive* operation, we can find more varied uses for it. For example, if you look at the way the ActiveRecord object-relational mapping (ORM) works, you can see a good example of a proper use for this convention.

Creating a user that doesn't pass validations does not raise an exception, but rather stores issues in an errors array, and allows you to check whether a record is valid:

```
>> a = User.create(:login => "joe")
=> #<User id: nil, login: "joe", ... >
>> a.valid?
=> false
```

By calling User.create!, we can cause ActiveRecord to raise an error:

```
>> a = User.create!(:login => "joe")
ActiveRecord::RecordInvalid: Validation failed: Password confirmation can't be
blank, Password can't be blank,
Password is too short (minimum is 7 characters), Password Must include at
least three of the following character types: upper case, lower case, numeric,
non alphanumeric, Email can't be blank, Email is too short (minimum is 3
characters)
```

These two methods are functionally equivalent otherwise, but the latter has a more severe response, which exactly fits the conditions under which this convention is useful. Essentially, when you see a ! at the end of a Ruby method, think "Pay attention!" rather than "You are on your way to destruction!" and you'll be fine.

Make Use of Custom Operators

Ruby allows you to define custom operators for your classes. This is especially easy in Ruby because most operators are actually just syntactic sugar for ordinary methods:

```
>> 1.+(3)
=> 4

>> [1,2,3].<<(4)
=> [1, 2, 3, 4]
```

We can thus define our operators as if they were ordinary methods. Here's a quick example of one of the most common operators to implement, the append operator (<<):

```
class Inbox

  attr_reader :unread_count

  def initialize
    @messages     = []
    @unread_count = 0
  end

  def <<(msg)
    @unread_count += 1
    @messages << msg
    return self
  end

end

>> i = Inbox.new
=> #<Inbox:0x603290 @messages=[], @unread_count=0>
>> i << "foo" << "bar" << "baz"
=> #<Inbox:0x603290 @messages=["foo", "bar", "baz"], @unread_count=3>
>> i.unread_count
=> 3
```

A good habit to get into is to have your << method return the object itself, so the calls can be chained, as just shown.

Another good operator to know about is the *spaceship operator* (<=>), mainly because it allows you to make use of Comparable, which gives you a host of comparison methods: <, <=, ==, !=, >=, >, and between?().

The spaceship operator should return -1 if the current object is less than the object it is being compared to, 0 if it is equal, and 1 if it is greater. Most of Ruby's core objects that can be meaningfully compared already have <=> implemented, so it's often simply a matter of delegating to them, as shown here:

```
class Tree

  include Comparable

  attr_reader :age

  def initialize(age)
    @age = age
  end

  def <=>(other_tree)
    age <=> other_tree.age
  end

end

>> a = Tree.new(2)
=> #<Tree:0x5c9ba8 @age=2>
>> b = Tree.new(3)
=> #<Tree:0x5c7fb0 @age=3>
>> c = Tree.new(3)
=> #<Tree:0x5c63b8 @age=3>

>> a < b
=> true
>> b == c
=> true
>> c > a
=> true
>> c != a
=> true
```

You can, of course, override some of the individual operators that Comparable provides, but its defaults are often exactly what you need.

Most operators you use in Ruby can be customized within your objects. Whenever you find yourself writing append() when you really want <<, or add() when you really want +, consider using your own custom operators.

None of the conventions mentioned here are set laws that need to be followed; in fact, you'll certainly run into situations where it'll make sense to violate some of them from time to time. However, generally these practices have become popular because they make your code better, and make it easier for someone who has never used your code before to get up and running. Here's a quick recap of some of the tips we've covered:

- Use attr_reader, attr_writer, and attr_accessor whenever possible, and avoid writing your own accessors unless it is necessary.
- Consider ending methods that are designed to be used in conditional statements with a question mark.

- If you have a method foo(), and a similar method that does nearly the same thing but requires the user to pay more attention to what's going on, consider calling it foo!().
- Don't bother creating a method foo!() if there is not already a method called foo() that does the same thing with less severe consequences.
- If it makes sense to do so, define custom operators for your objects.

Conclusions

The difficulty of designing a solid API for a given problem depends largely on the problem itself. However, we've seen in this chapter that Ruby is pretty much happy to get out of your way and provide you with an enormous amount of flexibility so that you can more easily design what you had in mind, rather than what Matz thinks you should do.

When developing your interfaces, be sure to actually use them in order to drive them along. In this way, you are forced to eat your own dog food, and this ensures that the API ends up satisfying the goal of working nicely rather than simply looking nice from a distance. You can gain a lot of inspiration by looking at the way in which the core Ruby objects are designed, API-wise. The best way to make your code more Rubyish is to make it work like core Ruby objects do whenever you can. Of course, like anything else, trying to stretch this idea too far can be disastrous. In moderation, however, this general approach combined with the technical details in this chapter should put you on your way to writing solid Ruby libraries in no time, or, failing that, should clean up your existing code a bit and make it easier to work with.

## CHAPTER 3

Mastering the Dynamic Toolkit

If you've done even a little bit of Ruby, you probably have a sense of the great flexibility and power that it offers as a language. This chapter is designed to underscore that point, specifically by showing you what can be accomplished when you unleash the power of Ruby onto itself. When you hear that everything is an object in Ruby, it's easy to forget that classes, modules, and methods all fall into that category as well. With enough imagination, we can think of all sorts of interesting applications that fall out of this elegant design.

Take the fact that all of our programmatic constructs can be represented as first-order data objects and combine it with the ability to modify any of them at runtime. Then mix in the idea that everything from defining a new function to calling a method that does not exist can be detected and handled by custom code. Top this off with first-rate reflection capabilities and you'll find that Ruby is a perfect foundation for writing highly dynamic applications.

On the surface, these ideas may seem a bit esoteric or academic in nature. But when you get down to it, there are a lot of practical uses for having such a high degree of flexibility baked into Ruby. Because Ruby's dynamic nature is a huge part of what makes the language what it is, you'll find no shortage of real examples in this chapter. These run the gamut from dynamic interface generation to safely modifying preexisting code at runtime. But to get your feet wet, we'll dive in with the same head-first approach found in the rest of the chapters of this book. We're about to look at the code behind Jim Weirich's `BlankSlate` class, which provides an excellent case study of what can be accomplished with the dynamic toolkit that Ruby provides for us.

If you feel a bit overwhelmed at first, don't be discouraged—each individual topic will be discussed later on in this chapter in greater detail. For now, let's just try to have fun and see just how powerful Ruby really is.

BlankSlate: A BasicObject on Steroids

Although Ruby 1.9 has `BasicObject` as a very lightweight object designed to be used for implementing objects with dynamic interfaces and other similar tasks, Ruby 1.8

users weren't so lucky. In light of this, `BlankSlate` became a fairly common tool for those who needed an object that didn't do much of anything. One of the practical applications of this somewhat abstract object was in implementing the XML generator in the *builder* gem. In case you've not seen XML Builder before, it is a tool that turns Ruby code like this:

```
builder = Builder::XmlMarkup.new(:target=>STDOUT, :indent=>2)
builder.person { |b| b.name("Jim"); b.phone("555-1234") }
```

into XML output like this:

```
<person>
  <name>Jim</name>
  <phone>555-1234</phone>
</person>
```

Without going into too much detail, it is obvious from this example that `Builder::XmlMarkup` implements a dynamic interface that can turn your method calls into matching XML output. But if it had simply inherited from `Object`, you'd run into certain naming clashes wherever a tag had the same name as one of `Object`'s instance methods.

Builder works by capturing calls to missing methods, which means it has trouble doing its magic whenever a method is actually defined. For example: if `XmlMarkup` were just a subclass of `Object`, with no methods removed, you wouldn't be able produce the following XML, due to a naming conflict:

```
<class>
  <student>Greg Gibson</student>
</class>
```

The underlying issue here is that `Kernel#class` is already defined for a different purpose. Of course, if we instead inherit from an object that has very few methods to begin with, this greatly lessens our chance for a clash.

`BasicObject` certainly fits the bill, as you can see with a quick glance at its instance methods via *irb*:

```
>> BasicObject.instance_methods
=> [:==, :equal?, :!, :!=, :instance_eval, :instance_exec, :__send__]
```

These methods form the lowest common denominator for Ruby, so `BasicObject` is pretty reasonable in its offerings. The key thing to remember is that a `BasicObject` is fully defined by this limited set of features, so you shouldn't expect anything more than that. Although this makes perfect sense in Ruby 1.9's object hierarchy, it's somewhat interesting to see that `BlankSlate` takes an entirely different approach.

On Ruby 1.8, there was no `BasicObject` class to speak of, so instead of starting off with a tiny set of methods, `BlankSlate` had to do something to get rid of the significant baggage that rides along with Ruby's `Object` class. This is done in an especially clever way, and a quick *irb* session complete with the expected noise that results from removing potentially important methods shows the primary interesting features of BlankSlate:

```
>> class A < BlankSlate; end
=> nil
>> A.new
NoMethodError: undefined method 'inspect' for #<A:0x42ac34>
...
>> A.reveal(:inspect)
=> #<Proc:0x426558@devel/rbp_code/dynamic_toolkit/blankslate.rb:43 (lambda)>
>> A.new
NoMethodError: undefined method 'to_s' for #<A:0x425004>
...
>> A.reveal(:to_s)
=> #<Proc:0x422e30@devel/rbp_code/dynamic_toolkit/blankslate.rb:43 (lambda)>
>> A.new
=> #<A:0x425004>
>> A.new.methods
NoMethodError: undefined method 'methods' for #<A:0x425004>
        from (irb):8
        from /Users/sandal/lib/ruby19_1/bin/irb:12:in '<main>'
>> A.reveal(:methods)
=> #<Proc:0x41ed6c@devel/rbp_code/dynamic_toolkit/blankslate.rb:43 (lambda)>
>> A.new.methods
=> [:inspect, :to_s, :methods, :__id__, :instance_eval, :__send__]
```

After reading through this code, you should be able to get a sense of how it works. BlankSlate isn't really a blank slate at all; instead, it's an object that acts like a blank slate by hiding all of its methods until you tell them explicitly to reveal themselves. This clever bit of functionality allows BlankSlate's initial instance methods to be kept to the absolute minimum. Everything else can be explicitly revealed later, as needed.

BlankSlate does this per subclass, so you can have different customized minimal objects for different purposes in your system. Predictably, you can also rehide functions, including those that you add yourself:

```
>> A.new.foo
=> "Hi"
>> A.hide(:foo)
=> A
>> A.new.foo
NoMethodError: undefined method 'foo' for #<A:0x425004>
        from (irb):18
        from /Users/sandal/lib/ruby19_1/bin/irb:12:in '<main>'
>> A.hide(:inspect)
=> A
>> A.new
NoMethodError: undefined method 'inspect' for #<A:0x40a484>
...
```

All in all, although it is a bit more heavyweight than BasicObject, the BlankSlate class may have its uses even on Ruby 1.9, due to this ability to seamlessly hide and restore functionality on the fly. If you were thinking that this sounds like complicated stuff, you might be surprised. The core implementation of BlankSlate is relatively straightforward. Of course, the devil is in the details, but the most interesting bits can be understood with a little explanation:

```ruby
class BlankSlate
  class << self

    # Hide the method named +name+ in the BlankSlate class.  Don't
    # hide +instance_eval+ or any method beginning with "_".
    def hide(name)
      if instance_methods.include?(name) and
        name !~ /^(__|instance_eval)/
        @hidden_methods ||= {}
        @hidden_methods[name] = instance_method(name)
        undef_method name
      end
    end

    def find_hidden_method(name)
      @hidden_methods ||= {}
      @hidden_methods[name] || superclass.find_hidden_method(name)
    end

    # Redefine a previously hidden method so that it may be called on a blank
    # slate object.
    def reveal(name)
      unbound_method = find_hidden_method(name)
      fail "Don't know how to reveal method '#{name}'" unless unbound_method
      define_method(name, unbound_method)
    end
  end

  instance_methods.each { |m| hide(m) }
end
```

As you can see, the class is simply three short class methods, followed by the call that causes all of BlankSlate's instance methods to be hidden. Let's start by taking a closer look at the hide() method.

```ruby
def hide(name)
  if instance_methods.include?(name) && name !~ /^(__|instance_eval)/
    @hidden_methods ||= {}
    @hidden_methods[name] = instance_method(name)
    undef_method name
  end
end
```

Here you can see that BlankSlate first checks to make sure that the method name passed to hide() exists within the currently visible instance methods. Once it checks to make sure the method is not one of the special reserved methods, it begins the process of storing and hiding the specified method.

The technique used here is simply to initialize a @hidden_methods hash within the class, and then assign the method name as a key to the associated UnboundMethod object. An UnboundMethod can be thought of as roughly similar to a Proc object, but rather than being truly anonymous, it is later hooked up to an object that knows how to make use of the function, which is typically an object of the same class. As a trivial example, we can play around with `String#reverse` to illustrate this point:

```
>> a = String.instance_method(:reverse)
=> #<UnboundMethod: String#reverse>
>> a.bind("foo").call
=> "oof"
```

We'll take a closer look at this a little later, but suffice it to say that by grabbing the `UnboundMethod` before removing the method definition, we have a way of restoring the behavior in the future.

I assume you can get the gist of what's going on with `find_hidden_method()` just by inspection, so we can jump straight into the most interesting code in `BlankSlate`, the method that actually restores the old functionality:

```
# Redefine a previously hidden method so that it may be called on a blank
# slate object.
def reveal(name)
  unbound_method = find_hidden_method(name)
  fail "Don't know how to reveal method '#{name}'" unless unbound_method
  define_method(name, unbound_method)
end
```

Here, the `find_hidden_method()` helper is used to recall an `UnboundMethod` by name. If it doesn't manage to find a matching name in the `@hidden_methods` hash, an error is raised. However, assuming the lookup went according to plan, we can see that the method is redefined to call the newly rebound method. All the original arguments are passed on to the restored method call, so you end up with the original behavior restored.

Although we've shown the key components of `BlankSlate` here, we haven't gone into the full details yet. It's worth mentioning that because `BlankSlate` inherits from `Object` and not `BasicObject`, it has to do some additional magic to deal with module inclusion, and it also must handle methods added to `Object` and `Kernel`. We'll get to these a little later, in "Registering Hooks and Callbacks" on page 88. For now, let's just quickly review the concepts we've touched on.

In this initial exploration phase, we've caught a glimpse of `define_method`, `instance_methods`, `instance_method`, `undef_method`, and `UnboundMethod`. Or in English, we've seen an example of how to use reflection to determine the names of the instance methods on a class, copy their implementations into objects that could then be keyed by name in a hash, undefine them, and later restore them by building up a new definition programmatically. You have probably noticed that even though these concepts are very high-level, they're essentially ordinary Ruby code, without any sort of magic. The rest of this chapter will serve to reinforce that point.

Now that we've seen a few of these concepts in action, we'll slow down and discuss what each one of them actually means, while diving even deeper into dynamic Ruby territory. In this next example, we'll look at a favorite topic for budding Rubyists. I'm going to share the secrets behind building flexible interfaces that can be used for domain-specific applications. The heavy-handed term for this sort of thing is an "internal domain-specific language," but we don't need to be so fancy, as it can create misconceptions. The ability to build pleasant domain-specific interfaces is a key feature of Ruby, and deserves some discussion—no matter what you want to call it.

Building Flexible Interfaces

Heads up: you might start to feel a bit of déjà vu in this section. What we'll cover here is basically a recap of what was discussed in Chapter 2, *Designing Beautiful APIs*, mixed in with a little dynamic help here and there. Though each step may seem fairly inconsequential, the end result is quite powerful.

When implementing a flexible domain-specific interface, the idea is that we want to strip away as much boilerplate code as possible so that every line expresses something meaningful in the context of our domain. We also want to build up a vocabulary to work with, and express our intents in that vocabulary as much as possible. A domain-specific interface puts Ruby in the background: available when you need it, but not as in-your-face as ordinary programmatic interfaces tend to be. An easy comparison would be to look at the difference between some elementary `Test::Unit` code and its RSpec equivalent.[*]

First, we'll look at the vanilla `Test::Unit` code:

```
class NewAccountTest < Test::Unit

  def setup
    @account = Account.new
  end

  def test_must_start_with_a_zero_balance
    assert_equal Money.new(0, :dollars), @account.balance
  end

end
```

To a Rubyist, this code might seem relatively clear, straightforward, and expressive. However, its defining characteristic is that it looks like any other Ruby code, with all the associated benefits and drawbacks. Others prefer a different approach, which you can clearly see in this RSpec code:

```
describe Account, " when first created" do

  before do
    @account = Account.new
  end
```

---

[*] This example is from the RSpec home page (*http://rspec.info*), with minor modifications.

```
it "should have a balance of $0" do
  @account.balance.should eql(Money.new(0, :dollars))
end

end
```

When we read RSpec code, it feels like we're reading specifications rather than Ruby code. Many people feel this is a major advantage, because it encourages us to express ourselves in a domain-specific context. When it comes to testing, this does create some controversy, because although the RSpec code is arguably more readable here, the `Test::Unit` code is certainly less magical. But in the interest of avoiding politics, I've shown this example to illustrate the difference between two styles, not to advocate one over the other.

Even though some particular uses of domain-specific interfaces can be a touchy subject, you'll find many cases where they come in handy. To help you get a feel for how they come together, we'll be looking at some problems and their solutions. We're about to walk through the lifecycle of wrapping a nice interface on top of Prawn's `Document` class. Don't worry about the particular domain; instead, focus on the techniques we use so that you can make use of them in your own projects.

Making instance_eval( ) Optional

In the previous chapter, we covered a common pattern for interface simplification, allowing you to turn code like this:

```
pdf = Prawn::Document.new
pdf.text "Hello World"
pdf.render_file "hello.pdf"
```

into something like this:

```
Prawn::Document.generate("hello.pdf") do
  text "Hello World"
end
```

As you'll recall, this trick is relatively straightforward to implement:

```
class Prawn::Document
  def self.generate(file, *args, &block)
    pdf = Prawn::Document.new(*args)
    pdf.instance_eval(&block)
    pdf.render_file(file)
  end
end
```

However, there is a limitation that comes with this sort of interface. Because we are evaluating the block in the context of a `Document` instance, we do not have access to anything but the local variables of our enclosing scope. This means the following code won't work:

```
class MyBestFriend

  def initialize
    @first_name = "Paul"
    @last_name  = "Mouzas"
  end

  def full_name
    "#{@first_name} #{@last_name}"
  end

  def generate_pdf
    Prawn::Document.generate("friend.pdf") do
      text "My best friend is #{full_name}"
    end
  end

end
```

It'd be a shame to have to revert to building this stuff up manually, and a bit messy to rely on storing things in local variables. Luckily, there is a middle-of-the-road option: we can optionally yield a Document object. Here's how we'd go about doing that:

```
class Prawn::Document
  def self.generate(file, *args, &block)
    pdf = Prawn::Document.new(*args)
    block.arity < 1 ? pdf.instance_eval(&block) : block.call(pdf)
    pdf.render_file(file)
  end
end
```

This new code preserves the old instance_eval behavior, but allows a new approach as well. We can now write the following code without worry:

```
class MyOtherBestFriend

  def initialize
    @first_name = "Pete"
    @last_name  = "Johansen"
  end

  def full_name
    "#{@first_name} #{@last_name}"
  end

  def generate_pdf
    Prawn::Document.generate("friend.pdf") do |doc|
      doc.text "My best friend is #{full_name}"
    end
  end

end
```

Here, the code is an ordinary closure, and as such, can access the instance methods and variables of the enclosing scope. Although we need to go back to having an explicit

---

receiver for the PDF calls, our `Document.generate` method can still do its necessary setup and teardown for us, salvaging some of its core functionality.

The feature that makes this all possible is `Proc#arity`. This method tells you how many arguments, if any, the code block was given. Here's a few examples as an illustration:

```
>> lambda { |x| x + 1 }.arity
=> 1
>> lambda { |x,y,z| x + y + z }.arity
=> 3
>> lambda { 1 }.arity
=> 0
```

As you can see, because `Proc` objects are just objects themselves, we can do some reflective inquiry to find out how many arguments they're expecting to process. Although not strictly related to our task, it's worth mentioning that you can accomplish the same thing with methods as well:

```
>> Comparable.instance_method(:between?).arity
=> 2
>> Fixnum.instance_method(:to_f).arity
=> 0
```

Although our use of an `arity` check was confined to a relatively simple task here, the technique is general. Any time you want to conditionally handle something based on how many block arguments are present, you can use this general approach.

That having been said, even if you never use this trick for anything else, knowing how to selectively `instance_eval` a block is important. As you'll see through the rest of this section, a key part of developing a pleasant domain-specific interface is maintaining flexibility. If you limit yourself to an all-or-nothing choice between your sexy shortcuts and the bland, low-level API, frustration is inevitable. Of course, because Ruby is so dynamic, you should never be forced to make this decision.

We'll now move on to another key component of flexible interface design: the use of `method_missing` and `send` to dynamically route messages within your objects.

Handling Messages with method_missing( ) and send( )

Continuing on a theme, we can look at more Prawn code to see how to make things a bit more dynamic. We'll be looking at elementary drawing operations here, but you can substitute your own problem mentally. As in other examples, the actual domain does not matter.

In Prawn, there are two ordinary ways to generate some shapes and then draw them onto the page. The first is the most simple—just drawing the paths, and then calling one of `stroke`, `fill`, or `fill_and_stroke`:

```
Prawn::Document.generate("shapes.pdf") do
  fill_color "ff0000"
```

```
# Fills a red circle
circle_at [100,100], :radius => 25
fill

# Strokes a transparent circle with a black border and a line extending
# from its center point
circle_at [300,300] :radius => 50
line [300,300], [350, 300]
stroke

# Fills and strokes a red hexagon with a black border
polygon [100, 250], [200, 300], [300, 250],
        [300, 150], [200, 100], [100, 150]
fill_and_stroke
end
```

This isn't too bad, but for some needs, a block form is better. This makes it clearer what paint operation is being used, and may be a bit easier to extend:

```
Prawn::Document.generate("shapes.pdf") do
  fill_color "ff0000"

  # Fills a red circle
  fill { circle_at [100,100], :radius => 25 }

  # Strokes a transparent circle with a black border and a line extending
  # from its center point
  stroke do
    circle_at [300,300] :radius => 50
    line [300,300], [350, 300]
  end

  fill_and_stroke do
    # Fills and strokes a red hexagon with a black border
    polygon [100, 250], [200, 300], [300, 250],
            [300, 150], [200, 100], [100, 150]
  end

end
```

This may be a bit more readable, especially the middle one, in which multiple paths need to be stroked. However, it still feels like more work than we'd really want. Wouldn't things be nicer this way?

```
Prawn::Document.generate("shapes.pdf") do
  fill_color "ff0000"

  fill_circle_at [100,100], :radius => 25

  stroke_circle_at [300,300] :radius => 50
  stroke_line [300,300], [350, 300]

  fill_and_stroke_polygon [100, 250], [200, 300], [300, 250],
                          [300, 150], [200, 100], [100, 150]
end
```

This has a nice, declarative feel to it. Obviously though, we don't want to define four methods for every graphics drawing operation. This is especially true when you think of the nature of what each of these would look like. Let's take **stroke** for example:

```
def stroke_some_method(*args)
  some_method(*args)
  stroke
end
```

Repeat that ad nauseam for every single drawing method, and keep up this pattern every time a new one is added? No way! Maybe this sort of repetition would be tolerated over in Java-land, but in Ruby, we can do better. The answer lies in dynamically interpreting method calls.

When you attempt to call a method that doesn't exist in Ruby, you see an exception raised by default. However, Ruby provides a way to hook into this process and intercept the call before an error can be raised. This is done through the method `method_missing`.

To give a very brief introduction to how it works, let's take a quick spin in *irb*:

```
>> def method_missing(name, *args, &block)
>>   puts "You tried to call #{name} with #{args.inspect}"
>>   puts "Epic Fail!"
>> end
=> nil
>> 1.fafsafs
You tried to call fafsafs with []
Epic Fail!
=> nil
>> "kitten".foo("bar", "baz")
You tried to call foo with ["bar", "baz"]
Epic Fail!
```

By including a `method_missing` hook at the top level, all unknown messages get routed through our new method and print out our message. As you can see, the name of the message as well as the arguments are captured. Of course, this sort of global change is typically a very bad idea, and serves only as an introduction. But if you're feeling ambitious, take a moment to think about how this technique could be used to solve the problem we're working on here, before reading on.

Did you have any luck? If you did attempt this exercise, what you would find is that `method_missing` isn't very useful on its own. Typically, it is used to do part of a job and then route the work to another function. The way we do this is by making use of `Kernel#send`, which allows us to call a method by just passing a symbol or string, followed by any arguments:

```
>> "foo".send(:reverse)
=> "oof"
>> [1,2,3].send("join", "|")
=> "1|2|3"
```

Does this clue make things a bit clearer? For those who didn't try to build this on their own, or if you attempted it and came up short, here's how to make it all work:

```
# Provides the following shortcuts:
#
#    stroke_some_method(*args) #=> some_method(*args); stroke
#    fill_some_method(*args) #=> some_method(*args); fill
#    fill_and_stroke_some_method(*args) #=> some_method(*args); fill_and_stroke
#
def method_missing(id,*args,&block)
  case(id.to_s)
  when /^fill_and_stroke_(.*)/
    send($1,*args,&block); fill_and_stroke
  when /^stroke_(.*)/
    send($1,*args,&block); stroke
  when /^fill_(.*)/
    send($1,*args,&block); fill
  else
    super
  end
end
```

As the documentation describes, this hook simply extracts the paint command out from the method call, and then sends the remainder as the function to execute. All arguments (including an optional block) are forwarded on to the real method. Then, when it returns, the specified paint method is called.

It's important to note that when the patterns do not match, `super` is called. This allows objects up the chain to do their own `method_missing` handling, including the default, which raises a `NoMethodError`. This prevents something like `pdf.the_shiny_kitty` from failing silently, as well as the more subtle `pdf.fill_circle`.

Although this is just a single example, it should spark your imagination for all the possibilities. But it also hints at the sort of looseness that comes with this approach. Prawn will happily accept `pdf.fill_and_stroke_start_new_page` or even `pdf.stroke_stroke_stroke_line` without complaining. Any time you use the `method_missing` hook, these are the trade-offs you must be willing to accept. Of course, by making your hooks more robust, you can get a bit more control, but that starts to defeat the purpose if you take it too far.

The best approach is to use `method_missing` responsibly and with moderation. Be sure to avoid accidental silent failures by calling `super` for any case you do not handle, and don't bother using it if you want things to be ironclad. In cases where there is a relatively small set of methods you want to generate dynamically, a solution using `define_method` might be preferred. That having been said, when used as a shortcut alternative to a less pleasant interface, `method_missing` can be quite helpful, especially in cases where the messages you'll need to accept are truly dynamic.

The techniques described so far combined with some of the methods shown in the previous chapter will get you far in building a domain-specific interface. We're about to move on to other dynamic Ruby topics, but before we do that, we'll cover one more cheap trick that leads to clean and flexible interfaces.

Dual-Purpose Accessors

One thing you will notice when working with code that has an `instance_eval`-based interface is that using ordinary setters can be ugly. Because you need to disambiguate between local variables and method calls, stuff like this can really cramp your style:

```ruby
Prawn::Document.generate("accessors.txt") do

  self.font_size = 10
  text "The font size is now #{font_size}"

end
```

It's possible to make this look much nicer, as you can see:

```ruby
Prawn::Document.generate("accessors.txt") do

  font_size 10
  text "The font size is now #{font_size}"

end
```

The concept here isn't a new one; we covered it in the previous chapter. We can use Ruby's default argument syntax to determine whether we're supposed to be getting or setting the attribute:

```ruby
class Prawn::Document

  def font_size(size = nil)
    return @font_size unless size
    @font_size = size
  end

  alias_method :font_size=, :font_size

end
```

As I said before, this is a relatively cheap trick with not much that is special to it. But the first time you forget to do it and find yourself typing `self.foo = bar` in what is supposed to be a domain-specific interface, you'll be sure to remember this technique.

One thing to note is that you shouldn't break the normal behavior of setters from the outside. We use `alias_method` here instead of `attr_writer` to ensure down the line that there won't be any difference between the following two lines of code:

```ruby
pdf.font_size = 16
pdf.font_size(16)
```

Though not essential, this is a nice way to avoid potential headaches at a very low cost, so it's a good habit to get into when using this technique.

When we combine all the tactics we've gone over so far, we've got all the essential components for building flexible domain-specific interfaces. Before we move on to the next topic, let's review the main points to remember about flexible interface design:

- As mentioned in the previous chapter, using `instance_eval` is a good base for writing a domain-specific interface, but has some limitations.

- You can use a `Proc#arity` check to provide the user with a choice between `instance_eval` and yielding an object.

- If you want to provide shortcuts for certain sequences of method calls, or dynamic generation of methods, you can use `method_missing` along with `send()`.

- When using `method_missing`, be sure to use `super()` to pass unhandled calls up the chain so they can be handled properly by other code, or eventually raise a `NoMethodError`.

- Normal attribute writers don't work well in `instance_eval`-based interfaces. Offer a dual-purpose reader/writer method, and then alias a writer to it, and both external and internal calls will be clear.

With these tips in mind, let's move on to another topic. It's time to shift gears from per-class dynamic behavior to individual objects.

Implementing Per-Object Behavior

An interesting aspect of Ruby is that not only can objects have per-class method definitions, but they can also have per-object behaviors. What this means is that each and every object carries around its own unique identity, and that the class definition is simply the blueprint for the beginning of an object's lifecycle.

Let's start with a simple *irb* session to clearly illustrate this concept:

```
>> a = [1,2,3]
=> [1, 2, 3]
>> def a.secret
>>   "Only this object knows the secrets of the world"
>> end
=> nil
>> a.secret
=> "Only this object knows the secrets of the world"
>> [1,2,3,4,5].secret
NoMethodError: undefined method 'secret' for [1, 2, 3, 4, 5]:Array
        from (irb):17
        from :0
>> [1,2,3].secret
NoMethodError: undefined method 'secret' for [1, 2, 3]:Array
        from (irb):18
        from :0
```

Here, using a familiar method definition syntax, we add a special method called `secret` to the array we've assigned to `a`. The remaining examples show that only `a` gets this new method definition. If the last one surprised you a bit, remember that most objects in Ruby are not immediate values, so two arrays set to [1,2,3] are not the same object, even if they contain the same data. More concisely:

```
>> [1,2,3].object_id
=> 122210
>> a.object_id
=> 159300
```

So when we talk about each object having its own behavior, we mean exactly that here. You may be wondering at this point what uses there might be for such a feature. An interesting abstract example might be to note that class methods are actually just per-object behavior on an instance of the class Class, but I think it'd be more productive to give you a concrete example to sink your teeth into.

We're going to take a look at how to build a simple stubbing system for use in testing. In the testing chapter, I recommended *flexmock* for this purpose, and I still do, but going through the process of building a tiny stubbing framework will show a good use case for our current topic.

Our goal is to create a system that will generate canned responses to certain method calls, without modifying their original classes. This is an important feature, because we don't want our stubbed method calls to have a global effect during testing. Our target interface will be something like this:

```
user = User.new
Stubber.stubs(:logged_in?, :for => user, :returns => true)
user.logged_in? #=> true
```

We'll start with a very crude approach in *irb* to get a feel for the problem:

```
>> class User; end
=> nil
>> user = User.new
=> #<User:0x636b4>
>> def user.logged_in?
>>   true
>> end
=> nil
>> user.logged_in?
=> true
>> another_user = User.new
=> #<User:0x598d0>
>> another_user.logged_in?
NoMethodError: undefined method 'logged_in?' for #<User:0x598d0>
        from (irb):40
        from :0
```

This is essentially the behavior we want to capture: per-object customization that doesn't affect the class definition generally. Of course, to do this dynamically takes a little more work than the manual version. Our first hurdle is that the technique used in the earlier BlankSlate example doesn't work out of the box here:

```
>> user.define_method(:logged_in?) { true }
NoMethodError: undefined method 'define_method' for #<User:0x40ed90>
        from (irb):17
        from /Users/sandal/lib/ruby19_1/bin/irb:12:in '<main>'
```

As it turns out, each object hides its individual space for method definitions (called a singleton class) from plain view. However, we can reveal it by using a special syntax:

```
>> singleton = class << user; self; end
=> #<Class:#<User:0x40ed90>>
```

My earlier clues about class methods being per-object behavior on an instance of Class should come to mind here. We often use this syntax when we need to define a few class methods:

```
class A
  class << self
    def foo
      "hi"
    end

    def bar
      "bar"
    end
  end
end
```

The possible new thing here is that self can be replaced by any old object. So when you see class << user; self; end, what's really going on is we're just asking our object to give us back its singleton class. Once we have that in hand, we can define methods on it. Well, almost:

```
>> singleton.define_method(:logged_in?) { true }
NoMethodError: private method 'define_method' called for #<Class:#<User:0x40ed90>>
        from (irb):19
        from /Users/sandal/lib/ruby19_1/bin/irb:12:in '<main>'
```

Because what we're doing is not exactly business as usual, Ruby is throwing some red flags up reminding us to make sure we know what we're doing. But because we do, we can use send to bypass the access controls:

```
>> singleton.send(:define_method, :logged_in?) { true }
=> #<Proc:0x3fc1f4@(irb):20 (lambda)>
>> user.logged_in?
=> true
>> User.new.logged_in?
NoMethodError: undefined method 'logged_in?' for #<User:0x3f62f4>
        from (irb):22
        from /Users/sandal/lib/ruby19_1/bin/irb:12:in '<main>'
```

Perfect! Now our dynamic approach matches our manual one, and we can proceed to building a Stubber module. We'll be a bit flexible and assume that any stubbed method can take any number of arguments, rather than assuming a certain amount or none at all. Beyond that, the definition is just a compilation of what we've done so far:

```
module Stubber
  extend self

  def stubs(method, options={})
    singleton(options[:for]).send(:define_method, method) do |*a|
      options[:returns]
    end
  end


  def singleton(obj)
    class << obj; self; end
  end
end
```

With this simple implementation, we're in business, doing everything we set out for in the beginning:

```
>> user = User.new
=> #<User:0x445bec>
>> Stubber.stubs(:logged_in?, :for => user, :returns => true)
=> #<Proc:0x43faa8@(irb):28 (lambda)>
>> user.logged_in?
=> true
>> User.new.logged_in?
NoMethodError: undefined method 'logged_in?' for #<User:0x439fe0>
        from (irb):40
        from /Users/sandal/lib/ruby19_1/bin/irb:12:in '<main>'
```

Beyond what we've already discussed, another important thing to remember is that the block passed to `define_method()` is a closure, which allows us to access the local variables of the enclosing scope. This is why we can pass the return value as a parameter to `Stubber.stubs()` and have it returned from our dynamically defined method.

This is a general feature of `define_method`, and is not restricted to singleton objects. Here's a quick demonstration to emphasize this point:

```
class Statistics
  def self.stat(attribute, value)
    define_method(attribute) { value }
  end

  stat :foo, :bar
  stat :baz, :quux
end

stats = Statistics.new
stats.foo #=> :bar
stats.baz #=> :quux
```

Be sure to remember this about `define_method`. It is pretty much the only clean way to dynamically define a method with a custom return value.

Returning to the core topic, we see that `Stubber`'s main trick is that it makes use of customized behaviors for individual objects. However, to do this, we need to temporarily jump into the scope of the special space reserved for this purpose in our object, so that we can pull back a reference to it. This is what the whole `class << obj; self; end` is about. Once we have this object, we can dynamically define methods on it using `define_method()` as we would in a class definition, but we need to access it via `send()` because this method is made private on singleton classes. Once we do this, we take advantage of the fact that `define_method()`'s block argument is a closure with access to the enclosing `scope`'s local variables. We set the return value this way, and complete our task of per-object stubbing.

Although this is only a single example, it demonstrates a number of key concepts about per-object behavior in Ruby:

- Using per-object behavior usually makes the most sense when you don't want to define something at the per-class level.
- Objects in Ruby may have individually customized behaviors that can replace, supplement, or amend the functionality provided by their class definitions.
- Per-object behavior (known as singleton methods), can be implemented by gaining access to the singleton class of an object using the `class << obj` notation.
- `define_method` is made private on singleton classes, so `send()` is needed to utilize it.
- When implementing nondynamic per-object behavior, the familiar `def obj.some_method` syntax may be used.

All that we've discussed so far about per-object behavior is sort of a special case of a more general topic. Ruby's open class system allows us to amend and modify the behavior of pretty much everything we can imagine, in a number of ways. This is one of the fairly unique aspects of Ruby, so there is a whole lot we can discuss here. We'll start with an anecdote and then move into some more focused details.

Extending and Modifying Preexisting Code

When I introduce Ruby to new students, my first example is often meant to shake them up a little. It is relatively unremarkable, but to those who have not worked in languages with an open class system before, it can be quite alarming:

```ruby
class Fixnum

  def +(other)
    42
  end

end
```

The implications typically don't sink in until I fire up *irb*:

```
>> 2 + 2
=> 42
```

This demonstration is typically followed by a firm "never do this" reminder, but I continue to use it because it opens people's eyes to just how different Ruby is from most other languages. The standard response to this example is a flurry of questions about how Rubyists manage to make heads or tails of things when people can go all willy-nilly with extending classes as they see fit. That's what this section is all about.

We're going to talk about two related but somewhat distinct topics here. The first is extending Ruby classes with new behaviors by reopening classes; the second is actually modifying existing behaviors to fit new requirements. What separates the two is primarily the level of controversy, and hence the necessary level of care.

Because adding new functionality is the less dangerous of the two, we'll start with that and go over some of the specifics.

Adding New Functionality

In Chapter 1, *Driving Code Through Tests*, I mentioned and made use of a small extension to `Test::Unit` that dynamically defines test methods for us. As previously mentioned, we've borrowed this functionality from the granddaddy of Ruby extensions, ActiveSupport. We glossed over the implementation details before, but now that we're on the topic, this serves as a good example of the sorts of things you can accomplish by extending preexisting classes. We still don't need to worry about how it works; the focus is on how it extends `TestCase`:

```ruby
module Test::Unit
  class TestCase

    def self.must(name, &block)
      test_name = "test_#{name.gsub(/\s+/,'_')}".to_sym
      defined = instance_method(test_name) rescue false
      raise "#{test_name} is already defined in #{self}" if defined
      if block_given?
        define_method(test_name, &block)
      else
        define_method(test_name) do
          flunk "No implementation provided for #{name}"
        end
      end
    end

  end
end
```

To recap, the purpose of the `must()` method is to allow you to write your test cases a bit more cleanly. Here's an example from a board game I've been working on:

```ruby
class TestStone < Test::Unit::TestCase
  def setup
    @board = Pressman::Board.new
    @stone = Pressman::Stone.new(:black, :board   => @board,
                                         :position => [3,3] )
```

```
    end

    must "have a color" do
      assert_equal :black, @stone.color
    end

    must "have a default status of active" do
      assert_equal :active, @stone.status
    end

    must "be able to deactivate" do
      @stone.deactivate
      assert_equal :inactive, @stone.status
    end
  end
```

Without this extension, you would need to write the full test method names out in the traditional way:

```
class TestStone < Test::Unit::TestCase
  def setup
    @board = Pressman::Board.new
    @stone = Pressman::Stone.new(:black, :board   => @board,
                                         :position => [3,3] )
  end

  def test_must_have_a_color
    assert_equal :black, @stone.color
  end

  def test_must_be_active_by_default
    assert_equal :active, @stone.status
  end

  def test_must_be_able_to_deactivate
    @stone.deactivate
    assert_equal :inactive, @stone.status
  end
end
```

Although this code might be a bit more conceptually simple, it is also a bit less readable and doesn't have the same shortcuts that must() provides. For example, if you just write a single line like this:

```
must "do something eventually"
```

The extension will create a failing test for you. For those familiar with RSpec, this is similar to the pending test functionality you'd find there. Of course, by tweaking Test::Unit a bit for our own needs, we can focus on adding only the functionality we're missing, rather than jumping ship and moving to a whole other system. This is a key benefit of Ruby's open class system.

From what we've seen so far, it seems like adding functionality to a class definition is as easy as defining a new class. It uses the same syntax without any additional overhead. However, that is not to say it is without dangers.

If you can extend predefined objects for your own needs, so can everyone else, including any of the libraries you may depend on. Though we'll discuss safe techniques for combining partial definitions a little later, the technique shown here of simply opening up a class and defining a new method can result in naming clashes.

Consider two fictional units libraries, one of which converts things like `12.in` and `15.ft` into meters. We'll call this *metrics_conversions.rb*:

```
class Numeric
  def in
    self * 0.0254
  end

  def ft
    self.in * 12
  end
end
```

Our other library converts them into PDF points (1/72 of an inch). We'll call this *pdf_conversions.rb*:

```
class Numeric
  def in
    self * 72
  emd

  def ft
    self.in * 12
  end
end
```

If we load both libraries in, which one gets used? Let's ask *irb*:

```
>> require "metrics_conversions"
=> true
>> 1.in
=> 0.0254
>> require "pdf_conversions"
=> true
>> 1.in
=> 72
```

As you can see, whatever code is loaded last takes precedence. The way we have written it, the old definitions are completely clobbered and there is no easy way to recover them.

Because we'd almost never want two competing units systems loaded at the same time, it'd be better to see an error rather than a silent failure here. We can do that with the PDF conversion code and see what it looks like:

```
class Numeric

  [:in, :ft].each do |e|
    if instance_methods.include?(e)
      raise "Method '#{e}' exists, PDF Conversions will not override!"
    end
  end

  def in
    self * 72
  end

  def ft
    self.in * 12
  end

end
```

Loaded in on its own, this code runs without issue:

```
>> require "pdf_conversions"
=> true
>> 1.in
=> 72
>> 1.ft
=> 864
```

But when we revisit the original name clash problem, we have a much more explicit indicator of this issue:

```
>> require "metrics_conversions"
=> true
>> require "pdf_conversions"
RuntimeError: Method 'in' exists, PDF Conversions will not override!
    ...
```

Of course, if we do not modify *metrics_conversions.rb* as well, it will silently override *pdf_conversions.rb*. The ideal situation is for both libraries to use this technique, because then, regardless of the order in which they are required, the incompatibility between dependencies will be quickly spotted.

It is worth mentioning that it is possible for the library that is loaded first to detect the second library's attempt to override its definitions and act upon that, but this is generally considered aggressive and also results in fairly convoluted code, so it's better to address your own problems than the problems of others when it comes to extending an object's functionality.

So far, we've been talking about adding new functionality and dealing with accidental clashes. However, there are going to be times when you intentionally want to modify other code, while preserving some of its initial functionality. Ruby provides a number of ways to do that, so let's examine a few of them and weigh their risks and benefits.

Modification via Aliasing

We've used `alias_method` before for the purpose of making a new name point at an old method. This of course is where the feature gets its name: allowing you to create aliases for your methods.

But another interesting aspect of `alias_method` is that it doesn't simply create a new name for a method—it makes a copy of it. The best way to show what this means is through a trivial code example:

```
# define a method
class Foo
  def bar
    "baz"
  end
end

f = Foo.new
f.bar #=> "baz"


# Set up an alias
class Foo
  alias_method :kittens, :bar
end

f.kittens #=> "baz"

# redefine the original method
class Foo
  def bar
    "Dog"
  end
end

f.bar     #=> "Dog"
f.kittens #=> "baz"
```

As you can see here, even when we override the original method `bar()`, the alias `kittens()` still points at the original definition. This turns out to be a tremendously useful feature.

Because I like to keep contrived examples to a minimum, we're going to take a look at a real use of this technique in code that we use every day, RubyGems.

When RubyGems is loaded, it provides access to the libraries installed through its package manager. However, we typically don't need to load these packages through some alternative interface, we just use `Kernel#require`, as we do when we're loading in our own application files. The reason this is possible is because RubyGems patches `Kernel#require` using the exact technique we've been talking about here. This is what the code looks like for *custom_require.rb*:

```
module Kernel

  ##
  # The Kernel#require from before RubyGems was loaded.

  alias_method :gem_original_require, :require

  def require(path) # :doc:
    gem_original_require path
  rescue LoadError => load_error
    if load_error.message =~ /#{Regexp.escape path}\z/ and
        spec = Gem.searcher.find(path) then
      Gem.activate(spec.name, "= #{spec.version}")
      gem_original_require path
    else
      raise load_error
    end
  end

end
```

This code first makes a copy of the original **require** method, then begins to define its enhanced one. It first tries to call the original method to see whether the requested file can be loaded that way. If it can, then it is exactly equivalent to before RubyGems was loaded, and no further processing is needed.

However, if the original require fails to find the requested library, the error it raises is rescued, and then the RubyGems code goes to work looking for a matching gem to activate and add to the loadpath. If it finds one, it then goes back to the original **require**, which will work this time around because the necessary files have been added to the path.

If the code fails to find a gem that can be loaded, the original **LoadError** is raised. So this means that in the end, it reverts to the same failure condition as the original **require** method, making it completely invisible to the user.

This is a great example of responsible modification to a preexisting method. This code does not change the signature of the original method, nor does it change the possible return values or failure states. All it does is add some new intermediate functionality that will be transparent to the user if it is not needed.

However, this concept of copying methods via **alias_method** might seem a bit foreign to some folks. It also has a bit of a limitation, in that you need to keep coming up with new aliases, as aliases are subject to collision just the same as ordinary methods are.

For example, although this code works fine:

```
class A

  def count
    "one"
  end
```

```
alias_method :one, :count

def count
  "#{one} two"
end

alias_method :one_and_two, :count

def count
  "#{one_and_two} three"
end

end

A.new.count #=> "one two three"
```

if we rewrote it this way, we'd blow the stack:

```
class A

  def count
    "one"
  end

  alias_method :old_count, :count

  def count
    "#{old_count} two"
  end

  alias_method :old_count, :count

  def count
    "#{old_count} three"
  end

end
```

Accidentally introducing infinite recursion by aliasing an old method twice to the same name is definitely not fun. Although this problem is rarer than you might think, it's important to know that there is a way around it.

Per-Object Modification

If we move our modifications from the per-class level to the per-object level, we end up with a pretty nice solution that gets rid of aliasing entirely, and simply leverages Ruby's ordinary method resolution path. Here's how we'd do it:

```
class A
  def count
    "one"
  end
end
```

```ruby
module AppendTwo
  def count
    "#{super} two"
  end
end

module AppendThree
  def count
    "#{super} three"
  end
end

a = A.new
a.extend(AppendTwo)
a.extend(AppendThree)
a.count #=> "one two three"
```

Here, we have mixed two modules in an instance of A, each of them relying on a call to super(). Each method redefinition gets to use the same name, so we don't need to worry about naming clashes. Each call to super goes one level higher, until it reaches the top-level instance method as defined in the class.

Provided that all the code used by your application employs this approach instead of aliased method chaining, you end up with two main benefits: a pristine original class and no possibility for collisions. Because the amended functionality is included at the instance level, rather than in the class definition, you don't risk breaking other people's code as easily, either.

Note that not every single object can be meaningfully extended this way. Any objects that do not allow you to access their singleton space cannot take advantage of this technique. This mostly applies to things that are immediate values, such as numbers and symbols. But more generally, if you cannot use a call to new() to construct your object, chances are that you won't be able to use these tricks. In those cases, you'd need to revert to aliasing.

Even with this limitation, you can get pretty far with this approach. I don't want to end the section without one more practical example, so we'll look at a fun trick that earlier versions of Ruport did to manage a memory consumption issue in PDF::Writer.

Back before I maintained the Ruby PDF project, it went through a couple years of being relatively unsupported. However, when I ran into problems with it, Austin Ziegler was often willing to help me find workarounds for my own needs, even if he wasn't able to find the time to get them into a maintenance release for PDF::Writer.

One such fix resolved a memory consumption issue by setting up a hook for transaction_simple in PDF::Writer. I won't go into the details of how this works, but here is the module that implements it:

```
module PDFWriterMemoryPatch #:nodoc:
  unless self.class.instance_methods.include?("_post_transaction_rewind")
    def _post_transaction_rewind
      @objects.each { |e| e.instance_variable_set(:@parent,self) }
    end
  end
end
```

When people use Ruport, they use `PDF::Writer` indirectly through the object we instantiate for them. Because of this, it was easy to use the techniques described in this section. The following code should look similar to our earlier abstract examples:

```
class Ruport::Formatter::PDF

  # other implementation details omitted.

  def pdf_writer
    @pdf_writer ||= PDF::Writer.new( :paper       => paper_size || "LETTER",
                                     :orientation => paper_orientation || :portrait)
    @pdf_writer.extend(PDFWriterMemoryPatch)
  end
end
```

This code dynamically fixed an issue for Ruport users without making a global change that might conflict with other patches. Of course, it was no substitute for fixing the issue at its source, which eventually did happen, but it was a good stopgap procedure that made our users happy. When used appropriately, the power to resolve issues in other codebases whether or not you have direct access to the original code can really come in handy.

Here are the key points to remember from this section:

- All classes in Ruby are open, which means that object definitions are never finalized, and new behaviors can be added at runtime.
- To avoid clashes, conditional statements utilizing reflective features such as `instance_methods` and friends can be used to check whether a method is already defined before overwriting it.
- When intentionally modifying code, `alias_method` can be used to make a copy of the original method to fall back on.
- Whenever possible, per-object behavior is preferred. The `extend()` method comes in handy for this purpose.

So far, we've talked about extending objects others have created, as well as handling dynamic calls to objects we've created ourselves. But we can take this a step further by noticing that `Class` and `Module` are objects themselves, and as such, can be dynamically generated and molded to our needs.

Building Classes and Modules Programmatically

When I first started to get into higher-level Ruby, one of the most exciting finds was *why the lucky stiff*'s tiny web framework, Camping. This little package was packed with all sorts of wild techniques I had never seen before, including a way to write controllers to handle URL routing that just seemed out of this world:

```ruby
module Camping::Controllers

  class Edit < R '/edit/(\d+)'
    def get(id)
      # ...
    end
  end

end
```

It didn't even occur to me that such things could be syntactically possible in Ruby, but upon seeing how it worked, it all seemed to make sense. We're not going to look at the real implementation here, but I can't resist pulling back the curtain just a little so that you can see the basic mechanics of how something like this might work.

The key secret here is that `R` is actually just a method, `Camping::Controllers::R()`. This method happens to return a class, so that means you can inherit from it. Obviously, there are a few more tricks involved, as the class you inherit from would need to track its children, but we'll get to those topics later.

For now, let's start with a simple example of how parameterized subclassing might work, and then move on to more examples of working with anonymous classes and modules in general.

First, we need a method that returns some classes. We'll call it `Mystery()`:

```ruby
def Mystery(secret)
  if secret == "chunky bacon"
    Class.new do
      def message
        "You rule!"
      end
    end
  else
    Class.new do
      def message
        "Don't make me cry"
      end
    end
  end
end
```

Notice here that we call `Class.new()` with a block that serves as its class definition. New anonymous classes are generated on every call, which means they're basically throwaway here. That is, until we make use of them via subclassing:

```
class Win < Mystery "chunky bacon"

  def who_am_i
    "I am win!"
  end

end

class EpicFail < Mystery "smooth ham"

  def who_am_i
    "I am teh fail"
  end

end
```

Now, when we build up some instances, you can see what all of this bought us:

```
a = Win.new
a.message  #=> "You rule!"
a.who_am_i #=> "I am win!"

b = EpicFail.new
b.message  #=> "Don't make me cry"
b.who_am_i #=> "I am teh fail"
```

Even though this example doesn't really do anything useful on its own, the key concepts are still ripe for the picking. We can see that `Mystery()` conditionally chooses which class to inherit from. Furthermore, the classes generated by `Mystery()` are anonymous, meaning they don't have some constant identifier out there somewhere, and that the method is actually generating class objects, not just returning references to preexisting definitions. Finally, we can see that the subclasses behave ordinarily, in the sense that you can add custom functionality to them as needed.

When you put all of these ideas together, you might already have plans for how you could make use of this technique. Then again, it can't hurt to go over some more real-world code.

We're going to do a quick walk-through of the abstract formatting system at the heart of Ruport 2.0, called Fatty.[†] Despite the name, the implementation is quite slim and fairly easy to explain.

The main thing this library does is cleanly split out format-specific code, while handling parameter passing and validations. A simple example of using Fatty to just print out a greeting to someone in PDF and plain text might look like this:

```
options = { :first_name => "Chenoa", :last_name  => "Siegenthaler" }
MyReport.render_file("foo.pdf", options)
puts MyReport.render(:txt, options)
```

---

† Format abstraction toolkit-ty. See *http://github.com/sandal/fatty*.

We have support for a nonmagical interface, which—even without seeing the underlying implementation—shouldn't surprise anyone:

```ruby
class MyReport < Fatty::Formatter
  module Helpers
    def full_name
      "#{params[:first_name]} #{params[:last_name]}"
    end
  end

  class Txt < Fatty::Format
    include MyReport::Helpers

    def render
      "Hello #{full_name} from plain text"
    end
  end

  # use a custom Fatty::Format subclass for extra features
  class PDF < Prawn::FattyFormat
    include MyReport::Helpers

    def render
      doc.text "Hello #{full_name} from PDF"
      doc.render
    end
  end

  formats.update(:txt => Txt, :pdf => PDF)
end
```

This looks almost entirely like ordinary Ruby subclassing and module inclusion. The only tricky thing might be the `formats()` class method, but it just points at a hash that links file extensions to the classes that handle them.

All in all, this doesn't look too bad. But it turns out that we can clean up the interface substantially if we use a bit of dynamic creativity. The following code is functionally equivalent to what you've just seen:

```ruby
class MyReport < Fatty::Formatter
  required_params :first_name, :last_name

  helpers do
    def full_name
      "#{params[:first_name]} #{params[:last_name]}"
    end
  end

  format :txt do
    def render
      "Hello #{full_name} from plain text"
    end
  end
```

```
format :pdf, :base => Prawn::FattyFormat do
  def render
    doc.text "Hello #{full_name} from PDF"
    doc.render
  end
end
```

```
end
```

Our class definitions have been transformed into a domain-specific interface for format abstraction. Aside from having nicer names for things and a more pleasant syntax, we have gained some side benefits. We no longer need to manually map file extensions to class names: the format() method handles that for us. We also don't need to manually include our helper module; that is taken care of as well. As these are the two things that fit well with this topic, let's take a look at how both of them are handled.

First, we'll take a look at the format() helper, which is a simple one-liner:

```
def format(name, options={}, &block)
  formats[name] = Class.new(options[:base] || Fatty::Format, &block)
end
```

When this class method is called with just a block, it generates an anonymous subclass of Fatty::Format, and then stores this subclass keyed by extension name in the formats hash. In most cases, this is enough to do the trick. However, sometimes you will want to inherit from a base class that implements some additional helpers, as we did with Prawn::FattyFormat. This is why options[:base] is checked first. This one line of code with its two possible cases covers how the class definitions are created and stored.

We can now turn our eyes to the helpers() method, which is another one-liner. This one has two possible uses as well, but we showed only one in our example:

```
def helpers(helper_module=nil, &block)
  @helpers = helper_module || Module.new(&block)
end
```

As you can see here, modules can also be built up anonymously using a block. This code gives the user a choice between doing that or providing the name of a module like this:

```
class MyReport < Fatty::Formatter

  helpers MyHelperModule

  #...
end
```

Of course, the more interesting case is when you use the block form, but only marginally so. The real work happens in render():

```
def render(format, params={})
  validate(format, params)

  format_obj = formats[format].new    ❶
  format_obj.extend(@helpers) if @helpers    ❷
  format_obj.params = params
  format_obj.validate
  format_obj.render
end
```

I've marked the two lines we're interested in:

❶ This line uses the `formats` hash to look up our anonymous class by extension name.

❷ This line mixes in our helper module, whether it's a reference to an explicitly defined module or, as in our example, a block that defines the anonymous module's body.

The rest of the method is fairly self-explanatory but inconsequential. It was the dynamic class/module creation we were interested in—the rest is just mundane detail particular to Fatty's implementation.

With just a few lines of code, we've been able to show just how powerful Ruby is when you programmatically generate higher-level objects such as classes and modules. In this particular example, we've used this technique for interface cleanup and the associated organizational benefits. You may find a lot of other uses, or none at all, depending on your work.

Like with many other concepts in this chapter, we've truly been cooking with gas here. Let's go over a few tips to help you avoid getting burned, then hit one more short topic before finishing up:

- Classes and modules can be instantiated like any other object. Both constructors accept a block that can be used to define methods as needed.
- To construct an anonymous subclass, call `Class.new(MySuperClass)`.
- Parameterized subclassing can be used to add logic to the subclassing process, and essentially involves a method returning a class object, either anonymous or explicitly defined.

Registering Hooks and Callbacks

In the very beginning of the chapter, we looked at the `BlankSlate` class, and I had mentioned that there was some additional work that needed to be done to deal with things such as new method definitions on `Object` or module inclusion.

To recap the situation, `BlankSlate` is supposed to be a "naked" base class we can inherit from that doesn't reveal any of its methods until we tell it to. We have already covered the ins and outs of how `BlankSlate` hides its initial instance methods and how it can selectively reveal them. The problem that remains to be solved is how to accommodate for changes that happen at runtime.

Detecting Newly Added Functionality

As we've seen, due to the open class system, Ruby object definitions are never really finalized. As a consequence, if you add a method to `Object`, it becomes available immediately to every object in the system except instances of `BasicObject`. To put words into code, here's what that means:

```
>> a  = "foo"
=> "foo"
>> b = [1,2,3]
=> [1, 2, 3]
>> class C; end
=> nil
>> c = C.new
=> #<C:0x42a400>
>> class Object
>>   def party
>>      "wooohoo!"
>>   end
>> end
=> nil
>> a.party
=> "wooohoo!"
>> b.party
=> "wooohoo!"
>> c.party
=> "wooohoo!"
```

Now everyone is partying, except `BlankSlate`. Or more accurately, `BlankSlate` is being forced to party when it doesn't want to. The solution is to set up a hook that watches for newly defined methods and hides them:

```ruby
class Object
  class << self
    alias_method :blank_slate_method_added, :method_added

    # Detect method additions to Object and remove them in the
    # BlankSlate class.
    def method_added(name)
      result = blank_slate_method_added(name)
      return result if self != Object
      BlankSlate.hide(name)
      result
    end

  end
end
```

This code uses techniques discussed earlier in this chapter to modify the behavior of a core Ruby function, `Object.method_added()`, while remaining transparent for the ordinary use cases. Classes inherited from `Object` will not affect `BlankSlate`, so this code is set to short-circuit in those cases. However, if `self` happens to be `Object`, the code tells

BlankSlate to hide it and then returns the results of the original method_added() function that has been aliased here.

You'd think that would do the trick, but as it turns out, Object includes the module Kernel. This means we need to track changes over there too, using nearly the same approach:

```ruby
module Kernel
  class << self
    alias_method :blank_slate_method_added, :method_added

    # Detect method additions to Kernel and remove them in the
    # BlankSlate class.
    def method_added(name)
      result = blank_slate_method_added(name)
      return result if self != Kernel
      BlankSlate.hide(name)
      result
    end
  end
end
```

There isn't much new here, so it's safe to say that if you understood how this worked on Object, you can assume this is just more of the same stuff. However, it does give a hint about another problem: inclusion of modules into Object at runtime.

First, another quick illustration of the issue:

```ruby
>> module A
>>   def foo
>>     "bar"
>>   end
>> end
=> nil
>> a = Object.new
=> #<Object:0x428ca4>
>> a.extend(A)
=> #<Object:0x428ca4>
>> a.foo
=> "bar"
>> module A
>>   def kittens
>>     "meow"
>>   end
>> end
=> nil
>> a.kittens
=> "meow"
```

Every module included in an object is like a back door for future expansion. When you first fire up Ruby, the only module you need to worry about is Kernel, but after that, all bets are off. So we end up jumping up one level higher to take care of module inclusion dynamically:

```
class Module
  alias blankslate_original_append_features append_features
  def append_features(mod)
    result = blankslate_original_append_features(mod)
    return result if mod != Object
    instance_methods.each do |name|
      BlankSlate.hide(name)
    end
    result
  end
end
```

In this example, `mod` is the class that was modified by a module inclusion. As in the other hooks, `BlankSlate` makes an alias of the original, calls it, and simply returns its result if the modified object isn't `Object` itself. In the case where a module is mixed into `Object`, `BlankSlate` needs to wipe out the instance methods added to its own class definition. After this, it returns the result of the original `append_features()` call.

This pretty much describes the key aspects of capturing newly added functionality at the top level. You can of course apply these hooks to individual classes lower in the chain and make use of them in other ways.

Tracking Inheritance

When you write unit tests via `Test::Unit`, you typically just subclass `Test::Unit::Test Case`, which figures out how to find your tests for you. Though we won't look at the details for how that is actually implemented, we can take a naive shot at it on our own using the `Class#inherited` hook.

We're going to implement the code to make this example functional:

```
class SimpleTest < SimpleTestHarness

  def setup
    puts "Setting up @string"
    @string = "Foo"
  end

  def test_string_must_be_foo
    answer = (@string == "Foo" ? "yes" : "no")
    puts "@string == 'Foo': " << answer
  end

  def test_string_must_be_bar
    answer = (@string == "bar" ? "yes" : "no")
    puts "@string == 'bar': " << answer
  end

end

class AnotherTest < SimpleTestHarness
```

```
    def test_another_lame_example
      puts "This got called, isn't that good enough?"
    end

    def helper_method
      puts "But you'll never see this"
    end

    def a_test_method
      puts "Or this"
    end

  end

  SimpleTestHarness.run
```

We must first identify each subclass as a test case, and store it in an array until
SimpleTestHarness.run is called. Like Test::Unit and other common Ruby testing
frameworks, we'll wipe the slate clean by reinstantiating our tests for each test method,
running a setup method if it exists. We will follow the Test::Unit convention and run
only the methods whose names begin with test_. We haven't implemented any assertions or anything like that, because it's not really the point of this exercise.

The task can easily be broken down into two parts: detecting the subclasses, and later
manipulating them. The first part is where we use the inherited hook, as you can see:

```
  class SimpleTestHarness

    class << self

      def inherited(base)
        tests << base
      end

      def tests
        @tests ||= []
      end

    end

  end
```

Surprisingly enough, that was relatively painless. Each time a new subclass is derived
from SimpleTestHarness, the inherited() hook is called, passing in the subclass as
base. If we just store these in an array at class level, that's all we need for writing a test
runner. Adding in SimpleTestHarness.run, our full class looks like this:

```
  class SimpleTestHarness
    class << self

      def inherited(base)
        tests << base
      end
```

```
      def tests
        @tests ||= []
      end

      def run
        tests.each do |t|
          t.instance_methods.grep(/^test_/).each do |m|
            test_case = t.new
            test_case.setup if test_case.respond_to?(:setup)
            test_case.send(m)
          end
        end
      end
   end

  end
```

This code walks over each class in the **tests** array, and then filters out the names of the instance methods that begin with **test_**. For each of these methods, it creates a new instance of the test case, calls **setup** if it exists, and then uses **send** to dynamically invoke the individual test. With this class definition in place, the original set of tests for which we were trying to implement this functionality can actually run, resulting in the following output:

```
Setting up @string
@string == 'Foo': yes
Setting up @string
@string == 'bar': no
This got called, isn't that good enough?
```

Pretty cool, huh? These hooks essentially provide an event system, giving you a way to handle changes to Ruby in a dynamic way. If you've ever had to do GUI programming or anything else that involved dynamic callbacks, you already grasp the core ideas behind this concept. The only difference is that rather than capturing a button press, you're capturing an inheritance event or an added method. When used appropriately, this can be a very powerful technique.

We're about to wrap things up here, but before we do, it's worth showing the equivalent of what we just did, but for modules. There happens to be a fairly standard Ruby idiom that takes advantage of that hook, so it's one you shouldn't skip over.

Tracking Mixins

You probably already know that if you use **include** to mix a module into a class, the methods become available at the instance level, and that if you use **extend**, they become available at the class level. However, an issue comes up when you want to provide both class and instance methods from a single module.

A naive workaround might look like this:

```ruby
module MyFeatures

  module ClassMethods
    def say_hello
      "Hello"
    end

    def say_goodbye
      "Goodbye"
    end
  end

  def say_hello
    "Hello from #{self}!"
  end

  def say_goodbye
    "Goodbye from #{self}"
  end
end


class A
  include MyFeatures
  extend MyFeatures::ClassMethods
end
```

If we test this out in *irb*, we see that it does work:

```ruby
?> A.say_hello
=> "Hello"
>> obj = A.new
=> #<A:0x1ee628>
>> obj.say_hello
=> "Hello from #<A:0x1ee628>!"
>> obj.say_goodbye
=> "Goodbye from #<A:0x1ee628>"
>> A.say_goodbye
=> "Goodbye"
```

Having to manually do the extend call seems a bit ugly, though. It's not terrible when we are writing it ourselves, but it would be a little weird to do this any time you used a third-party module. Of course, that's where a nice little hook comes in handy. The following code is functionally equivalent to our previous example:

```ruby
module MyFeatures

  module ClassMethods
    def say_hello
      "Hello"
    end

    def say_goodbye
      "Goodbye"
    end
  end
```

```
  def self.included(base)
    base.extend(ClassMethods)
  end

  def say_hello
    "Hello from #{self}!"
  end

  def say_goodbye
    "Goodbye from #{self}"
  end

end # MyFeatures

class A
  include MyFeatures
end
```

Here, we were able to get rid of the manual extend call and automate it through the included hook. This hook gets called every time the module is included into a class, and passes the class object as the base object. From here, we simply call extend as before; it is just now wrapped up in the hook rather than manually specified in the class definition. Although this may seem like a small change, having a single entry point to the module's features is a major win, as it keeps implementation details off the mind as much as possible when simply including the module.

Although we could dig up more and more hooks provided by Ruby, we've already covered most of the ones that are used fairly often. There are certainly plenty that we didn't cover, and you might want to read over the core Ruby documentation a bit to discover some of the more obscure ones if you're either curious or have an uncommon need.

For the hooks we did cover, here are some things to remember:

• If you are making changes to any hooks at the top level, be sure to safely modify them via aliasing, so as not to globally break their behavior.

• Hooks can be implemented on a particular class or module, and will catch everything below them.

• Most hooks either capture a class, a module, or a name of a method and are executed after an event takes place. This means that it's not really possible to intercept an event before it happens, but it is usually possible to undo one once it is.

And with that, we can wrap up this intense chapter with some closing notes and a final challenge to the adventurous.

Conclusions

I found myself getting physically tired writing this chapter. If you feel that way after reading it, I don't really blame you. People will tell you again and again that this sort of coding is extremely hard or fueled by some sort of magic. Others will tell you it's the bee's knees and that you should use it all the time, everywhere, whenever you can. Neither statement is true.

The truth of the matter is that taken individually, each of Ruby's dynamic features is relatively straightforward, and can be a valuable tool if used properly. But looking at all of this stuff and trying to use it as much as possible in your code would be absolutely overwhelming.

My general rule of thumb is to ignore all of these advanced Ruby features until my code illustrates a need for them. If I write several method calls that appear to do almost the same thing with a different name, I might be able to leverage `method_missing`. If I want to endow certain objects with some handy shortcuts, but leave the option of instantiating a simple, unadorned core object, I might look into mixing in some singleton methods using `extend`. By the end of the day, in a large or complicated application, I may end up using a large subset of the techniques discussed here. But if I started out by thinking about what dynamic features my code needed rather than what requirements it must satisfy, development would come to a confusing, grinding halt.

So here's my advice about making use of the information in this chapter: just make a mental note of what you've learned here, and then wait until some code jumps out at you and seems to be begging to be cleaned up using one of the techniques shown here. If it works out well, you've probably made a good decision. If it seems like more trouble than it's worth, bail out and wait for the next bit of code to alert you again. Keep repeating this process and you'll find a good balance for how dynamic your code really needs to be.

Because this chapter is focused on a series of topics that are sort of a rite of passage as far as Ruby development goes, I'd like to end with a bit of code that might challenge your understanding a bit.

What follows is a simplistic approximation of Camping's routing magic. It is meant to help you learn, but is left without comments so that you can figure it out on your own. It does not introduce any new concepts beyond what was discussed in this chapter, so if you can figure out how it works, you can be sure that you have a fairly solid grasp of what we've been talking about here.

Enjoy!

```ruby
module NaiveCampingRoutes

  extend self

  def R(url)
    route_lookup = routes

    klass = Class.new
    meta  = class << klass; self; end
    meta.send(:define_method, :inherited) do |base|
      raise "Already defined" if route_lookup[url]
      route_lookup[url] = base
    end
    klass
  end

  def routes
    @routes ||= {}
  end

  def process(url, params={})
    routes[url].new.get(params)
  end
end

module NaiveCampingRoutes
  class Hello < R '/hello'
    def get(params)
      puts "hello #{params[:name]}"
    end
  end

  class Goodbye < R '/goodbye'
    def get(params)
      puts "goodbye #{params[:name]}"
    end
  end
end

NaiveCampingRoutes.process('/hello', :name => "greg")
NaiveCampingRoutes.process('/goodbye', :name => "joe")
```

## CHAPTER 4

Text Processing and File Management

Ruby fills a lot of the same roles that languages such as Perl and Python do. Because of this, you can expect to find first-rate support for text processing and file management. Whether it's parsing a text file with some regular expressions or building some *nix-style filter applications, Ruby can help make life easier.

However, much of Ruby's I/O facilities are tersely documented at best. It is also relatively hard to find good resources that show you general strategies for attacking common text-processing tasks. This chapter aims to expose you to some good tricks that you can use to simplify your text-processing needs as well as sharpen your skills when it comes to interacting with and managing files on your system.

As in other chapters, we'll start off by looking at some real open source code—this time, a simple parser for an Adobe Font Metrics (AFM) file. This example will expose you to text processing in its setting. We'll then follow up with a number of detailed sections that look at different practices that will help you master basic I/O skills. Armed with these techniques, you'll be able to take on all sorts of text-processing and file-management tasks with ease.

Line-Based File Processing with State Tracking

Processing a text document line by line does not mean that we're limited to extracting content in a uniform way, treating each line identically. Some files have more structure than that, but can still benefit from being processed linearly. We're now going to look over a small parser that illustrates this general idea by selecting different ways to extract our data based on what section of a file we are in.

The code in this section was written by James Edward Gray II as part of Prawn's AFM support. Though the example itself is domain-specific, we won't get hung up in the particular details of this parser. Instead, we'll be taking a look at the general approach for how to build a state-aware parser that operates on an efficient line-by-line basis. Along the way, you'll pick up some basic I/O tips and tricks as well as see the important role that regular expressions often play in this sort of task.

Before we look at the actual parser, we can take a glance at the sort of data we're dealing with. AFM files are essentially font glyph measurements and specifications, so they tend to look a bit like a configuration file of sorts. Some of these things are simply straight key/value pairs, such as:

```
CapHeight 718
XHeight 523
Ascender 718
Descender -207
```

Others are organized sets of values within a section, as in the following example:

```
StartCharMetrics 315
C 32 ; WX 278 ; N space ; B 0 0 0 0 ;
C 33 ; WX 278 ; N exclam ; B 90 0 187 718 ;
C 34 ; WX 355 ; N quotedbl ; B 70 463 285 718 ;
C 35 ; WX 556 ; N numbersign ; B 28 0 529 688 ;
C 36 ; WX 556 ; N dollar ; B 32 -115 520 775 ;
....
EndCharMetrics
```

Sections can be nested within each other, making things more interesting. The data across the file does not fit a uniform format, as each section represents a different sort of thing. However, we can come up with patterns to parse data in each section that we're interested in, because they are consistent within their sections. We also are interested in only a subset of the sections, so we can safely ignore some of them. This is the essence of the task we needed to accomplish, but as you may have noticed, it's a fairly abstract pattern that we can reuse. Many documents with a simple section-based structure can be worked with using the approach shown here.

The code that follows is essentially a simple finite state machine that keeps track of what section the current line appears in. It attempts to parse the opening or closing of a section first, and then it uses this information to determine a parsing strategy for the current line. We simply skip the sections that we're not interested in parsing.

We end up with a very straightforward solution. The whole parser is reduced to a simple iteration over each line of the file, which manages a stack of nested sections, while determining whether and how to parse the current line.

We'll see the parts in more detail in just a moment, but here is the whole AFM parser that extracts all the information we need to properly render Adobe fonts in Prawn:

```
def parse_afm(file_name)
  section = []

  File.foreach(file_name) do |line|
    case line
    when /^Start(\w+)/
      section.push $1
      next
    when /^End(\w+)/
      section.pop
      next
```

```
      end

      case section
      when ["FontMetrics", "CharMetrics"]
        next unless line =~ /^CH?\s/

        name                  = line[/\bN\s+(\.?\w+)\s*;/, 1]
        @glyph_widths[name]   = line[/\bWX\s+(\d+)\s*;/, 1].to_i
        @bounding_boxes[name] = line[/\bB\s+([^;]+);/, 1].to_s.rstrip
      when ["FontMetrics", "KernData", "KernPairs"]
        next unless line =~ /^KPX\s+(\.?\w+)\s+(\.?\w+)\s+(-?\d+)/
        @kern_pairs[[$1, $2]] = $3.to_i
      when ["FontMetrics", "KernData", "TrackKern"], ["FontMetrics", "Composites"]
        next
      else
        parse_generic_afm_attribute(line)
      end
    end
  end
```

You could try to understand the particular details if you'd like, but it's also fine to black-box the expressions used here so that you can get a sense of the overall structure of the parser. Here's what the code looks like if we do that for all but the patterns that determine the section nesting:

```
def parse_afm(file_name)
  section = []

  File.foreach(file_name) do |line|
    case line
    when /^Start(\w+)/
      section.push $1
      next
    when /^End(\w+)/
      section.pop
      next
    end

    case section
    when ["FontMetrics", "CharMetrics"]
      parse_char_metrics(line)
    when ["FontMetrics", "KernData", "KernPairs"]
      parse_kern_pairs(line)
    when ["FontMetrics", "KernData", "TrackKern"], ["FontMetrics", "Composites"]
      next
    else
      parse_generic_afm_attribute(line)
    end
  end
end
```

With these simplifications, it's very clear that we're looking at an ordinary finite state machine that is acting upon the lines of the file. It also makes it easier to notice what's actually going on.

The first **case** statement is just a simple way to check which section we're currently looking at, updating the stack as necessary as we move in and out of sections:

```
case line
when /^Start(\w+)/
  section.push $1
  next
when /^End(\w+)/
  section.pop
  next
end
```

If we find a section beginning or end, we skip to the next line, as we know there is nothing else to parse. Otherwise, we know that we have to do some real work, which is done in the second **case** statement:

```
case section
when ["FontMetrics", "CharMetrics"]
  next unless line =~ /^CH?\s/

  name                  = line[/\bN\s+(\.?\w+)\s*;/, 1]
  @glyph_widths[name]   = line[/\bWX\s+(\d+)\s*;/, 1].to_i
  @bounding_boxes[name] = line[/\bB\s+([^;]+);/, 1].to_s.rstrip
when ["FontMetrics", "KernData", "KernPairs"]
  next unless line =~ /^KPX\s+(\.?\w+)\s+(\.?\w+)\s+(-?\d+)/
  @kern_pairs[[$1, $2]] = $3.to_i
when ["FontMetrics", "KernData", "TrackKern"], ["FontMetrics", "Composites"]
  next
else
  parse_generic_afm_attribute(line)
end
```

Here, we've got four different ways to handle our line of text. In the first two cases, we process the lines that we need to as we walk through the section, extracting the bits of information we need and ignoring the information we're not interested in.

In the third case, we identify certain sections to skip and simply resume processing the next line if we are currently within that section.

Finally, if the other cases fail to match, our last **case** scenario assumes that we're dealing with a simple key/value pair, which is handled by a private helper method in Prawn. Because it does not provide anything different to look at than the first two sections of this **case** statement, we can safely ignore how it works without missing anything important.

However, the interesting thing that you might have noticed is that the first case and the second case use two different ways of extracting values. The code that processes CharMetrics uses String#[ ], whereas the code handling KernPairs uses Perl-style global match variables. The reason for this is largely convenience. The following two lines of code are equivalent:

```
name = line[/\bN\s+(\.?\w+)\s*;/, 1]
name = line =~ /\bN\s+(\.?\w+)\s*;/ && $1
```

There are still other ways to handle your captured matches (such as `MatchData` via `String#match`), but we'll get into those later. For now, it's simply worth knowing that when you're trying to extract a single matched capture, `String#[]` does the job well, but if you need to deal with more than one, you need to use another approach. We see this clearly in the second case:

```
next unless line =~ /^KPX\s+(\.?\w+)\s+(\.?\w+)\s+(-?\d+)/
@kern_pairs[[$1, $2]] = $3.to_i
```

This code is a bit clever, as the line that assigns the values to `@kern_pairs` gets executed only when there is a successful match. When the match fails, it will return `nil`, causing the parser to skip to the next line for processing.

We could continue studying this example, but we'd then be delving into the specifics, and those details aren't important for remembering this simple general pattern.

When dealing with a structured document that can be processed by discrete rules for each section, the general approach is simple and does not typically require pulling the entire document into memory or doing multiple passes through the data.

Instead, you can do the following:

- Identify the beginning and end markers of sections with a pattern.
- If sections are nested, maintain a stack that you update before further processing of each line.
- Break up your extraction code into different cases and select the right one based on the current section you are in.
- When a line cannot be processed, skip to the next one as soon as possible, using the `next` keyword.
- Maintain state as you normally would, processing whatever data you need.

By following these basic guidelines, you can avoid overthinking your problem, while still saving clock cycles and keeping your memory footprint low. Although the code here solves a particular problem, it can easily be adapted to fit a wide range of basic document processing needs.

This introduction has hopefully provided a taste of what text processing in Ruby is all about. The rest of the chapter will provide many more tips and tricks, with a greater focus on the particular topics. Feel free to jump around to the things that interest you most, but I'm hoping all of the sections have something interesting to offer—even to seasoned Rubyists.

Regular Expressions

At the time of writing this chapter, I was spending some time watching the Dow Jones Industrial Average, as the world was in the middle of a major financial meltdown. If you're wondering what this has to do with Ruby or regular expressions, take a quick look at the following code:

```
require "open-uri"
loop do
  puts( open("http://finance.google.com/finance?cid=983582").read[
  /<span class="\w+" id="ref_983582_c">([+-]?\d+\.\d+)/m, 1] )
  sleep(30)
end
```

In just a couple of lines, I was able to throw together a script that would poll Google Finance and pull down the current average price of the Dow. This sort of "find a needle in the haystack" extraction is what regular expressions are all about.

Of course, the art of constructing regular expressions is often veiled in mystery. Even simple patterns such as this one might make some folks feel a bit uneasy:

```
/<span class="\w+" id="ref_983582_c">([+-]?\d+\.\d+)/m
```

This expression is simple by comparison to some other examples we can show, but it still makes use of a number of regular expression concepts. All in one line, we can see the use of character classes (both general and special), escapes, quantifiers, groups, and a switch that enables multiline matching.

Patterns are dense because they are written in a special syntax, which acts as a sort of domain language for matching and extracting text. The reason that it may be considered daunting is that this language is made up of so few special characters:

```
\ [ ] . ^ $ ? * + { } | ( )
```

At its heart, regular expressions are nothing more than a facility to do find and replace operations. This concept is so familiar that anyone who has used a word processor has a strong grasp on it. Using a regex, you can easily replace all instances of the word "Mitten" with "Kitten", just like your favorite text editor or word processor can:

```
some_string.gsub(/\bMitten\b/,"Kitten")
```

Many programmers get this far and stop. They learn to use regex as if it were a necessary evil rather than an essential technique. We can do better than that. In this section, we'll look at a few guidelines for how to write effective patterns that do what they're supposed to without getting too convoluted. I'm assuming you've done your homework and are at least familiar with regex basics as well as Ruby's pattern syntax. If that's not the case, pick up your favorite language reference and take a few minutes to review the fundamentals.

As long as you can comfortably read the first example in this section, you're ready to move on. If you can convince yourself that writing regular expressions is actually much easier than people tend to think it is, the tips and tricks to follow shouldn't cause you to break a sweat.

Don't Work Too Hard

Despite being such a compact format, it's relatively easy to write bloated patterns if you don't consciously remember to keep things clean and tight. We'll now take a look at a couple sources of extra fat and see how to trim them down.

Alternation is a very powerful regex tool. It allows you to match one of a series of potential sequences. For example, if you want to match the name "James Gray" but also match "James gray", "james Gray", and "james gray", the following code will do the trick:

```
>> ["James Gray", "James gray", "james gray", "james Gray"].all? { |e|
?>   e.match(/James|james Gray|gray/) }
=> true
```

However, you don't need to work so hard. You're really talking about possible alternations of simply two characters, not two full words. You could write this far more efficiently using a character class:

```
>> ["James Gray", "James gray", "james gray", "james Gray"].all? { |e|
?>   e.match(/[Jj]ames [Gg]ray/) }
=> true
```

This makes your pattern clearer and also will result in a much better optimization in Ruby's regex engine. So in addition to looking better, this code is actually faster.

In a similar vein, it is unnecessary to use explicit character classes when a shortcut will do. To match a four-digit number, we could write:

```
/[0-9][0-9][0-9][0-9]/
```

which can of course be cleaned up a bit using repetitions:

```
/[0-9]{4}/
```

However, we can do even better by using the special class built in for this:

```
/\d{4}/
```

It pays to learn what shortcuts are available to you. Here's a quick list for further study, in case you're not already familiar with them:

```
. \s \S \w \W \d \D
```

Each one of these shortcuts corresponds to a literal character class that is more verbose when written out. Using shortcuts increases clarity and decreases the chance of bugs creeping in via ill-defined patterns. Though it may seem a bit terse at first, you'll be able to sight-read them with ease over time.

Anchors Are Your Friends

One way to match my name in a string is to write the following simple pattern:

```
string =~ /Gregory Brown/
```

However, consider the following:

```
>> "matched" if "Mr. Gregory Browne".match(/Gregory Brown/)
=> "matched"
```

Oftentimes we mean "match this phrase," but we write "match this sequence of characters." The solution is to make use of anchors to clarify what we mean.

Sometimes we want to match only if a string starts with a phrase:

```
>> phrases = ["Mr. Gregory Browne", "Mr. Gregory Brown is cool",
              "Gregory Brown is cool", "Gregory Brown"]

>> phrases.grep /\AGregory Brown\b/
=> ["Gregory Brown is cool", "Gregory Brown"]
```

Other times we want to ensure that the string contains the phrase:

```
>> phrases.grep /\bGregory Brown\b/
=> ["Mr. Gregory Brown is cool", "Gregory Brown is cool", "Gregory Brown"]
```

And finally, sometimes we want to ensure that the string matches an exact phrase:

```
>> phrases.grep /\AGregory Brown\z/
=> ["Gregory Brown"]
```

Although I am using English names and phrases here for simplicity, this can of course be generalized to encompass any sort of matching pattern. You could be verifying that a sequence of numbers fits a certain form, or something equally abstract. The key thing to take away from this is that when you use anchors, you're being much more explicit about how you expect your pattern to match, which in most cases means that you'll have a better chance of catching problems faster, and an easier time remembering what your pattern was supposed to do.

An interesting thing to note about anchors is that they don't actually match characters. Instead, they match between characters to allow you to assert certain expectations about your strings. So when you use something like \b, you are actually matching between one of \w\W, \W\w, \A, \z. In English, that means that you're transitioning from a word character to a nonword character, or from a nonword character to a word character, or you're matching the beginning or end of the string. If you review the use of \b in the previous examples, it should now be very clear how anchors work.

The full list of available anchors in Ruby is \A, \Z, \z, ^, $, and \b. Each has its own merits, so be sure to read up on them.

Use Caution When Working with Quantifiers

One of the most common antipatterns I picked up when first learning regular expressions was to make use of .* everywhere. Though this practice may seem innocent, it is similar to my bad habit of using `rm -Rf` on the command line all the time instead of just `rm`. Both can result in catastrophe when used incorrectly.

But maybe you're not as crazy as I am. Instead, maybe you've been writing innocent things like /(\d*)Foo/ to match any number of digits prepended to the word "Foo":

For some cases, this works great:

```
>> "1234Foo"[/(\d*)Foo/,1]
=> "1234"
```

But does this surprise you?

```
>> "xFoo"[/(\d*)Foo/,1]
=> ""
```

It may not, but then again, it may. It's relatively common to forget that * always matches. At first glance, the following code seems fine:

```
if num = string[/(\d*)Foo/,1]
  Integer(num)
end
```

However, because the match will capture an empty string in its failure case, this code will break. The solution is simple. If you really mean "at least one," use + instead:

```
if num = string[/(\d+)Foo/,1]
  Integer(num)
end
```

Though more experienced folks might not easily be trapped by something so simple, there are more subtle variants. For example, if we intend to match only "Greg" or "Gregory", the following code doesn't quite work:

```
>> "Gregory"[/Greg(ory)?/]
=> "Gregory"
>> "Greg"[/Greg(ory)?/]
=> "Greg"
>> "Gregor"[/Greg(ory)?/]
=> "Greg"
```

Even if the pattern looks close to what we want, we can see the results don't fit. The following modifications remedy the issue:

```
>> "Gregory"[/\bGreg(ory)?\b/]
=> "Gregory"
>> "Greg"[/\bGreg(ory)?\b/]
=> "Greg"
>> "Gregor"[/\bGreg(ory)?\b/]
=> nil
```

Notice that the pattern now properly matches Greg or Gregory, but no other words. The key thing to take away here is that unbounded zero-matching quantifiers are tautologies. They can never fail to match, so you need to be sure to account for that.

A final gotcha about quantifiers is that they are greedy by default. This means they'll try to consume as much of the string as possible before matching. The following is an example of a greedy match:

```
>> "# x # y # z #"[/#(.*)#/,1]
=> " x # y # z "
```

As you can see, this code matches everything between the first and last # character. But sometimes, we want processing to happen from the left and end as soon as we have a match. To do this, append a ? to the repetition:

```
>> "# x # y # z #"[/#(.*?)#/,1]
=> " x "
```

All quantifiers can be made nongreedy this way. Remembering this will save a lot of headaches in the long run.

Though our treatment of regular expressions has been by no means comprehensive, these few basic tips will really carry you a long way. The key things to remember are:

- Regular expressions are nothing more than a special language for find-and-replace operations, built on simple logical constructs.

- There are lots of shortcuts built in for common regular expression operations, so be sure to make use of special character classes and other simplifications when you can.

- Anchors provide a way to set up some expectation about where in a string you want to look for a match. These help with both optimization and pattern correctness.

- Quantifiers such as * and ? will always match, so they should not be used without sufficient boundaries.

- Quantifiers are greedy by default, and can be made nongreedy via ?.

By following these guidelines, you'll write clearer, more accurate, and faster regular expressions. As a result, it'll be a whole lot easier to revisit them when you run into them in your own old code a few months down the line.

A final note on regular expressions is that sometimes we are seduced by their power and overlook other solutions that may be more robust for certain needs. In both the stock ticker and AFM parsing examples, we were working within the realm where regular expressions are a quick, easy, and fine way to go.

However, as documents take on more complex structures, and your needs move from extracting some values to attempting to fully parse a document, you will probably need to look to other techniques that involve full-blown parsers such as Treetop, Ghost Wheel, or Racc. These libraries can solve problems that regular expressions can't solve, and if you find yourself with data that's hard to map a regex to, it's worth looking at these alternative solutions.

Of course, your mileage will vary based on the problem at hand, so don't be afraid of trying a regex-based solution first before pulling out the big guns.

Working with Files

There are a whole slew of options for doing various file management tasks in Ruby. Because of this, it can be difficult to determine what the best approach for a given task might be. In this section, we'll cover two key tasks while looking at three of Ruby's standard libraries.

First, you'll learn how to use the *pathname* and *fileutils* libraries to traverse your filesystem using a clean cross-platform approach that rivals the power of popular *nix shells without sacrificing compatibility. We'll then move on to how to use *tempfile* to automate handling of temporary file resources within your scripts. These practical tips will help you write platform-agnostic Ruby code that'll work out of the box on more systems, while still managing to make your job easier.

Using Pathname and FileUtils

If you are using Ruby to write administrative scripts, it's nearly inevitable that you've needed to do some file management along the way. It may be quite tempting to drop down into the shell to do things like move and rename directories, search for files in a complex directory structure, and other common tasks that involve ferrying files around from one place to the other. However, Ruby provides some great tools to avoid this sort of thing.

The *pathname* and *fileutils* standard libraries provide virtually everything you need for file management. The best way to demonstrate their capabilities is by example, so we'll now take a look at some code and then break it down piece by piece.

To illustrate `Pathname`, we can take a look at a small tool I've built for doing local installations of libraries found on GitHub. This script, called *mooch*, essentially looks up and clones a git repository, puts it in a convenient place within your project (a *vendor/* directory), and optionally sets up a stub file that will include your vendored packages into the loadpath upon requiring it. Sample usage looks something like this:

```
$ mooch init lib/my_project
$ mooch sandal/prawn  0.2.3
$ mooch ruport/ruport 1.6.1
```

We can see the following will work without loading RubyGems:

```
>> require "lib/my_project/dependencies"
=> true
>> require "prawn"
=> true
>> require "ruport"
=> true
>> Prawn::VERSION
=> "0.2.3"
>> Ruport::VERSION
=> "1.6.1"
```

Although this script is pretty useful, that's not what we're here to talk about. Instead, let's focus on how this sort of thing is built, as it shows a practical example of using Pathname to manipulate files and folders. I'll start by showing you the whole script, and then we'll walk through it part by part:

```ruby
#!/usr/bin/env ruby
require "pathname"

WORKING_DIR = Pathname.getwd
LOADER = %Q{
  require "pathname"

  Pathname.glob("#{WORKING_DIR}/vendor/*/*/") do |dir|
    lib = dir + "lib"
    $LOAD_PATH.push(lib.directory? ? lib : dir)
  end
}

if ARGV[0] == "init"
  lib = Pathname.new(ARGV[1])
  lib.mkpath
  (lib + 'dependencies.rb').open("w") do |file|
    file.write LOADER
  end
else
  vendor = Pathname.new("vendor")
  vendor.mkpath
  Dir.chdir(vendor.realpath)
  system("git clone git://github.com/#{ARGV[0]}.git #{ARGV[0]}")
  if ARGV[1]
    Dir.chdir(ARGV[0])
    system("git checkout #{ARGV[1]}")
  end
end
```

As you can see, it's not a ton of code, even though it does a lot. Let's shine the spotlight on the interesting Pathname bits:

```ruby
WORKING_DIR = Pathname.getwd
```

Here we are simply assigning the initial working directory to a constant. We use this to build up the code for the *dependencies.rb* stub script that can be generated via mooch init. Here we're just doing quick-and-dirty code generation, and you can see the full stub as stored in LOADER:

```ruby
LOADER = %Q{
  require "pathname"

  Pathname.glob("#{WORKING_DIR}/vendor/*/*/") do |dir|
    lib = dir + "lib"
    $LOAD_PATH.push(lib.directory? ? lib : dir)
  end
}
```

This script does something fun. It looks in the working directory that `mooch init` was run in for a folder called *vendor*, and then looks for folders two levels deep fitting the GitHub convention of *username/project*. We then use a `glob` to traverse the directory structure, in search of folders to add to the loadpath. The code will check to see whether each project has a *lib* folder within it (as is the common Ruby convention), but will add the project folder itself to the loadpath if it is not present.

Here we notice a few of `Pathname`'s niceties. You can see we can construct new paths by just adding new strings to them, as shown here:

```
lib = dir + "lib"
```

In addition to this, we can check to see whether the path we've created actually points to a directory on the filesystem, via a simple `Pathname#directory?` call. This makes traversal downright easy, as you can see in the preceding code.

This simple stub may be a bit dense, but once you get the hang of `Pathname`, you can see that it's quite powerful. Let's look at a couple more tricks, focusing this time on the code that actually writes this snippet to file:

```
lib = Pathname.new(ARGV[1])
lib.mkpath
(lib + 'dependencies.rb').open("w") do |file|
    file.write LOADER
end
```

Before, the invocation looked like this:

```
$ mooch init lib/my_project
```

Here, `ARGV[1]` is *lib/my_project*. So, in the preceding code, you can see we're building up a relative path to our current working directory and then creating a folder structure. A very cool thing about `Pathname` is that it works in a similar way to `mkdir -p` on *nix, so `Pathname#mkpath` will actually create any necessary nesting directories as needed, and won't complain if the structure already exists, which are both results that we want here.

Once we build up the directories, we need to create our *dependencies.rb* file and populate it with the string in `LOADER`. We can see here that `Pathname` provides shortcuts that work in a similar fashion to `File.open()`.

In the code that actually downloads and vendors libraries from GitHub, we see the same techniques in use yet again, this time mixed in with some shell commands and `Dir.chdir`. As this doesn't introduce anything new, we can skip over the details.

Before we move on to discussing temporary files, we'll take a quick look at `FileUtils`. The purpose of this module is to provide a Unix-like interface to file manipulation tasks, and a quick look at its method list will show that it does a good job of this:

```
cd(dir, options)
cd(dir, options) {|dir| .... }
pwd()
mkdir(dir, options)
mkdir(list, options)
```

```
mkdir_p(dir, options)
mkdir_p(list, options)
rmdir(dir, options)
rmdir(list, options)
ln(old, new, options)
ln(list, destdir, options)
ln_s(old, new, options)
ln_s(list, destdir, options)
ln_sf(src, dest, options)
cp(src, dest, options)
cp(list, dir, options)
cp_r(src, dest, options)
cp_r(list, dir, options)
mv(src, dest, options)
mv(list, dir, options)
rm(list, options)
rm_r(list, options)
rm_rf(list, options)
install(src, dest, mode = <src's>, options)
chmod(mode, list, options)
chmod_R(mode, list, options)
chown(user, group, list, options)
chown_R(user, group, list, options)
touch(list, options)
```

You'll see a bit more of `FileUtils` later on in the chapter when we talk about atomic saves. But before we jump into advanced file management techniques, let's review another important foundational tool: the *tempfile* standard library.

The tempfile Standard Library

Producing temporary files is a common need in many applications. Whether you need to store something on disk to keep it out of memory until it is needed again, or you want to serve up a file but don't need to keep it lurking around after your process has terminated, odds are you'll run into this problem sooner or later.

It's quite tempting to roll our own `Tempfile` support, which might look something like the following code:

```
File.open("/tmp/foo.txt","w") do |file|
  file << some_data
end

# Then in some later code

File.foreach("/tmp/foo.txt") do |line|
  # do something with data
end

# Then finally
require "fileutils"
FileUtils.rm("/tmp/foo.txt")
```

This code works, but it has some drawbacks. The first is that it assumes that you're on a *nix system with a */tmp* directory. Secondly, we don't do anything to avoid file collisions, so if another application is using */tmp/foo.txt*, this will overwrite it. Finally, we need to explicitly remove the file, or risk leaving a bunch of trash around.

Luckily, Ruby has a standard library that helps us get around these issues. Using it, our example then looks like this:

```
require "tempfile"
temp = Tempfile.new("foo.txt")
temp << some_data

# then in some later code
temp.rewind
temp.each do |line|
  # do something with data
end

# Then finally
temp.close
```

Let's take a look at what's going on in a little more detail, to really get a sense of what the *tempfile* library is doing for us.

Automatic Temporary Directory Handling

The code looks somewhat similar to our original example, as we're still essentially working with an IO object. However, the approach is different. `Tempfile` opens up a file handle for us to a file that is stored in whatever your system's *tempdir* is. We can inspect this value, and even change it if we need to. Here's what it looks like on two of my systems:

```
>> Dir.tmpdir
=> "/var/folders/yH/yHvUeP-oFYamIyTmRPPoKE+++TI/-Tmp-"

>> Dir.tmpdir
=> "/tmp"
```

Usually, it's best to go with whatever this value is, because it is where Ruby thinks your temp files should go. However, in the cases where we want to control this ourselves, it is simple to do so, as shown in the following:

```
temp = Tempfile.new("foo.txt", "path/to/my/tmpdir")
```

Collision Avoidance

When you create a temporary file with `Tempfile.new`, you aren't actually specifying an exact filename. Instead, the filename you specify is used as a base name that gets a unique identifier appended to it. This prevents one temp file from accidentally overwriting another. Here's a trivial example that shows what's going on under the hood:

```
>> a = Tempfile.new("foo.txt")
=> #<File:/tmp/foo.txt.2021.0>
>> b = Tempfile.new("foo.txt")
=> #<File:/tmp/foo.txt.2021.1>
>> a.path
=> "/tmp/foo.txt.2021.0"
>> b.path
=> "/tmp/foo.txt.2021.1"
```

Allowing Ruby to handle collision avoidance is generally a good thing, especially if you don't normally care about the exact names of your temp files. Of course, we can always rename the file if we need to store it somewhere permanently.

Same Old I/O Operations

Because we're dealing with an object that delegates most of its functionality directly to File, we can use normal File methods, as shown in our example. For this reason, we can write to our file handle as expected:

```
temp << some_data
```

and read from it in a similar fashion:

```
# then in some later code
temp.rewind
temp.each do |line|
  # do something with data
end
```

Because we leave the file handle open, we need to rewind it to point to the beginning of the file rather than the end. Beyond that, the behavior is exactly the same as File#each.

Automatic Unlinking

Tempfile cleans up after itself. There are two main ways of unlinking a file; which one is correct depends on your needs. Simply closing the file handle is good enough, and it is what we use in our example:

```
temp.close
```

In this case, Ruby doesn't remove the temporary file right away. Instead, it will keep it around until all references to temp have been garbage-collected. For this reason, if keeping lots of open file handles around is a problem for you, you can actually close your handles without fear of losing your temp file, as long as you keep a reference to it handy.

However, in other situations, you may want to purge the file as soon as it has been closed. The change to make this happen is trivial:

```
temp.close!
```

Finally, if you need to explicitly delete a file that has already been closed, you can just use the following:

```
temp.unlink
```

In practice, you don't need to think about this in most cases. Instead, *tempfile* works as you might expect, keeping your files around while you need them and cleaning up after itself when it needs to. If you forget to close a temporary file explicitly, it'll be unlinked when the process exits. For these reasons, using the *tempfile* library is often a better choice than rolling your own solution.

There is more to be said about this very cool library, but what we've already discussed covers most of what you'll need day to day, so now is a fine time to go over what's been said and move on to the next thing.

We've gone over some of the tools Ruby provides for working with your filesystem in a platform-agnostic way, and we're about to get into some more advanced strategies for managing, processing, and manipulating your files and their contents. However, before we do that, let's review the key points about working with your filesystem and with temp files:

- There are a whole slew of options for file management in Ruby, including `FileUtils`, `Dir`, and `Pathname`, with some overlap between them.
- `Pathname` provides a high-level, modern Ruby interface to managing files and traversing your filesystem.
- `FileUtils` provides a *nix-style API to file management tools, but works just fine on any system, making it quite useful for porting shell scripts to Ruby.
- The *tempfile* standard library provides a convenient IO-like class for dealing with temp files in a system-independent way.
- The *tempfile* library also helps make things easier through things like name collision avoidance, automatic file unlinking, and other niceties.

With these things in mind, we'll see more of the techniques shown in this section later on in the chapter. But if you're bored with the basics, now is the time to look at higher-level strategies for doing common I/O tasks.

Text-Processing Strategies

Ruby makes basic I/O operations dead simple, but this doesn't mean it's a bad idea to pick up and apply some general approaches to text processing. Here we'll talk about two techniques that most programmers doing file processing will want to know about, and you'll see what they look like in Ruby.

Advanced Line Processing

The case study for this chapter showed the most common use of `File.foreach()`, but there is more to be said about this approach. This section will highlight a couple of tricks worth knowing about when doing line-by-line processing.

Using Enumerator

The following example shows code that extracts and sums the totals found in a file that has entries similar to these:

```
some
lines
of
text
total: 12

other
lines
of
text
total: 16

more
text
total: 3
```

The following code shows how to do this without loading the whole file into memory:

```
sum = 0
File.foreach("data.txt") { |line| sum += line[/total: (\d+)/,1].to_f }
```

Here, we are using `File.foreach` as a direct iterator, and building up our sum as we go. However, because `foreach()` returns an `Enumerator`, we can actually write this in a cleaner way without sacrificing efficiency:

```
enum = File.foreach("data.txt")
sum = enum.inject(0) { |s,r| s + r[/total: (\d+)/,1].to_f }
```

The primary difference between the two approaches is that when you use `File.foreach` directly with a block, you are simply iterating line by line over the file, whereas `Enumerator` gives you some more powerful ways of processing your data.

When we work with arrays, we don't usually write code like this:

```
sum = 0
arr.each { |e| sum += e }
```

Instead, we typically let Ruby do more of the work for us:

```
sum = arr.inject(0) { |s,e| s + e }
```

For this reason, we should do the same thing with files. If we have an `Enumerable` method we want to use to transform or process a file, we should use the enumerator provided by `File.foreach()` rather than try to do our processing within the block. This will allow

---

us to leverage the power behind Ruby's `Enumerable` module rather than doing the heavy lifting ourselves.

Tracking line numbers

If you're interested in certain line numbers, there is no need to maintain a manual counter. You simply need to create a file handle to work with, and then make use of the `File#lineno` method. To illustrate this, we can very easily implement the Unix command head:

```
def head(file_name,max_lines = 10)
  File.open(file_name) do |file|
    file.each do |line|
      puts line
      break if file.lineno == max_lines
    end
  end
end
```

For a more interesting use case, we can consider a file that is formatted in two line pairs, the first line a key, the second a value:

```
first name
gregory
last name
brown
email
gregory.t.brown@gmail.com
```

Using `File#lineno`, this is trivial to process:

```
keys   = []
values = []

File.open("foo.txt") do |file|
  file.each do |line|
    (file.lineno.odd? ? keys : values) << line.chomp
  end
end

Hash[*keys.zip(values).flatten]
```

The result of this code is a simple hash, as you might expect:

```
{ "first name" => "gregory",
  "last name"  => "brown",
  "email"      => "gregory.t.brown@gmail.com" }
```

Though there is probably more we can say about iterating over files line by line, this should get you well on your way. For now, there are other important I/O strategies to investigate, so we'll keep moving.

Atomic Saves

Although many file processing scripts can happily read in one file as input and produce another as output, sometimes we want to be able to do transformations directly on a single file. This isn't hard in practice, but it's a little bit less obvious than you might think.

It is technically possible to rewrite parts of a file using the "r+" file mode, but in practice, this can be unwieldy in most cases. An alternative approach is to load the entire contents of a file into memory, manipulate the string, and then overwrite the original file. However, this approach is wasteful, and is not the best way to go in most cases.

As it turns out, there is a simple solution to this problem, and that is simply to work around it. Rather than trying to make direct changes to a file, or store a string in memory and then write it back out to the same file after manipulation, we can instead make use of a temporary file and do line-by-line processing as normal. When we finish the job, we can rename our temp file so as to replace the original. Using this approach, we can easily make a backup of the original file if necessary, and also roll back changes upon error.

Let's take a quick look at an example that demonstrates this general strategy. We'll build a script that strips comments from Ruby files, allowing us to take source code such as this:

```ruby
# The best class ever
# Anywhere in the world
class Foo

  # A useless comment
  def a
     true
  end

  #Another Useless comment
  def b
    false
  end

end
```

and turn it into comment-free code such as this:

```ruby
class Foo

  def a
     true
  end

  def b
    false
  end

end
```

With the help of Ruby's *tempfile* and *fileutils* standard libraries, this task is trivial:

```
require "tempfile"
require "fileutils"
temp = Tempfile.new("working")
File.foreach(ARGV[0]) do |line|
  temp << line unless line =~ /^\s*#/
end

temp.close
FileUtils.mv(temp.path,ARGV[0])
```

We initialize a new `Tempfile` object and then iterate over the file specified on the command line. We append each line to the `Tempfile`, as long as it is not a comment line. This is the first part of our task:

```
temp = Tempfile.new("working")
File.foreach(ARGV[0]) do |line|
  temp << line unless line =~ /^\s*#/
end

temp.close
```

Once we've written our `Tempfile` and closed the file handle, we then use `FileUtils` to rename it and replace the original file we were working on:

```
FileUtils.mv(temp.path,ARGV[0])
```

In two steps, we've efficiently modified a file without loading it entirely into memory or dealing with the complexities of using the `r+` file mode. In many cases, the simple approach shown here will be enough.

Of course, because you are modifying a file in place, a poorly coded script could risk destroying your input file. For this reason, you might want to make a backup of your file. This can be done trivially with `FileUtils.cp`, as shown in the following reworked version of our example:

```
require "tempfile"
require "fileutils"

temp = Tempfile.new("working")
File.foreach(ARGV[0]) do |line|
  temp << line unless line =~ /^\s*#/
end

temp.close
FileUtils.cp(ARGV[0],"#{ARGV[0]}.bak")
FileUtils.mv(temp.path,ARGV[0])
```

This code makes a backup of the original file only if the temp file is successfully populated, which prevents it from producing garbage during testing.

Sometimes it will make sense to do backups; other times, it won't be essential. Of course, it's better to be safe than sorry, so if you're in doubt, just add the extra line of code for a bit more peace of mind.

The two strategies shown in this section will come up in practice again and again for those doing frequent text processing. They can even be used in combination when needed.

We're about to close our discussion on this topic, but before we do that, it's worth mentioning the following reminders:

- When doing line-based file processing, `File.foreach` can be used as an `Enumerator`, unlocking the power of `Enumerable`. This provides an extremely handy way to search, traverse, and manipulate files without sacrificing efficiency.

- If you need to keep track of which line of a file you are on while you are iterating over it, you can use `File#lineno` rather than incrementing your own counter.

- When doing atomic saves, the *tempfile* standard library can be used to avoid unnecessary clutter.

- Be sure to test any code that does atomic saves thoroughly, as there is real risk of destroying your original source files if backups are not made.

Conclusions

When dealing with text processing and file management in Ruby, there are a few things to keep in mind. Most of the pitfalls you can run into while doing this sort of work tend to have to do with performance, platform dependence, or code that doesn't clean up after itself.

In this chapter, we talked about a couple of standard libraries that can help keep things clean and platform-independent. Though Ruby is a fine language to write shell scripts in, there is often no need to resort to code that will run only on certain machines when a pure Ruby solution is just as clean. For this reason, using libraries such as *tempfile*, *pathname*, and *fileutils* will go a seriously long way toward keeping your code portable and maintainable down the line.

For issues of performance, you can almost always squeeze out extra speed and minimize your memory footprint by processing your data line by line rather than slurping everything into a single string. You can also much more effectively find a needle in the haystack if you form well-crafted regular expressions that don't make Ruby work too hard. The techniques we've shown here serve as reminders about common mistakes that even seasoned Rubyists tend to make, and provide good ways around them.

Text processing and file management can quickly become complex, but with a solid grasp of the fundamental strategies, you can use Ruby as an extremely powerful tool that works faster and more effectively than you might imagine.

## CHAPTER 5

Functional Programming Techniques

It doesn't take much time to realize that Ruby is a deeply object-oriented language that openly steals from the best of Smalltalk. But Matz is an equal-opportunity thief, and he has snatched features from various other languages as well, including Lisp. This means that although Ruby has its roots in object-oriented principles, we also have some of the high-level constructs that facilitate functional programming techniques.

Rightfully speaking, Ruby is not a functional programming language. Though it is possible to come close with great effort, Ruby simply lacks a number of the key aspects of functional languages. Virtually all state in Ruby is mutable, and because it is an object-oriented language, we tend to focus on state management rather than elimination of state. Ruby lacks tail call optimization,[*] making recursion highly inefficient. Beyond these key things, there are plenty of other subtleties that purists can discuss at length if you let them.

However, if you let Ruby be Ruby, you can benefit from certain functional techniques while still writing object-oriented code. This chapter will walk you through several practices that are inspired by functional languages and that have practical value for solving problems in Ruby. We'll look at things like lazy evaluation, memoization, infinite lists, higher-order procedures, and other stuff that has a nice academic ring to it. Along the way, I'll do my best to show you that this stuff isn't simply abstract and mathematical, but can meaningfully be used in day-to-day code.

Let's start by taking a look at how we're already using lazy evaluation whether we realize it or not, and then walk through a popular Ruby library that can simplify this for us. As in other chapters, we'll take a peek under the hood to see what's really going on.

Laziness Can Be a Virtue (A Look at lazy.rb)

If you've been writing Ruby for any amount of time, you've probably already written some code that makes use of lazy evaluation. Before we go further, let's look at a couple examples of lazy code that you will likely recognize on sight, if not by name.

---

[*] This can be enabled in YARV at compile time, but it is still experimental.

For starters, `Proc` objects are, by definition, lazy:

```ruby
a = lambda { File.read("foo.txt") }
```

When you create a `Proc` object using `lambda`, the code is not actually executed until you call the block. Therefore, a `Proc` is essentially a chunk of code that gets executed on demand, rather than in place. So if we actually wanted to read the contents of this file, we'd need to do this:

```ruby
b = a.call
```

In essence, code is said to be evaluated lazily if it is executed only at the time it is actually needed, not at the time it was defined. However, this behavior is not necessarily limited to blocks; we can do this with populating data for our objects as well. Let's take a look at a simplified model of Prawn's table cells for a more complete example:

```ruby
class Cell

  FONT_HEIGHT = 10
  FONT_WIDTH  = 8

  def initialize(text)
    @text = text
  end

  attr_accessor :text
  attr_writer :width, :height

  def width
    @width ||= calculate_width
  end

  def height
    @height ||= calculate_height
  end

  def to_s
    "Cell(#{width}x#{height})"
  end

  private

  def calculate_height
    @text.lines.count * FONT_HEIGHT
  end

  def calculate_width
    @text.lines.map { |e| e.length }.max * FONT_WIDTH
  end

end
```

In this example, `Cell#width` and `Cell#height` can be calculated based on the text in the cell, or they can be manually set. Because we don't need to know the exact dimensions of a cell until we render it, this is a perfect case for lazy evaluation. Even though the calculations may not be expensive on their own, they add up when dealing with thousands or hundreds of thousands of cells. Luckily, it's easy to avoid any unnecessary work.

By just looking at the core bits of this object, we can get a clearer sense of what's going on:

```ruby
class Cell
  attr_writer :width, :height

  def width
    @width ||= calculate_width
  end

  def height
    @height ||= calculate_height
  end
end
```

It should now be plain to see what's happening. If `@width` or `@height` have already been set, their calculations are never run. We also can see that these calculations will in the worst case be run exactly once, storing the return value as needed.

The idea here is that now we won't have to worry about calculating dimensions of preset `Cell` objects, and that those that calculate their dimensions will not need to repeat that calculation each time they are used. I am hoping that readers are familiar with this Ruby idiom already, but if you are struggling with it a little bit, just stop for a moment and toy with this in *irb* and it should quickly become clear how things work:

```ruby
>> cell = Cell.new("Chunky Bacon\nIs Very\nDelicious")
>> cell.width = 1000
=> 1000
>> cell.to_s
=> "Cell(1000x30)"
>> cell.height = 500
=> 500
>> cell.to_s
=> "Cell(1000x500)"
```

Though this process is relatively straightforward, we can probably make it better. It's sort of annoying to have to build special accessors for our `@width` and `@height` when what we're ultimately doing is setting default values for them, which is normally something we do in our constructor. What's more, our solution feels a little primitive in nature, at least aesthetically.

This is where MenTaLguY's *lazy.rb* comes in. It provides a method called `promise()` that does exactly what we want, in a much nicer way. The following code can be used to replace our original implementation:

```
require "lazy"

class Cell

  FONT_HEIGHT = 10
  FONT_WIDTH  = 8

  def initialize(text)
    @text   = text
    @width  = promise { calculate_width }
    @height = promise { calculate_height }
  end

  attr_accessor :text, :width, :height

  def to_s
    "Cell(#{width}x#{height})"
  end

  private

  def calculate_height
    @text.lines.count * FONT_HEIGHT
  end

  def calculate_width
    @text.lines.map { |e| e.length }.max * FONT_WIDTH
  end

end
```

Gone are our special accessors, and in their place, we have simple `promise()` calls in our constructor. This method returns a simple proxy object that wraps a block of code that is designed to be executed later. Once you call any methods on this object, it passes them along to whatever your block evaluates to. If this is tough to get your head around, again *irb* is your friend:

```
>> a = promise { 1 }
=> #<Lazy::Promise computation=#<Proc:0x3ce218@(irb):2>>
>> a + 3
=> 4
>> a
=> 1
```

`Lazy::Promise` objects are very cool, but a little bit sneaky. Because they essentially work the same as the evaluated object once the block is run once, it's hard to know that you're actually working with a proxy object. But if we dig deep, we can find the truth:

```
>> a.class
=> Fixnum
>> a.__class__
=> Lazy::Promise
```

If we try out the same examples we did before with `Cell`, you'll see it works as expected:

```
>> cell = Cell.new("Chunky Bacon\nIs Very\nDelicious")
>> cell.width = 1000
=> 1000
>> cell.to_s
=> "Cell(1000x30)"
>> cell.height = 500
=> 500
>> cell.to_s
=> "Cell(1000x500)"
```

Seeing that the output is the same, we can be satisfied knowing that our *lazy.rb* solution will do the trick, while making our code look a little cleaner. However, we shouldn't just pass the work that `promise()` is doing off as magic—it is worth looking at both for enrichment and because it's genuinely cool code.

I've gone ahead and simplified the implementation of `Lazy::Promise` a bit, removing some of the secondary features while still preserving the core functionality. We're going to look at the naive implementation, but please use this only for studying. The official version from MenTaLguY can handle thread synchronization and does much better error handling than what you will see here, so that's what you'll want if you plan to use *lazy.rb* in real code.

That all having been said, here's how you'd go about implementing a basic `Promise` object on Ruby 1.9:

```ruby
module NaiveLazy
  class Promise < BasicObject

    def initialize(&computation)
      @computation = computation
    end

    def __result__
      if @computation
        @result      = @computation.call
        @computation = nil
      end

      @result
    end

    def inspect
      if @computation
        "#<NaiveLazy::Promise computation=#{ @computation.inspect }>"
      else
        @result.inspect
      end
    end

    def respond_to?( message )
      message = message.to_sym
      [:__result__, :inspect].include?(message) ||
          __result__.respond_to? message
    end
```

```
    def method_missing(*a, &b)
      __result__.__send__(*a, &b)
    end

  end
end
```

Though compact, this might look a little daunting in one big chunk, so let's break it down. First, you'll notice that `NaiveLazy::Promise` inherits from `BasicObject` rather than `Object`:

```
module NaiveLazy
  class Promise < BasicObject

  end
end
```

`BasicObject` omits most of the methods you'll find on `Object`, making it so you don't need to explicitly remove those methods on your own in order to create a proxy object. This in effect gives you a blank slate object, which is exactly what we want for our current purposes.

The proxy itself works through `method_missing`, handing virtually all messages to the result of `Promise#__result__`:

```
module NaiveLazy
  class Promise < BasicObject
    def method_missing(*a, &b)
      __result__.__send__(*a, &b)
    end
  end
end
```

For the uninitiated, this code essentially just allows `promise.some_function` to be interpreted as `promise.__result__.some_function`, which makes sense when we recall how things worked in `Cell`:

```
>> cell.width
=> #<Lazy::Promise computation=#<Proc:...>>
>> cell.width + 10
=> 114
```

`Lazy::Promise` knew how to evaluate the computation and then pass your message to its result. This `method_missing` trick is how it works under the hood. When we go back and look at how `__result__` is implemented, this becomes even more clear:

```
module NaiveLazy
  class Promise < BasicObject

    def initialize(&computation)
      @computation = computation
    end
```

```
      def __result__
        if @computation
          @result      = @computation.call
          @computation  = nil
        end

        @result
      end

      def method_missing(*a, &b)
        __result__.__send__(*a, &b)
      end

    end
  end
```

When we create a new promise, it stores a code block to be executed later. Then, when you call a method on the promise object, method_missing runs the __result__ method. This method checks to see whether there is a Proc object in @computation that needs to be evaluated. If there is, it stores the return value of that code, and then wipes out the @computation. Further calls to __result__ return this value immediately.

On top of this, we add a couple of methods to make the proxy more well behaved, so that you can fully treat an evaluated promise as if it were just an ordinary value:

```
module NaiveLazy
  class Promise < BasicObject

    # ...

    def inspect
      if @computation
        "#<NaiveLazy::Promise computation=#{ @computation.inspect }>s"
      else
        @result.inspect
      end
    end

    def respond_to?( message )
      message = message.to_sym
      [:__result__, :inspect].include?(message) or
        __result__.respond_to? message
    end

    # ...
  end
end
```

I won't go into much detail about this code—both of these methods essentially just forward everything they can to the evaluated object, and are nothing more than underplumbing. However, because these round out the full object, you'll see them in action when we take our new NaiveLazy::Promise for a spin:

```
>> num = NaiveLazy::Promise.new { 3 }
=> #<NaiveLazy::Promise computation=#<Proc:0x3cfd98@(irb):2>
>> num + 100
=> 103
>> num
=> 3
>> num.respond_to?(:times)
=> true
>> num.class
=> Fixnum
```

So what we have here is an implementation of a proxy object that doesn't produce an exact value until it absolutely has to. This proxy is fully transparent, so even though num here is actually a `NaiveLazy::Promise` instance, not a `Fixnum`, other objects in your system won't know or care. This can be pretty handy when delaying your calculations until the last possible moment is important.

The reason I showed how to implement a `promise` is to give you a sense of what the primitive tools in Ruby are capable of doing. We've seen blocks used in a lot of different ways throughout Ruby, but this particular case might be easy to overlook. Another interesting factor here is that although this concept belongs to the functional programming paradigm, it is also easy to implement using Ruby's object-oriented principles.

As we move on to look at other techniques in this chapter, keep this general idea in mind. Much will be lost in translation if you try to directly convert functional concepts into Ruby, but by playing to Ruby's strengths, you can often preserve the idea without things feeling alien.

We're about to look at some other things that are handy to have in your tool belt, but before we do that, I'll reiterate some key points about lazy evaluation in Ruby:

- Lazy evaluation is useful when you have some code that may never need to be run, or would best be run as late as possible, especially if this code is expensive computationally. If you do not have this need, it is better to do without the overhead.

- All code blocks in Ruby are lazy, and are not executed until explicitly called.

- For simple needs, you can build attribute accessors for your objects that avoid running a calculation until they are called, storing the result in an instance variable once it is executed.

- MenTaLguY's *lazy.rb* provides a more comprehensive solution for lazy evaluation, which can be made to be thread-safe and is generally more robust than the naive example shown in this chapter.

We'll now move on to the sticky issue of state maintenance and side effects, as this is a key aspect of functional programming that goes a little against the grain of traditional Ruby code.

Minimizing Mutable State and Reducing Side Effects

Although Ruby is object-oriented, and therefore relies heavily on mutable state, we can write nondestructive code in Ruby. In fact, many of our `Enumerable` methods are inspired by this.

For a trivial example, we can consider the use case for `Enumerable#map`. We could write our own naive map implementation rather easily:

```
def naive_map(array)
  array.each_with_object([]) { |e, arr| arr << yield(e) }
end
```

When we run this code, it has the same results as `Enumerable#map`, as shown here:

```
>> a = [1,2,3,4]
=> [1, 2, 3, 4]
>> naive_map(a) { |x| x + 1 }
=> [2, 3, 4, 5]
>> a
=> [1, 2, 3, 4]
```

As you can see, a new array is produced, rather than modifying the original array. In practice, this is how we tend to write side-effect-free code in Ruby. We traverse our original data source, and then build up the results of a state transformation in a new object. In this way, we don't modify the original object. Because `naive_map()` doesn't make changes to anything outside of the function, we can say that this code is side-effect-free.

However, this code still uses mutable state to build up its return value. To truly make the code stateless, we'd need to build a new array every time we append a value to an array. Notice the difference between these two ways of adding a new element to the end of an array:

```
>> a
=> [1, 2, 3, 4]
>> a = [1,2,3]
=> [1, 2, 3]
>> b = a << 1
=> [1, 2, 3, 1]
>> a
=> [1, 2, 3, 1]

>> c = a + [2]
=> [1, 2, 3, 1, 2]
>> b
=> [1, 2, 3, 1]
>> a
=> [1, 2, 3, 1]
```

It turns out that `Array#<<` modifies its receiver, and `Array#+` does not. With this knowledge, we can rewrite `naive_map` to be truly stateless:

```
def naive_map(array, &block)
  return [] if array.empty?
  [ yield(array[0]) ] + naive_map(array[1..-1], &block)
end
```

This code works in a different way, building up the result set by calling itself repeatedly, resulting in something like this:

```
[1,2,3,4] => [2], [2,3,4] => [2] + [3], [3,4] => [2] + [3] + [4], [4] =>
    [2] + [3] + [4] + [5] => [2,3,4,5]
```

Depending on your taste for recursion, you may find this solution beautiful or scary. In Ruby, recursive solutions may look elegant and have appeal from a purist's perspective, but when it comes to their drawbacks, the pragmatists win out. Other languages optimize for this sort of thing, but Ruby does not, which is made obvious by this benchmark:

```
require "benchmark"

def naive_map(array, &block)
  new_array = []
  array.each { |e| new_array << block.call(e) }
  return new_array
end

def naive_map_recursive(array, &block)
  return [] if array.empty?
  [ yield(array[0]) ] + naive_map_recursive(array[1..-1], &block)
end

N = 100_000

Benchmark.bmbm do |x|
  a = [1,2,3,4,5]

  x.report("naive map") do
    N.times { naive_map(a) { |x| x + 1 } }
  end

  x.report("naive map recursive") do
    N.times { naive_map_recursive(a) { |x| x + 1 } }
  end
end

# Outputs:

sandal:fp $ ruby naive_map_bench.rb
Rehearsal --------------------------------------------------
naive map               0.370000   0.010000   0.380000 (  0.373221)
naive map recursive     0.530000   0.000000   0.530000 (  0.539722)
----------------------------------------- total: 0.910000sec

                            user     system      total        real
naive map               0.360000   0.000000   0.360000 (  0.369269)
naive map recursive     0.530000   0.000000   0.530000 (  0.538872)
```

Even though our functions are somewhat trivial, we see our recursive solution performing significantly slower than the iterative one. The reason behind this is the very high cost of method dispatch in Ruby. This means that despite the identical complexity between our iterative and recursive solutions, the latter can quickly become a performance nightmare. If we use a larger dataset, we can see this only exacerbates the problem:

```
N = 100_000

Benchmark.bmbm do |x|
  a = [1,2,3,4,5] * 20

  x.report("naive map") do
    N.times { naive_map(a) { |x| x + 1 } }
  end

  x.report("naive map recursive") do
    N.times { naive_map_recursive(a) { |x| x + 1 }  }
  end
end

# output

sandal:fp $ ruby naive_map_bench.rb
Rehearsal -----------------------------------------------------
naive map           4.360000   0.020000   4.380000 (  4.393069)
naive map recursive 9.420000   0.030000   9.450000 (  9.498580)
-------------------------------------------- total: 13.830000sec

                        user     system      total        real
naive map           4.350000   0.010000   4.360000 (  4.382038)
naive map recursive 9.420000   0.050000   9.470000 (  9.532602)
```

An important thing to remember is that any recursive solution can be rewritten iteratively. We can actually build an iterative, stateless, naive map without much extra effort:

```
def naive_map_via_inject(array, &block)
  array.inject([]) { |s,e| [ yield(e) ] + s }
end
```

Enumerable#inject is a favorite feature among Rubyists for accumulation. The way that it works is by passing two objects into the block: the base object and the current element. After each step through the iteration, the return value of the block becomes the new base. Essentially, this code is doing the same thing our recursive code did, without the recursion. We can take a quick look at the benchmarks now, expecting some improvement by cutting out all those expensive recursive method calls:

```
N = 100_000

Benchmark.bmbm do |x|
  a = [1,2,3,4,5] * 20

  x.report("naive map") do
    N.times { naive_map(a) { |x| x + 1 } }
  end
```

```
    x.report("naive map recursive") do
      N.times { naive_map_recursive(a) { |x| x + 1 }  }
    end

    x.report("naive map via inject") do
      N.times { naive_map_via_inject(a) { |x| x + 1 } }
    end
  end

# Output

sandal:fp $ ruby naive_map_bench.rb
Rehearsal -------------------------------------------------------
naive map                4.370000   0.030000   4.400000 (  4.458491)
naive map recursive      9.730000   0.090000   9.820000 ( 10.128538)
naive map via inject     7.550000   0.070000   7.620000 (  7.766988)
--------------------------------------------- total: 21.840000sec

                            user      system      total       real
naive map                4.360000   0.020000   4.380000 (  4.413264)
naive map recursive      9.480000   0.050000   9.530000 (  9.553978)
naive map via inject     7.420000   0.050000   7.470000 (  7.509197)
```

Do these numbers surprise you? As we expected, our `inject`-based solution is much faster than our recursive solution, but why is it so much slower than our dumb brute force and ignorance approach?

The reason behind this is one of the key roadblocks that prevent us from writing stateless code in Ruby. In order to solve this problem without modifying any objects, we need to create a new object every single time an element gets added to the array. As you may have guessed, objects are large in Ruby, and constructing them is a slow process. What's more, if we don't store any of these intermediate values, we risk getting the garbage collector churning frequently to kill off our discarded objects.

Avoiding side effects is different than avoiding mutable state entirely. That's the key point to take away from what we just looked at here. In Ruby, as long as it makes sense to do so, avoiding side effects is a good thing. It reduces the possibility for unexpected bugs much in the same way that avoiding the use of global variables does. However, avoiding the use of mutable state definitely depends more on your individual situation.

We showed two examples that avoided the use of mutable state, both of which might look appealing to people who enjoy functional programming style. However, we saw that their performance was abysmal, and because something like `Enumerable#map` tends to be used in a tight loop, this is a bad time to trade performance for aesthetic value.

However, in other situations, the trade-off may be tipped more in the other direction. If the stateless (possibly recursive) code looks better than other solutions, and performance is not a major concern, don't be afraid to write your code in the more elegant way.

In general, remember the following things:

- The simple way to avoid side effects in Ruby when transforming one object to another is to create a new object, and then populate it by iterating over your original object performing the necessary state transformations.

- You can write stateless code in Ruby by creating new objects every time you perform an operation, such as `Array#+`.

- Recursive solutions may aid in writing simple stateless solutions, but incur a major performance penalty in Ruby.

- Creating too many objects can create performance problems as well, so it is important to find the right balance, and to remember that side effects can be avoided without making things fully stateless.

We'll now move on from how you structure individual functions in your code to how you can organize the larger chunks. So let's take a look at what we can learn from modular organization, and how we can mix it in with our object-oriented code.

Modular Code Organization

In many functional languages, it is possible to group together your related functions using a module. However, we typically think of something different when we think of modules in Ruby:

```
class A

  include Enumerable

  def initialize(arr)
    @arr = arr
  end

  def each
    @arr.each { |e| yield(e) }
  end

end

>> A.new([1,2,3]).map { |x| x + 1 }
=> [2, 3, 4]
```

Here, we've included the `Enumerable` module into our class as a mixin. This enables shared implementation of functionality between classes, but is a different concept than modular code organization in general.

What we really want is a collection of functions unified under a single namespace. As it turns out, Ruby has that sort of thing, too! Although the `Math` module can be mixed into classes similar to the way we've used `Enumerable` here, you can also use it on its own:

```
>> Math.sin(Math::PI / 2)
=> 1.0
>> Math.sqrt(4)
=> 2.0
```

So, how'd they do that? One way is to use `module_function`:

```
module A
  module_function

  def foo
    "This is foo"
  end

  def bar
    "This is bar"
  end
end
```

We can now call these functions directly on the module, as you can see here:

```
>> A.foo
=> "This is foo"
>> A.bar
=> "This is bar"
```

You won't need anything more for most cases in which you want to execute functions on a module. However, this approach does come with some limitations, because it does not allow you to use private functions:

```
module A
  module_function

  def foo
    "This is foo calling baz: #{baz}"
  end

  def bar
    "This is bar"
  end

  private

  def baz
    "hi there"
  end
end
```

Though it seems like our code is fairly intuitive, we'll quickly run into an error once we try to call `A.foo`:

```
>> A.foo
NameError: undefined local variable or method 'baz' for A:Module
  from (irb):33:in 'foo'
  from (irb):46
  from /Users/sandal/lib/ruby19_1/bin/irb:12:in '<main>'
```

For some cases, not being able to access private methods might not be a big deal, but for others, this could be a major issue. Luckily, if we think laterally, there is an easy workaround.

Modules in Ruby, although they cannot be instantiated, are in essence ordinary objects. Because of this, there is nothing stopping us from mixing a module into itself:

```ruby
module A
  extend self

  def foo
    "This is foo calling baz: #{baz}"
  end

  def bar
    "This is bar"
  end

  private

  def baz
    "hi there"
  end
end
```

Once we do this, we get the same effect as `module_function` without the limitations:

```ruby
>> A.foo
=> "This is foo calling baz: hi there"
```

We aren't sacrificing encapsulation here, either. We will still get an error if we try to call `A.baz` directly:

```ruby
>> A.baz
NoMethodError: private method 'baz' called for A:Module
  from (irb):65
  from /Users/sandal/lib/ruby19_1/bin/irb:12:in '<main>'
```

Using this trick of extending a module with itself provides us with a structure that isn't too different (at least on the surface) from the sort of modules you might find in functional programming languages. But aside from odd cases such as the `Math` module, you might wonder when this technique would be useful.

For the most part, classes work fine for encapsulating code in Ruby. Traditional inheritance combined with the powerful mixin functionality of modules covers most of the bases just fine. However, there are definitely cases in which a concept isn't big enough for a class, but isn't small enough to fit in a single function.

I ran into this issue recently in a Rails app I was working on. I was implementing user authentication and needed to first test the database via ActiveRecord, and fall back to LDAP when a user didn't have an account set up in the application.

Without getting into too much detail, the basic structure for my authentication routine looked like this:

```
class User < ActiveRecord::Base

  # other model code omitted

  def self.authenticate(login, password)
    if u = find_by_login(login)
      u.authenticated?(password) ? u : nil
    else
      ldap_authenticate(login, password)
    end
  end

end
```

LDAP authentication was to be implemented in a private class method, which seemed like a good idea at first. However, as I continued to work on this, I found myself writing a very huge function that represented more than a page of code. As I knew there would be no way to keep this whole thing in my head easily, I proceeded to break things into more helper methods to make things clearer. Unfortunately, this approach didn't work as well as I had hoped.

By the end of this refactoring, I had racked up all sorts of strange routines on User, with names such as `initialize_ldap_conn`, `retrieve_ldap_user`, and so on. A well-factored object should do one thing and do it well, and my User model seemed to know much more about LDAP than it should have to. The solution was to break this code off into a module, which was only a tiny change to the User.`authenticate` method:

```
def self.authenticate(login, password)
  if u = find_by_login(login) # need to get the salt
    u.authenticated?(password) ? u : nil
  else
    LDAP.authenticate(login, password)
  end
end
```

By substituting the private method call on the User model with a modular function call on User::LDAP, I was able to define my function and its private helpers in a place that made more sense. The module ended up looking something like this:

```
module LDAP

  extend self

  def authenticate(username, password)
    connection = initialize_ldap_connection
    retrieve_ldap_user(username, password, connection)
  rescue Net::LDAP::LdapError => e
    ActiveRecord::Base.logger.debug "!!! LDAP Error: #{e.message} !!!"
    false
  end

  private
```

```
def initialize_ldap_connection
  #...
end

def retrieve_ldap_user(username, password, connection)
  #...
end

end
```

This definitely cleaned up the code and made it easier to follow, but it had additional benefits as well. It introduced a clear separation of concerns that helped make testing much easier. It also left room for future expansion and modification without tight coupling.

Of course, if we end up needing to do more than simply authenticate a user against the LDAP database, this module will need to go. As soon as you see the same argument being passed to a bunch of functions, you might be running into a situation where some persistence of state wouldn't hurt. You can probably see how we'd spend a lot of time passing around usernames and connection objects if this code grew substantially bigger.

The good news is, if need arises for expansion down the line, converting code that has been organized into a module is somewhat trivial. Here's how we'd do it with the LDAP module:

```
class LDAP

  def self.authenticate(username, password)
    user = new(username, password)
    user.authenticate(password)
  rescue Net::LDAP::LdapError => e
    ActiveRecord::Base.logger.debug "!!! LDAP Error: #{e.message} !!!"
    false
  end

  def initialize(username)
    @connection = initialize_ldap_connection
    @username   = username
  end

  def authenticate(password)
    #...
  end

  private

  def initialize_ldap_connection
    #...
  end

end
```

As you can see, the difference is somewhat minimal, and no changes need to be made to your user model. Object-oriented purists may even prefer this approach all around, but there is a certain appeal to the minimalism of the modular approach shown earlier.

Even though this latest iteration moves to a more object-oriented approach, there is still modular appeal to it. The ease of creating class methods in Ruby contributes highly to that, as it makes it possible for this to look like modular code even if it's building a new instance of the LDAP module each time.

Although it is not advisable to try extra hard to use this technique of modular code design in every possible situation, it is a neat organizational approach that is worth knowing about. Here are a few things to watch for that indicate this technique may be the right way to go:

- You are solving a single, atomic task that involves lots of steps that would be better broken out into helper functions.

- You are wrapping some functions that don't rely on much common state between them, but are related to a common topic.

- The code is very general and can be used standalone *or* the code is very specific but doesn't relate directly to the object that it is meant to be used by.

- The problem you are solving is small enough where object orientation does more to get in the way than it does to help you.

Because modular code organization reduces the amount of objects you are creating, it can potentially give you a decent performance boost. This offers an incentive to use this approach when it is appropriate.

Memoization

A typical "Hello World" program in functional programming languages is a recursive function that computes the Fibonacci sequence. In Ruby, the trivial implementation looks like this:

```
def fib(n)
  return n if (0..1).include? n
  fib(n-1) + fib(n-2)
end
```

However, you'll feel the pain that is relying on deep recursion in Ruby if you compute even modest values of n. On my machine, `fib(30)` computes within a few seconds, but I'm too impatient to even give you a time for `fib(40)`. However, there is a special characteristic of functions like this that makes it possible to speed them up drastically.

In mathematics, a function is said to be well defined if it consistently maps its input to exactly one output. This is obviously true for `fib(n)`, as `fib(6)` will always return `8`, no matter how many times you compute it. This sort of function is distinct from one that is not well defined, such as the following:

```
def mystery(n)
  n + rand(1000)
end
```

If we run this code a few times with the same n, we see there isn't a unique relationship between its input and output:

```
>> mystery(6)
=> 928
>> mystery(6)
=> 671
>> mystery(6)
=> 843
```

When we have a function like this, there isn't much we can assume about it. However, well-defined functions such as fib(n) can get a massive performance boost almost for free. Can you guess how?

If your mind wandered to tail-call optimization or rewriting the function iteratively, you're thinking too hard. However, the idea of reducing the amount of recursive calls is on track. As it stands, this code is a bad dream, as fib(n) is called five times when n=3 and nine times when n=4, with this trend continuing upward as n gets larger.

The key realization is what I mentioned before: fib(6) is always going to be 8, and fib(10) is always going to be 55. Because of this, we can store these values rather than calculate them repeatedly. Let's give that a shot and see what happens:

```
def fib(n)
  @series[n] ||= fib(n-1) + fib(n-2)
end
```

Huzzah! By simply storing our precalculated values in an array, we can now calculate much deeper into the sequence:

```
>> fib(1000)
=> 43466557686937456435688527675040625802560466051737178040248172908953655541
79490518904038798400792551692959225930803226347752096896232398733224711616416
299644090653318793829896964992851600370447613779516684922887 5
```

What we have done is used a technique called *memoization* to cache the return values of our function based on its input. Because we were caching a sequence, it's reasonable to use an array here, but in other cases in which the data is more sparse, a hash may be more appropriate. Let's take a look at some real code where that is the case, to help illustrate the point.

In my PDF generation library Prawn, I provide helper methods that convert from HTML colors to an array of RGB values and back again. Though they're nothing particularly exciting, this is what they look like in action:

```
>> rgb2hex([100,25,254])
=> "6419fe"

>> hex2rgb("6419fe")
=> [100, 25, 254]
```

The implementations of these functions are somewhat simple, and not nearly as computationally expensive as our recursive Fibonacci implementation:

```
def rgb2hex(rgb)
  rgb.map { |e| "%02x" % e }.join
end

def hex2rgb(hex)
  r,g,b = hex[0..1], hex[2..3], hex[4..5]
  [r,g,b].map { |e| e.to_i(16) }
end
```

Although these methods aren't especially complicated, they represent a decent use case for caching via memoization. Colors are likely to be reused frequently and, after they have been translated once, will never change. Therefore, `rgb2hex()` and `hex2rgb()` are well-defined functions.

As it turns out, Ruby's `Hash` is a truly excellent cache object. Before we get into the specifics, take a look at the memoized versions and see if you can figure out for yourself what's going on:

```
def rgb2hex_manual_cache(rgb)
  @rgb2hex ||= Hash.new do |colors, value|
    colors[value] = value.map { |e| "%02x" % e }.join
  end

  @rgb2hex[rgb]
end

def hex2rgb_manual_cache(hex)
  @hex2rgb ||= Hash.new do |colors, value|
    r,g,b = value[0..1], value[2..3], value[4..5]
    colors[value] = [r,g,b].map { |e| e.to_i(16) }
  end

  @hex2rgb[hex]
end
```

Does this example make much sense? If you look at it closely, you can see that the core implementation is still the same—we've just added some extra code to do the caching for us. To do this, we use the block form of `Hash.new`.

You may have used `Hash.new` to define a default value when an unknown key is used. This trick is a relatively simple way to do all sorts of things, including constructing a hash of arrays, or creating a hash for counting things:

```
>> a = Hash.new { |h,k| h[k] = [] }
=> {}
>> a[:foo] << 1
=> [1]
>> a[:foo] << 2
=> [1, 2]
>> a[:bar]
=> []
```

```
>> b = Hash.new { |h,k| h[k] = 0 }
=> {}
>> [:foo, :bar, :foo, :bar, :bar, :bar, :foo].each { |e| b[e] += 1 }
=> [:foo, :bar, :foo, :bar, :bar, :bar, :foo]
>> b
=> {:foo=>3, :bar=>4}
```

However, if we can compute our value based on the key to our hash, we can do more than simply provide default values. For example, it would be easy to create a hash that would multiply any key passed into it by 2:

```
>> doubler = Hash.new { |h,k| h[k] = k * 2 }
=> {}
>> doubler[2]
=> 4
>> doubler[5]
=> 10
>> doubler[10]
=> 20
```

With this in mind, it should be easier to understand the caching in our color conversion code upon a second glance:

```
def rgb2hex_manual_cache(rgb)
  @rgb2hex ||= Hash.new do |colors, value|
    colors[value] = value.map { |e| "%02x" % e }.join
  end

  @rgb2hex[rgb]
end

def hex2rgb_manual_cache(hex)
  @hex2rgb ||= Hash.new do |colors, value|
    r,g,b = value[0..1], value[2..3], value[4..5]
    colors[value] = [r,g,b].map { |e| e.to_i(16) }
  end

  @hex2rgb[hex]
end
```

Here we can see that the input to the function is being used to build up our `Hash`. We initialize the `Hash` once, and then we simply index into it to populate the values. The block is run exactly once per key, and then the cached values are returned thereafter. As a result, we have greatly sped up our function. Let's take a look at some benchmarks to see how much of a boost we get by writing things this way:

```
require "benchmark"

N = 500_000

Benchmark.bmbm do |x|
```

```
    x.report("rgb2hex_uncached") do
      N.times { rgb2hex([100,25,50]) }
    end
    x.report("rgb2hex_manual_cache") do
      N.times { rgb2hex_manual_cache([100,25,50]) }
    end

    x.report("hex2rgb_uncached") do
      N.times { hex2rgb("beaded") }
    end
    x.report("hex2rgb_manual_cache") do
      N.times { hex2rgb_manual_cache("beaded") }
    end

  end

  sandal:fp $ ruby rgb2hex.rb
  Rehearsal ---------------------------------------------------------
  rgb2hex_uncached       3.560000   0.030000   3.590000 (  3.656217)
  rgb2hex_manual_cache   1.030000   0.000000   1.030000 (  1.063319)
  hex2rgb_uncached       1.220000   0.010000   1.230000 (  1.240591)
  hex2rgb_manual_cache   0.280000   0.000000   0.280000 (  0.303417)
  ------------------------------------------ total: 6.130000sec

                          user       system     total        real
  rgb2hex_uncached       3.570000   0.040000   3.610000 (  3.733938)
  rgb2hex_manual_cache   1.040000   0.010000   1.050000 (  1.055863)
  hex2rgb_uncached       1.210000   0.010000   1.220000 (  1.248148)
  hex2rgb_manual_cache   0.280000   0.000000   0.280000 (  0.284613)
```

As you can see, the results are pretty convincing. The cached version of the code is several times faster than the uncached one. This means that when running under a tight loop, the memoization can really make a big difference in these functions, and may be worth the minimal noise introduced by adding a Hash into the mix.

You might have noticed that the process for doing memoization isn't really case-specific. In nearly every situation, you're going to want to create a simple hash that maps from the input to the output, and you'll want to return that value rather than recalculate it if it exists. Ruby wouldn't be Ruby if we couldn't hack our way around repetition like this, and luckily James Gray is one of the folks who has done exactly that.

James wrote a nice little module called Memoizable, which is designed to abstract the task of creating a cache to the point at which you simply mark each function that should be memoized similar to the way you mark something public or private.

Let's take a look at this in action, before digging deeper:

```
include Memoizable

def rgb2hex(rgb)
  rgb.map { |e| "%02x" % e }.join
end
```

```
memoize :rgb2hex

def hex2rgb(hex)
  r,g,b = hex[0..1], hex[2..3], hex[4..5]
  [r,g,b].map { |e| e.to_i(16) }
end

memoize :hex2rgb
```

That's really all there is to it. `Memoizable` works by making a copy of your function, renaming it as `__unmemoized_method_name__`, and then injects its automatic caching in place of the original function. That means that when we call `rgb2hex()` or `hex2rgb()`, we'll now be hitting the cached versions of the functions.

This is pretty exciting, as it means that for well-defined functions, you can use `Memoizable` to get a performance boost without even modifying your underlying implementation. Let's take a look at how this approach stacks up performance-wise when compared to the manual caching from before:

```
require "benchmark"

N = 500_000

Benchmark.bmbm do |x|

  x.report("rgb2hex (Memoizable)") do
    N.times { rgb2hex([100,25,50]) }
  end
  x.report("rgb2hex_manual_cache") do
    N.times { rgb2hex_manual_cache([100,25,50]) }
  end
  x.report("rgb2hex_uncached") do
    N.times { __unmemoized_rgb2hex__([100,25,50]) }
  end

  x.report("hex2rgb (Memoizable)") do
    N.times { hex2rgb("beaded") }
  end
  x.report("hex2rgb_manual_cache") do
    N.times { hex2rgb_manual_cache("beaded") }
  end
  x.report("hex2rgb_uncached") do
    N.times { __unmemoized_hex2rgb__("beaded") }
  end

end
```

```
sandal:fp $ ruby rgb2hex.rb
Rehearsal --------------------------------------------------
rgb2hex (Memoizable)    1.750000   0.010000   1.760000 (  1.801235)
rgb2hex_manual_cache    1.040000   0.010000   1.050000 (  1.067790)
rgb2hex_uncached        3.580000   0.020000   3.600000 (  3.680780)
hex2rgb (Memoizable)    0.990000   0.010000   1.000000 (  1.021821)
hex2rgb_manual_cache    0.280000   0.000000   0.280000 (  0.287521)
```

```
hex2rgb_uncached       1.210000  0.010000  1.220000 (  1.247875)
-------------------------------------------- total: 8.910000sec

                          user     system    total      real
rgb2hex (Memoizable)    1.760000  0.010000  1.770000 (  1.803120)
rgb2hex_manual_cache    1.040000  0.000000  1.040000 (  1.066625)
rgb2hex_uncached        3.600000  0.030000  3.630000 (  3.871221)
hex2rgb (Memoizable)    0.990000  0.010000  1.000000 (  1.017367)
hex2rgb_manual_cache    0.280000  0.000000  0.280000 (  0.283920)
hex2rgb_uncached        1.220000  0.010000  1.230000 (  1.248152)
```

Although `Memoizable` is predictably slower than our raw implementation, it is still cooking with gas when compared to the uncached versions of our functions. What we are seeing here is the overhead of an additional method call per request, so as the operation becomes more expensive, the cost of `Memoizable` actually gets lower. Also, if we look at things in terms of work versus payout, `Memoizable` is the clear winner, due to its ability to transparently hook itself into your functions.

I could stop here and move on to the next topic, but similar to when we looked into the belly of *lazy.rb* earlier in this chapter, I can't resist walking through and explaining some cool code. I am hoping that as you read through this book, you will find that things that seem magical on the surface have a clear and easy-to-understand implementation under the hood, and `Memoizable` is a perfect example for that.

Here is the full implementation of the module:

```
module Memoizable
  def memoize( name, cache = Hash.new )
    original = "__unmemoized_#{name}__"

    ([Class, Module].include?(self.class) ? self : self.class).class_eval do
      alias_method original, name
      private        original
      define_method(name) { |*args| cache[args] ||= send(original, *args) }
    end
  end
end
```

We see that the `memoize()` method takes a method name and an optional cache object, which defaults to an empty `Hash` if none is provided. The code then does some logic to determine whether you are using the top-level object (as we were), or just working in the context of an ordinary object. Once it figures that out, what remains is a simple `class_eval` block, which does what we talked about before. The original method is renamed, and then a new method is created that caches the return values of the original function based on the input arguments. Despite how powerful this code is, we see that it is of only marginally higher complexity than our handwritten caching.

Of course, this doesn't have a whole lot to do with functional programming techniques, except for showing you how you can abstract them into reusable constructs. In case this distracted you a bit, here are the things to remember about memoization before moving on to the next section:

- Functions that are well defined, where a single input consistently produces the same output, can be cached through memoization.

- Memoization often trades CPU time for memory, storing results rather than recalculating them. As a result, memoization is best used when memory is cheap and CPU time is costly, and not the other way around. In some cases, even when the memory consumption is negligible, the gains can be substantial. We can see this in the fib(n) example, which is transformed from an exponential algorithm to a linear one simply by storing the intermediate calculations.

- When coding your own solution, Hash.new's block form can be a very handy way of putting together a simple caching object.

- James Gray's Memoizable module makes it trivial to introduce memoization to well-defined functions without directly modifying their implementations, but incurs a small cost of indirection over an explicit caching strategy.

When dealing with sequences that can be generated from previous values, memoization isn't the only game in town. We're now going to take a look at how to build upon the concept of lazy evaluation to form very interesting structures known as infinite lists.

Infinite Lists

Infinite lists (also known as lazy streams) provide a way to represent arbitrary sequences that can be traversed by applying a certain function that gets to you the next element for any given element in the list. For example, if we start with any even number, we can get to the next one in the sequence by simply adding 2 to our original element.

Before we look at more complicated examples, let's take a look at how we can represent the even sequence of numbers this way, using a simple Ruby object:

```ruby
module EvenSeries
  class Node
    def initialize(number=0)
      @value = number
      @next  = lambda { Node.new(number + 2) }
    end

    attr_reader :value

    def next
      @next.call
    end
  end
end

e = EvenSeries::Node.new(30)
10.times do
  p e.value
  e = e.next
end
```

When we run this code, we get the following output:

```
30
32
34
36
38
40
42
44
46
48
```

The implementation should be mostly self-explanatory. An `EvenSeries::Node` is nothing more than a number and a `Proc` that is designed to add 2 to that number and construct a new `Node`. What we end up with is something that looks similar to a linked list, and we can clearly see what happens when we take 10 steps forward from 30 through the even numbers.

The key innovation is that we've turned an external iteration and state transformation into an internal one. The benefits of this technique will become more clear in later examples, but for now, it's worth noting that this is the key motivation for creating such a construct.

Although this example shows you the simplest thing that could possibly work when it comes to infinite lists, we can benefit from using a more generalized, more feature-complete structure for this task. Rather than rolling our own, I'm going to walk you through some of the examples for James Gray's `LazyStream` implementation, many of which you may have already seen in his Higher-Order Ruby blog series (*http://blog .grayproductions.net/categories/higherorder_ruby*). His focus was on showing how to build an infinite list structure; mine will be on how to make use of them.

The following is a trivial example of using *lazy_stream.rb*, doing simple iteration over a range of numbers:

```ruby
require "lazy_stream"

def upto( from, to )
  return if from > to
  lazy_stream(from) { upto(from + 1, to) }
end
upto(3, 6).show  # => 3 4 5 6

def upfrom( start )
  lazy_stream(start) { upfrom(start + 1) }
end
upfrom(7).show(10)  # => 7 8 9 10 11 12 13 14 15 16
```

As you can see here, `lazy_stream()` is just creating recursive calls that build up new elements that in turn know how to get to their next element. What is neat is that as the name suggests, these things are evaluated lazily. When we call `upto(3, 6)`, a `Proc` is set up to carry out this task for us, but it's not actually executed until we tell it to show us the results. Something similar is happening when we call `upfrom(7)`. Though this example is fairly basic, it gives us a jumping point into `lazy_stream`. We can make things more interesting by introducing classes into the mix:

```
require "lazy_stream"

class Upto < LazyStream::Node
  def initialize( from, to )
    if from > to
      super(nil, &nil)
    else
      super(from) { self.class.new(from + 1, to) }
    end
  end
end
Upto.new(3, 6).show  # => 3 4 5 6

class Upfrom < LazyStream::Node
  def initialize( from )
    super(from) { self.class.new(from + 1) }
  end
end
Upfrom.new(7).show(10)  # => 7 8 9 10 11 12 13 14 15 16
```

Though this code looks a bit more complex, it is also more flexible. What we have done is created our own custom `LazyStream::Node` objects, which, as you can see, accomplish the same thing as we did before but without relying on a generic constructor.

`LazyStream::Node` objects are enumerable, and this lets us do all sorts of fun stuff. The following code illustrates this by constructing a simple step iterator:

```
require "lazy_stream"

class Step < LazyStream::Node
  def initialize( step, start = 1 )
    super(start) { self.class.new(step, start + 1) }

    @step = step
  end

  def next_group( count = 10 )
    limit!(count).map { |i| i * @step }
  end
end

evens = Step.new(2)

puts "The first ten even numbers are:"
puts evens.next_group.join(" ")  # => 2 4 6 8 10 12 14 16 18 20

# later...

puts
puts "The next ten even numbers are:"
puts evens.next_group.join(" ")  # => 22 24 26 28 30 32 34 36 38 40
```

```
puts
puts "The current index for future calculations is:"
puts evens.current # => 21
```

Here is where the benefit of an internal iterator becomes clear. When we work with a Step object once it's been set up, we don't really care what its underlying function is from element to element. However, we can still work with it and pull out groups of elements as needed, keeping track of where we are in the list as we go along.

If we wanted to jump up in steps of three instead of two, you can see that the code changes are minimal:

```
threes = Step.new(3)

puts "The first ten multiples of 3 are"
puts threes.next_group.join(" ")   # => 3 6 9 12 15 18 21 24 27 30

# later...

puts
puts "The next ten are:"
puts threes.next_group.join(" ")   # => 33 36 39 42 45 48 51 54 57 60

puts
puts "The current index for future calculations is:"
puts threes.current # => 21
```

Though this stuff is pretty cool, things get a whole lot more interesting when you mix filters and transforms into the mix:

```
require "lazy_stream"

def letters( letter )
  lazy_stream(letter) { letters(letter.succ) }
end

letters("a").filter(/[aeiou]/).show(10)       # => a e i o u aa ab ac ad ae
letters("a").filter { |l| l.size == 2 }.show(3)   # => aa ab ac

letters("a").transform { |l| l + "..." }.show(3)  # => a... b... c...
```

Here, we're walking over successive ASCII string values. In the very first example, we ask lazy_stream to nab us the first 10 values that contain a vowel. In the second example, we ask for the first three strings of length two. In the third example, we ask to show the first three values with ... appended to them. In all three cases, lazy_stream is happy to provide us with what we'd expect.

To really get a sense for how nice this is, go ahead and write out a solution to these three problems using normal iterators and conditionals. Then compare your solution to using lazy_stream. What you will most likely find is that because lazy_stream internalizes a lot of the logic for us, it is more pleasant to work with and generally more expressive.

Before we move on, I'd like to show one more trick that `lazy_stream` has up its sleeve, and that is the ability to build up an infinite list recursively:

```
require "lazy_stream"

class Powers < LazyStream::Node
  def initialize( of, start = 1 )
    super(start) { self.class.new(of, start * of) }
  end
end

powers_of_two = Powers.new(2)
powers_of_two.show(10)  # => 1 2 4 8 16 32 64 128 256 512
```

We have caught glimpses of this technique in other examples, but this one shows clearly how you can build up a list based on its previous values. Here we construct the powers of two by repeatedly constructing new `LazyStream::Node` objects with values twice as much as their predecessors.

This turns out to be a simple, expressive way to traverse, filter, and transform lists that are linked together by a function that binds one element to the next. However, if this stuff is making your head hurt, you need to remember just the following things:

- Infinite lists essentially consist of nodes that contain a value along with a procedure that will transform that value into the next element in the sequence.
- Infinite lists are lazily evaluated, and thus are sometimes called lazy streams.
- An infinite list might be an appropriate structure to use when you need to iterate over a sequential list in groups at various points in time, or if you have a general function that can be tweaked by some parameters to fit your needs.
- For data that is sparse, memoization might be a better technique than using an infinite list.
- When you need to do filtering or state transformation on a long sequence of elements that have a clear relationship from one to the next, a lazy stream might be the best way to go.
- JEG2's *lazy_stream.rb* provides a generalized implementation of infinite lists that is worth taking a look at if you have a need for this sort of thing.

If you're still hanging on this far into the chapter, you're either really enjoying this weird functional stuff, or you're a very determined reader. Either way, you will be happy to know that all of the hard parts are over. Before we close the chapter and make some conclusions, let's take a quick look at one of the most simple but fundamentally useful things Ruby has borrowed from its functional peers: higher-order procedures.

Higher-Order Procedures

Throughout this whole chapter, we've been taking something for granted that not all languages can: in Ruby, a `Proc` is just another object. This means we can sling these chunks of code around as if they were any other value, which results in a whole lot of powerful functionality.

This feature is so ingrained in Ruby development, and so well integrated into the system, that it's easy to overlook. However, I could not in good conscience wrap up a chapter on functional programming techniques without at least showing a simple example of higher-order procedure.

A function is said to be a higher-order function if it accepts another function as input or returns a function as its output. We see a lot of the former in Ruby; basically, we'd see this any time we provide a code block to a method. But functions that return functions might be a bit less familiar to those who are new to the language.

Through closures, we can use a function to essentially build up customized procedures on the fly. I could show some abstract examples or academically exciting functionality such as `Proc#curry`, but instead, I decided that I wanted to show you something I use fairly frequently.

If you used Rails before Ruby 1.9, you probably were familiar with the "innovation" of `Symbol#to_proc`. What some smart folks realized is that Ruby's `&block` mechanism actually calls a hook on the underlying object, which could be self-defined. Though `Symbol#to_proc` exists in Ruby 1.9 by default, let's look at what a simple implementation of it would look like in Ruby:

```ruby
class Symbol
  def to_proc
    lambda { |x| x.send(self) }
  end
end
```

As you probably know, this feature allows for some nice syntactic sugar:

```ruby
>> %w[foo bar baz].map(&:capitalize)
=> ["Foo", "Bar", "Baz"]
```

The way that it works should be easy to see from the implementation shown here, but in essence, what happens is that `&:capitalize` invokes `Symbol#to_proc` and then constructs a block like this:

```ruby
lambda { |x| x.send(:capitalize) }
```

This in turn is then treated as a code block, making it functionally identical to the following code:

```ruby
>> %w[foo bar baz].map { |x| x.capitalize }
```

Of course, you've probably seen a hundred blog posts about this feature, so this is not what I'm really trying to show you. What I'd like you to know, and eventually take advantage of, is that `Object#to_proc` is a generic hook. This means `Symbol#to_proc` isn't special, and we can build our own custom objects that do even cooler tricks than it does.

The place I use this functionality all the time is in Rails applications where I need to build up filter mechanisms that do some of the work in SQL, and the rest in Ruby.

Though my filter objects typically grow to be long, complicated, and nasty, their back-bone always lies upon something somewhat simple. Here is the general pattern I usually start with:

```ruby
class Filter
  def initialize
    @constraints = []
  end

  def constraint(&block)
    @constraints << block
  end

  def to_proc
    lambda { |e| @constraints.all? { |fn| fn.call(e) } }
  end
end
```

We can then construct a `Filter` object and assign constraints to it on the fly:

```ruby
filter = Filter.new
filter.constraint { |x| x > 10 }
filter.constraint { |x| x.even? }
filter.constraint { |x| x % 3 == 0 }
```

Now, when dealing with an `Enumerable` object, it is easy to filter the data based on our constraints:

```ruby
p (8..24).select(&filter) #=> [12,18,24]
```

As we add more constraints, new blocks are generated for us, so things work as expected:

```ruby
filter.constraint { |x| x % 4 == 0 }
```

```ruby
p (8..24).select(&filter) #=> [12,24]
```

As you can see, `Symbol#to_proc` isn't the only game in town. Any object that can meaningfully be reduced to a function can implement a useful **to_proc** method.

Of course, higher-order procedures are not limited to **to_proc** hacks. There are lots of other good uses for functions that return functions, though it is often a relatively rare use case, so it's hard to give you a list of must-have techniques when it comes to this topic.

Because this example was short and sweet, we don't need to go over various guidelines as we have in previous sections. Just keep this trick in the back of your mind, and use it to improve the readability and flexibility of your code.

We've covered a lot of ground here, so it's about time to wrap up this chapter.

Conclusions

Although we covered a number of "functional programming techniques" throughout this chapter, it's fairly plain to see that Ruby isn't a functional programming language. Even if we can force Ruby into being pretty much whatever we want it to be, it's generally not an advisable thing to do.

Nevertheless, we've covered some interesting and useful tricks here that were inspired by techniques used in other languages. By letting Ruby be Ruby and not striving too hard for a direct translation, we end up with code that is actually practical and suitable for use in everyday applications.

My general feeling about applying functional programming techniques in Ruby is mainly that they can be a true source of elegance and simplicity when appropriate. However, judging when it's the right time to bust out some functional goodness rather than going with the more vanilla approach can be difficult, even among seasoned developers. It is entirely possible to make your code too clever, and this often has real penalties in performance or in the ability of other developers to easily learn your code.

Many functional programming techniques result in code that is highly readable at the expense of learnability, at least in the context of Ruby. If you keep an eye on that balance and make it fit within your working environment, you'll be just fine.

Even if some of the techniques seen in this chapter cannot be readily used in a direct way in many cases, there is a lot to be said for thinking differently and looking at your code from another angle. Hopefully, this chapter has helped you do that.

## CHAPTER 6

When Things Go Wrong

Unfortunately, neither this book nor a lifetime of practice can cause you to attain Ruby programming perfection. However, a good substitute for never making a mistake is knowing how to fix your problems as they arise. The purpose of this chapter is to provide you with the necessary tools and techniques to prepare you for Ruby search-and-rescue missions.

We will start by walking through a simple but real bug-hunting session to get a basic outline of how to investigate issues in your Ruby projects. We'll then dive into some more specific tools and techniques for helping refine this process. What may surprise you is that we'll do all of this without ever talking about using a debugger. This is mainly because most Rubyists can and do get away without the use of a formal debugging tool, via various lightweight techniques that we'll discuss here.

One skill set you will need in order to make the most out of what we'll discuss here is a decent understanding of how Ruby's built-in unit testing framework works. That means if you haven't yet read Chapter 1, *Driving Code Through Tests*, you may want to go ahead and do that now.

What you will notice about this chapter is that it is much more about the process of problem solving in the context of Ruby than it is about solving any particular problem. If you keep this goal in mind while reading through the examples, you'll make the most out of what we'll discuss here.

Now that you know what to expect, let's start fixing some stuff.

A Process for Debugging Ruby Code

Part of becoming masterful at anything is learning from your mistakes. Because Ruby programming is no exception, I want to share one of my embarrassing moments so that others can benefit from it. If the problems with the code that I am about to show are immediately obvious to you, don't worry about that. Instead, focus on the problem-solving strategies used, as that's what is most important here.

We're going to look at a simplified version of a real problem I ran into in my day-to-day work. One of my Rails gigs involved building a system for processing scholarship applications online. After users have filled out an application once, whether it was accepted or rejected, they are presented with a somewhat different application form upon renewal. Although it deviates a bit from our real-world application, here's some simple code that illustrates that process:

```ruby
if gregory.can_renew?
  puts "Start the application renewal process"
else
  puts "Edit a pending application or submit a new one"
end
```

At first, I thought the logic for this was simple. As long as all of the user's applications had a status of either accepted or rejected, it was safe to say that they could renew their application. The following code provides a rough model that implements this requirement:

```ruby
Application = Struct.new(:state)

class User
  def initialize
    @applications = []
  end

  attr_reader :applications

  def can_renew?
    applications.all? { |e| [:accepted, :rejected].include?(e.state) }
  end
end
```

Using this model, we can see that the output of the following code is Start the application renewal process:

```ruby
gregory = User.new
gregory.applications << Application.new(:accepted)
gregory.applications << Application.new(:rejected)

if gregory.can_renew?
  puts "Start the application renewal process"
else
  puts "Edit a pending application or submit a new one"
end
```

If we add a pending application into the mix, we see that the other case is triggered, outputting Edit a pending application or submit a new one:

```ruby
gregory = User.new
gregory.applications << Application.new(:accepted)
gregory.applications << Application.new(:rejected)
gregory.applications << Application.new(:pending)

if gregory.can_renew?
  puts "Start the application renewal process"
```

```
    else
      puts "Edit a pending application or submit a new one"
    end
```

So far everything has been going fine, but the next bit of code exposes a nasty edge case:

```
gregory = User.new

if gregory.can_renew?
  puts "Start the application renewal process"
else
  puts "Edit a pending application or submit a new one"
end
```

I fully expected this to print out `Edit a pending application or submit a new one`, but it managed to print the other message instead!

Popping open *irb*, I tracked down the root of the problem:

```
>> gregory = User.new
=> #<User:0x2618bc @applications=[]>
>> gregory.can_renew?
=> true

>> gregory.applications
=> []
>> gregory.applications.all? { false }
=> true
```

Of course, the trouble here was due to an incorrect use of the `Enumerable#all?` method. I had been relying on Ruby to do what I meant rather than what I actually asked it to do, which is usually a bad idea. For some reason I thought that calling `all?` on an empty array would return `nil` or `false`, but instead, it returned `true`. To fix it, I'd need to rethink `can_renew?` a little bit.

I could have fixed the issue immediately by adding a special case involving `applications.empty?`, but I wanted to be sure this bug wouldn't have a chance to crop up again. The easiest way to do this was to write some tests, which I probably should have done in the first place.

The following simple test case clearly specified the behavior I expected, splitting it up into three cases as we did before:

```
require "test/unit"

class UserTest < Test::Unit::TestCase
  def setup
    @gregory = User.new
  end

  def test_a_new_applicant_cannot_renew
    assert_block("Expected User#can_renew? to be false for a new applicant") do
      not @gregory.can_renew?
    end
  end
```

```
def test_a_user_with_pending_applications_cannot_renew
  @gregory.applications << app(:accepted) << app(:pending)

  msg = "Expected User#can_renew? to be false when user has pending applications"
  assert_block(msg) do
    not @gregory.can_renew?
  end
end

def test_a_user_with_only_accepted_and_rejected_applications_can_renew
  @gregory.applications << app(:accepted) << app(:rejected) << app(:accepted)
  msg = "Expected User#can_renew? to be true when all applications " +
        "are accepted or rejected"
  assert_block(msg) { @gregory.can_renew? }
end

private

def app(name)
  Application.new(name)
end

end
```

When we run the tests, we can clearly see the failure that we investigated manually a little earlier:

```
1) Failure:
test_a_new_applicant_cannot_renew(UserTest) [foo.rb:24]:
Expected User#can_renew? to be false for a new applicant

3 tests, 3 assertions, 1 failures, 0 errors
```

Now that we've successfully captured the essence of the bug, we can go about fixing it. As you may suspect, the solution is simple:

```
def can_renew?
  return false if applications.empty?
  applications.all? { |e| [:accepted, :rejected].include?(e.state) }
end
```

Running the tests again, we see that everything passes:

```
3 tests, 3 assertions, 0 failures, 0 errors
```

If we went back and ran our original examples that print some messages to the screen, we'd see that those now work as expected as well. We could have used those on their own to test our attempted fix, but by writing automated tests, we have a safety net against regressions, which may be one of the main benefits of unit tests.

Though the particular bug we squashed may be a bit boring, what we have shown is a repeatable procedure for bug hunting, without ever firing up a debugger or combing through logfiles. To recap, here's the general plan for how things should play out:

1. First, identify the different scenarios that apply to a given feature.

2. Enumerate over these scenarios to identify which ones are affected by defects and which ones work as expected. This can be done in many ways, ranging from printing debugging messages on the command line to logfile analysis and live application testing. The important thing is to identify and isolate the cases affected by the bug.

3. Hop into *irb* if possible and take a look at what your objects actually look like under the hood. Experiment with the failing scenarios in a step-by-step fashion to try to dig down and uncover the root cause of problems.

4. Write tests to reproduce the problems you are having, along with what you expect to happen when the issue is resolved.

5. Implement a fix that passes the tests, and then repeat the process until all issues are resolved.

Sometimes, it's possible to condense this process into two steps simply by writing a test that reproduces the bug and then introducing a fix that passes the tests. However, most of the time the extra legwork will pay off, as understanding the root cause of the problem will allow you to treat your application's disease all at once rather than addressing its symptoms one by one.

Given this basic outline of how to isolate and resolve issues within our code, we can now focus on some specific tools and techniques that will help improve the process for us.

Capturing the Essence of a Defect

Before you can begin to hunt down a bug, you need to be able to reproduce it in isolation. The main idea is that if you remove all the extraneous code that is unrelated to the issue, it will be easier to see what is really going on. As you continue to investigate an issue, you may discover that you can reduce the example more and more based on what you learn. Because I have a real example handy from one of my projects, we can look at this process in action to see how it plays out.

What follows is some Prawn code that was submitted as a bug report. The problem it's supposed to show is that every text span() resulted in a page break happening, when it wasn't supposed to:

```
Prawn::Document.generate("span.pdf") do

  span(350, :position => :center) do
    text "Here's some centered text in a 350 point column. " * 100
  end

  text "Here's my sentence."

  bounding_box([50,300], :width => 400) do
    text "Here's some default bounding box text. " * 10
    span(bounds.width,
```

```
        :position => bounds.absolute_left - margin_box.absolute_left) do
      text "The rain in Spain falls mainly on the plains. " * 300
    end
  end

  text "Here's my second sentence."

end
```

Without a strong knowledge of Prawn, this example may already seem fairly reduced. After all, the text represents a sort of abstract problem definition rather than some code that was ripped out of an application, and that is a good start. But upon running this code, I noticed that the defect was present whenever a span() call was made. This allowed me to reduce the example substantially:

```
Prawn::Document.generate("span.pdf") do

  span(350) do
    text "Here's some text in a 350pt wide column. " * 20
  end

  text "This text should appear on the same page as the spanning text"

end
```

Whether or not you have any practical experience in Prawn, the issue stands out better in this revised example, simply because there is less code to consider. The code is also a bit more self-documenting, which makes buggy output harder to miss. Many bug reports can be reduced in a similar fashion. Of course, not everything compacts so well, but every little bit of simplification helps.

Most bugs aren't going to show up in the first place you look. Instead, they'll often be hidden farther down the chain, stashed away in some low-level helper method or in some other code that your feature depends on. As this is so common, I've developed the habit of mentally tracing the execution path that my example code follows, in hopes of finding some obvious mistake along the way. If I notice anything suspicious, I start the next iteration of bug reproduction.

Using this approach, I found that the problem with span() wasn't actually in span() at all. Although the details aren't important, it turns out that the core problem was in a lower-level function called canvas(), which span() relies on. This method was incorrectly setting the text cursor on the page to the very bottom of the page after executing its block argument. I used the following example to confirm this was the case:

```
Prawn::Document.generate("canvas_sets_y_to_0.pdf") do
  canvas { text "Some text at the absolute top left of the page" }

  text "This text should not be after a pagebreak"
end
```

When I saw that I was able to reproduce the problem, I went on to formally specify what was wrong in the form of tests, feeling reasonably confident that this was the root defect.

Whenever you are hunting for bugs, the practice of reducing your area of interest first will help you avoid dead ends and limit the number of possible places in which you'll need to look for problems. Before doing any formal investigation, it's a good idea to check for obvious problems so that you can get a sense of where the real source of your defect is. Some bugs are harder to catch on sight than others, but there is no need to overthink the easy ones.

If a defect can be reproduced in isolation, you can usually narrow it down to a specific deviation from what you expected to happen. We'll now take a look at how to go from an example that reproduces a bug to a failing test that fully categorizes it.

The main benefit of an automated test is that it will explode when your code fails to act as expected. It is important to keep in mind that even if you have an existing test suite, when you encounter a bug that does not cause any failures, you need to update your tests. This helps prevent regressions, allowing you to fix a bug once and forget about it.

Continuing with our example, here is a simple but sufficient test to corner the bug:

```ruby
class CanvasTest < Test::Unit::TestCase

  def setup
    @pdf = Prawn::Document.new
  end

  def test_canvas_should_not_reset_y_to_zero
    after_text_position = nil

    @pdf.canvas do
      @pdf.text "Hello World"
      after_text_position = @pdf.y
    end

    assert_equal after_text_position, @pdf.y
  end
end
```

Here, we expect the *y* coordinate after the **canvas** block is executed to be the same as it was just after the text was rendered to the page. Running this test reproduces the problem we created an example for earlier:

```
  1) Failure:test_canvas_should_not_reset_y_to_zero(CanvasTest) [---]
<778.128> expected but was
<0.0>.
```

Here, we have converted our simplified example into something that can become a part of our automated test suite. The simpler an example is, the easier this is to do. More complicated examples may need to be broken into several chunks, but this process is straightforward more often than not.

Once we write a test that reproduces our problem, the way we fix it is to get our tests passing again. If other tests end up breaking in order to get our new test to pass, we know that something is still wrong. If for some reason our problem isn't solved when we get all the tests passing again, it means that our reduced example probably didn't cover the entirety of the problem, so we need to go back to the drawing board in those cases. Even still, not all is lost. Each test serves as a significant reduction of your problem space. Every passing assertion eliminates the possibility of that particular issue from being the root of your problem. Sooner or later, there won't be any place left for your bugs to hide.

For those who need a recap, here are the keys to producing a good reduced example:

- Remove as much extraneous code as possible from your example, and the bug will be clearer to see.
- Try to make your example self-describing, so that even someone unfamiliar with the core issue can see at a glance whether something is wrong. This helps others report regressions even if they don't fully understand the internals of your project.
- Continue to revise your examples until they reach the root cause of the problem. Don't throw away any of the higher-level examples until you verify that fixing a general problem solves the specific issue that you ran into as well.
- When you understand the root cause of your problem, code up a failing test that demonstrates how the code should work. When it passes, the bug should be gone. If it fails again, you'll know there has been a regression.

Scrutinizing Your Code

When things aren't working the way you expect them to, you obviously need to find out why. There are certain tricks that can make this task a lot easier on you, and you can use them without ever needing to fire up the debugger.

Utilizing Reflection

Many bugs come from using an object in a different way than you're supposed to, or from some internal state deviating from your expectations. To be able to detect and fix these bugs, you need to be able to get a clear picture of what is going on under the hood in the objects you're working with.

I'll assume that you already know that `Kernel#p` and `Object#inspect` exist, and how to use them for basic needs. However, when left to their default behaviors, using these tools to debug complex objects can be too painful to be practical. We can take an unadorned `Prawn::Document`'s `inspect` output for an example:

```
#<Prawn::Document:0x12cf17c @page_content=#<Prawn::Reference:0x12cecf4
@data={:Length=>0}, @gen=0, @identifier=4, @stream="0.000 0.000 0.000 r
g\n0.000 0.000 0.000 RG\nq\n", @compressed=false>, @info=
#<Prawn::Reference:0x12cf0c8 @data={:Creator=>"Prawn", :Producer=>"Prawn"},
@gen=0, @identifier=1, @compressed=false>
, @root=#<Prawn::Reference:0x12cf064 @data={:Type=>:Catalog, :Pages=>
#<Prawn::Reference:0x12cf08c @data={:Count=>1, :Kids=>[#<Prawn::Reference:0x12ceca4
@data={:Contents=>#<Prawn::Reference:0x12cecf4
@data={:Length=>0}, @gen=0, @identifier=4, @stream="0.000 0.000 0.000 rg\n0.000
0.000 0.000 RG\nq\n",

<< ABOUT 50 MORE LINES LIKE THIS >>

#<Prawn::Reference:0x12cf08c @data={:Count=>1, :Kids=>[#<Prawn::Reference:0x12ceca4
...>], :Type=>:Pages}, @gen=0, @identifier=2, @compressed=false>,
:MediaBox=>[0, 0, 612.0, 792.0]}, @gen=0, @identifier=5, @compressed=false>],
@margin_box=#<Prawn::Document::BoundingBox:0x12ced30 @width=540.0,
@y=756.0, @x=36, @parent=#<Prawn::Document:0x12cf17c ...>, @height=720.0>,
@fill_color="000000", @current_page=#<Prawn::Reference:0x12ceca4 @data={:Contents=>
#<Prawn::Reference:0x12cecf4 @data={:Length=>0}, @gen=0, @identifier=4,
@stream="0.000 0.000 0.000 rg\n0.000 0.000 0.000 RG\nq\n", @compressed=false>,
:Type=>:Page, :Parent=>#<Prawn::Reference:0x12cf08c @data={:Count=>1,
:Kids=>[#<Prawn::Reference:0x12ceca4 ...>], :Type=>:Pages},
@gen=0, @identifier=2, @compressed=false>, :MediaBox=>[0, 0, 612.0, 792.0]},
@gen=0, @identifier=5, @compressed=false>, @skip_encoding=nil,
@bounding_box=#<Prawn::Document::BoundingBox:0x12ced30 @width=540.0, @y=756.0, @x=36,
@parent=#<Prawn::Document:0x12cf17c ...>, @height=720.0>, @page_size="LETTER",
@stroke_color="000000" , @text_options={}, @compress=false, @margins={:top=>36,
:left=>36, :bottom=>36, :right=>36}>
```

Although this information sure is thorough, it probably won't help us quickly identify what page layout is being used or what the dimensions of the margins are. If we aren't familiar with the internals of this object, such verbose output is borderline useless. Of course, this doesn't mean we're simply out of luck. In situations like this, we can infer a lot about an object by using Ruby's reflective capabilities:

```
>> pdf.class
=> Prawn::Document

>> pdf.instance_variables
=> [:@objects, :@info, :@pages, :@root, :@page_size, :@page_layout, :@compress,
:@skip_encoding, :@background, :@font_size, :@text_options, :@margins, :@margin_box,
:@bounding_box, :@page_content, :@current_page, :@fill_color, :@stroke_color, :@y]

>> Prawn::Document.instance_methods(inherited_methods=false).sort
=> [:bounding_box, :bounds, :bounds=, :canvas, :compression_enabled?, :cursor,
:find_font, :font, :font_families, :font_registry, :font_size, :font_size=,
:margin_box, :margin_box=, :margins, :mask, :move_down, :move_up, :pad, :pad_bottom,
:pad_top, :page_count, :page_layout, :page_size, :render, :render_file, :save_font,
:set_font, :span, :start_new_page, :text_box, :width_of, :y, :y=]

>> pdf.private_methods(inherited_methods=false)
=> [:init_bounding_box, :initialize, :build_new_page_content, :generate_margin_box]
```

Now, even if we haven't worked with this particular object before, we have a sense of what is available, and it makes queries like the ones mentioned in the previous paragraph much easier:

```
>> pdf.margins
=> {:left=>36, :right=>36, :top=>36, :bottom=>36}

>> pdf.page_layout
=> :portrait
```

If we want to look at some lower-level details, such as the contents of some instance variables, we can do so via `instance_variable_get`:

```
>> pdf.instance_variable_get(:@current_page)
=> #<Prawn::Reference:0x4e5750 @identifier=5, @gen=0, @data={:Type=>:Page,
:Parent=>#<Prawn::Reference:0x4e5b60 @identifier=2, @gen=0, @data={:Type=>:Pages,
:Count=>1, :Kids=>[#<Prawn::Reference:0x4e5750 ...>]}, @compressed=false,
@on_encode=nil>, :MediaBox=>[0, 0, 612.0, 792.0],
:Contents=>#<Prawn::Reference:0x4e57a0 @identifier=4, @gen=0, @data={:Length=>0},
@compressed=false, @on_encode=nil,
@stream="0.000 0.000 0.000 rg\n0.000 0.000 0.000 RG\nq\n">}, @compressed=false,
@on_encode=nil>
```

Using these tricks, we can easily determine whether we've accidentally got the name of a variable or method wrong. We can also see what the underlying structure of our objects are, and repeat this process to drill down and investigate potential problems.

Improving inspect Output

Of course, the whole situation here would be better if we had easier-to-read `inspect` output. There is actually a standard library called *pp* that improves the formatting of `inspect` while operating in a very similar fashion. I wrote a whole section in Appendix B about this library, including some of its advanced capabilities. You should definitely read up on what `pp` offers you when you get the chance, but here I'd like to cover some alternative approaches that can also come in handy.

As it turns out, the output of `Kernel#p` can be improved on an object-by-object basis. This may be obvious if you have used `Object#inspect` before, but it is also a severely underused feature of Ruby. This feature can be used to turn the mess we saw in the previous section into beautiful debugging output:

```
>> pdf = Prawn::Document.new
=> < Prawn::Document:0x27df8a:
        @background: nil
        @compress: false
        @fill_color: "000000"
        @font_size: 12
        @margins: {:left=>36, :right=>36, :top=>36, :bottom=>36}
        @page_layout: :portrait
        @page_size: "LETTER"
        @skip_encoding: nil
        @stroke_color: "000000"
```

```
@text_options: {}
@y: 756.0

@bounding_box -> Prawn::Document::BoundingBox:0x27dd64
@current_page -> Prawn::Reference:0x27dd1e
@info -> Prawn::Reference:0x27df44
@margin_box -> Prawn::Document::BoundingBox:0x27dd64
@objects -> Array:0x27df6c
@page_content -> Prawn::Reference:0x27dd46
@pages -> Prawn::Reference:0x27df26
@root -> Prawn::Reference:0x27df12 >
```

I think you'll agree that this looks substantially easier to follow than the default
`inspect` output. To accomplish this, I put together a template that allows you to pass
in a couple of arrays of symbols that point at instance variables:

```
module InspectTemplate

  def __inspect_template(objs, refs)
    obj_output = objs.sort.each_with_object("") do |v,out|
      out << "\n        #{v}: #{instance_variable_get(v).inspect}"
    end

    ref_output = refs.sort.each_with_object("") do |v,out|
      ref = instance_variable_get(v)
      out << "\n        #{v} -> #{__inspect_object_tag(ref)}"
    end

    "< #{__inspect_object_tag(self)}: #{obj_output}\n#{ref_output} >"
  end

  def __inspect_object_tag(obj)
    "#{obj.class}:0x#{obj.object_id.to_s(16)}"
  end

end
```

After mixing this into `Prawn::Document`, I need only to specify which variables I want
to display the entire contents of, and which I want to just show as references. Then, it
is as easy as calling `__inspect_template` with these values:

```
class Prawn::Document

  include InspectTemplate

  def inspect
    objs = [ :@page_size, :@page_layout, :@margins, :@font_size, :@background,
             :@stroke_color, :@fill_color, :@text_options, :@y, :@compress,
             :@skip_encoding ]
    refs = [ :@objects, :@info, :@pages, :@bounding_box, :@margin_box,
             :@page_content, :@current_page, :@root]
    __inspect_template(objs,refs)
  end
end
```

Once we provide a customized `inspect` method that returns a string, both `Kernel#p` and *irb* will pick up on it, yielding the nice results shown earlier.

Although my `InspectTemplate` can easily be reused, it carries the major caveat that you become 100% responsible for exposing your variables for debugging output. Anything not explicitly passed to `__inspect_template` will not be rendered. However, there is a middle-of-the-road solution that is far more automatic.

The *yaml* data serialization standard library has the nice side effect of producing highly readable representations of Ruby objects. Because of this, it actually provides a `Kernel#y` method that can be used as a stand-in replacement for p. Although this may be a bit strange, if you look at it in action, you'll see that it has some benefits:

```
>> require "yaml"
=> true

>> y Prawn::Document.new
--- &id007 !ruby/object:Prawn::Document
background:
bounding_box: &id002 !ruby/object:Prawn::Document::BoundingBox
  height: 720.0
  parent: *id007
  width: 540.0
  x: 36
  y: 756.0
compress: false
info: &id003 !ruby/object:Prawn::Reference
  compressed: false
  data:
    :Creator: Prawn
    :Producer: Prawn
  gen: 0
  identifier: 1
  on_encode:
margin_box: *id002
margins:
  :left: 36
  :right: 36
  :top: 36
  :bottom: 36
page_content: *id005
page_layout: :portrait
page_size: LETTER
pages: *id004
root: *id006
skip_encoding:
stroke_color: "000000"
text_options: {}

y: 756.0
=> nil
```

I truncated this file somewhat, but the basic structure shines through. You can see that YAML nicely shows nested object relations, and generally looks neat and tidy. Interestingly enough, YAML automatically truncates repeated object references by referring to them by ID only. This turns out to be especially good for tracking down a certain kind of Ruby bug:

```
>> a = Array.new(6)
=> [nil, nil, nil, nil, nil, nil]
>> a = Array.new(6,[])
=> [[], [], [], [], [], []]
>> a[0] << "foo"
=> ["foo"]
>> a
=> [["foo"], ["foo"], ["foo"], ["foo"], ["foo"], ["foo"]]
>> y a
---
- &id001
  - foo
- *id001
- *id001
- *id001
- *id001
- *id001
```

Here, it's easy to see that the six subarrays that make up our main array are actually just six references to the same object. And in case that wasn't the goal, we can see the difference when we have six distinct objects very clearly in YAML:

```
>> a = Array.new(6) { [] }
=> [[], [], [], [], [], []]
>> a[0] << "foo"
=> ["foo"]
>> a
=> [["foo"], [], [], [], [], []]
>> y a
---
- - foo
- []

- []

- []

- []

- []
```

Although this may not be a problem you run into every day, it's relatively easy to forget to deep-copy a structure from time to time, or to accidentally create many copies of a reference to the same object when you're trying to set default values. When that happens, a quick call to y will make a long series of references to the same object appear very clearly.

Of course, the YAML output will come in handy when you encounter this problem by accident or if it is part of some sort of deeply nested structure. If you already know exactly where to look and can easily get at it, using pure Ruby works fine as well:

```
>> a = Array.new(6) { [] }
=> [[], [], [], [], [], []]
>> a.map { |e| e.object_id }
=> [3423870, 3423860, 3423850, 3423840, 3423830, 3423820]
>> b = Array.new(6,[])
=> [[], [], [], [], [], []]
>> b.map { |e| e.object_id }
=> [3431570, 3431570, 3431570, 3431570, 3431570, 3431570]
```

So far, we've been focusing very heavily on how to inspect your objects. This is mostly because a great deal of Ruby bugs can be solved by simply getting a sense of what objects are being passed around and what data they really contain. But this is, of course, not the full extent of the problem; we also need to be able to work with code that has been set in motion.

Finding Needles in a Haystack

Sometimes it's impossible to pull up a defective object easily to directly inspect it. Consider, for example, a large dataset that has some occasional anomalies in it. If you're dealing with tens or hundreds of thousands of records, an error like this won't be very helpful after your script churns for a while and then goes right off the tracks:

```
>> @data.map { |e|Integer(e[:amount]) }
ArgumentError: invalid value for Integer: "157,000"
        from (irb):10:in 'Integer'
        from (irb):10
        from (irb):10:in 'inject'
        from (irb):10:in 'each'
        from (irb):10:in 'inject'
        from (irb):10
        from :0
```

This error tells you virtually nothing about what has happened, except that somewhere in your giant dataset, there is an invalidly formatted integer. Let's explore how to deal with situations like this, by creating some data and introducing a few problems into it.

When it comes to generating fake data for testing, you can't get easier than the *faker* gem. Here's a sample of creating an array of hash records containing 5,000 names, phone numbers, and payments:

```
>> data = 5000.times.map do
?>   { name: Faker::Name.name, phone_number: Faker::PhoneNumber.phone_number,
?>     payment: rand(10000).to_s }
>> end

>> data.length
=> 5000
>> data[0..2]
```

```
=> [{:name=>"Joshuah Wyman", :phone_number=>"393-258-6420", :payment=>"6347"},
   {:name=>"Kraig Jacobi", :phone_number=>"779-295-0532", :payment=>"9186"},
   {:name=>"Jevon Harris", :phone_number=>"985.169.0519", :payment=>"213"}]
```

Now, we can randomly corrupt a handful of records, to give us a basis for this example. Keep in mind that the purpose of this demonstration is to show how to respond to unanticipated problems, rather than a known issue with your data.

```
5.times { data[rand(data.length)][:payment] << ".25" }
```

Now if we ask a simple question such as which records have an amount over 1,000, we get our familiar and useless error:

```
>> data.select { |e| Integer(e[:payment]) > 1000 }
ArgumentError: invalid value for Integer: "1991.25"
```

At this point, we'd like to get some more information about where this problem is actually located in our data, and what the individual record looks like. Because we presumably have no idea how many of these records there are, we might start by rescuing a single failure and then reraising the error after printing some of this data to the screen. We'll use a begin...rescue construct here as well as Enumerable#with_index:

```
>> data.select.with_index do |e,i|
?>   begin
?>     Integer(e[:payment]) > 1000
>>   rescue ArgumentError
>>     p [e,i]
>>     raise
>>   end
>> end
[{:name=>"Mr. Clotilde Baumbach", :phone_number=>"(608)779-7942",
:payment=>"1991.25"}, 91]
ArgumentError: invalid value for Integer: "1991.25"
        from (irb):67:in 'Integer'
        from (irb):67:in 'block in irb_binding'
        from (irb):65:in 'select'
        from (irb):65:in 'with_index'
        from (irb):65
        from /Users/sandal/lib/ruby19_1/bin/irb:12:in '<main>'
```

So now we've pinpointed where the problem is coming from, and we know what the actual record looks like. Aside from the payment being a string representation of a Float instead of an Integer, it's not immediately clear that there is anything else wrong with this record. If we drop the line that reraises the error, we can get a full report of records with this issue:

```
>> data.select.with_index do |e,i|
?>   begin
?>     Integer(e[:payment]) > 1000
>>   rescue ArgumentError
>>     p [e,i]
>>   end
>> end; nil
[{:name=>"Mr. Clotilde Baumbach", :phone_number=>"(608)779-7942",
:payment=>"1991.25"}, 91]
```

```
[{:name=>"Oceane Cormier", :phone_number=>"658.016.1612", :payment=>"7361.25"}, 766]
[{:name=>"Imogene Bergnaum", :phone_number=>"(573)402-6508",
:payment=>"1073.25"}, 1368]
[{:name=>"Jeramy Prohaska", :phone_number=>"928.266.5508 x97173",
:payment=>"6109.25"}, 2398]
[{:name=>"Betty Gerhold", :phone_number=>"250-149-3161", :payment=>"8668.25"}, 2399]
=> nil
```

As you can see, this change recovered all the rows with this issue. Based on this information, we could probably make a decision about what to do to fix the issue. But because we're just interested in the process here, the actual solution doesn't matter that much. Instead, the real point to remember is that when faced with an opaque error after iterating across a large dataset, you can go back and temporarily rework things to allow you to analyze the problematic data records.

You'll see variants on this theme later on in the chapter, but for now, let's recap what to remember when you are looking at your code under the microscope:

- Don't rely on giant, ugly `inspect` statements if you can avoid it. Instead, use introspection to narrow your search down to the specific relevant objects.

- Writing your own `#inspect` method allows customized output from `Kernel#p` and within *irb*. However, this means that you are responsible for adding new state to the debugging output as your objects evolve.

- YAML provides a nice `Kernel#y` method that provides a structured, easy-to-read representation of Ruby objects. This is also useful for spotting accidental reference duplication bugs.

- Sometimes stack traces aren't enough. You can `rescue` and then reraise an error after printing some debugging output to help you find the root cause of your problems.

So far, we've talked about solutions that work well as part of the active debugging process. However, in many cases it is also important to passively collect error feedback for dealing with later. It is possible to do this with Ruby's logging system, so let's shift gears a bit and check it out.

Working with Logger

I'm not generally a big fan of logfiles. I much prefer the immediacy of seeing problems directly reported on the screen as soon as they happen. If possible, I actually want to be thrown directly into my problematic code so I can take a look around. However, this isn't always an option, and in certain cases, having an audit trail in the form of logfiles is as good as it's going to get.

Ruby's standard library *logger* is fairly full-featured, allowing you to log many different kinds of messages and filter them based on their severity. The API is reasonably well documented, so I won't be spending a ton of time here going over a feature-by-feature summary of what this library offers. Instead, I'll show you how to replicate a bit of functionality that is especially common in Ruby's web frameworks: comprehensive error logging.

If I pull up a log from one of my Rails applications, I can easily show what I'm talking about. The following is just a small section of a logfile, in which a full request and the error it ran into have been recorded:

```
Processing ManagerController#call_in_sheet (for 127.0.0.1 at 2009-02-13 16:38:42)
  [POST] Session ID: BAh7CCIJdXNlcmkiOg5yZXR1cm5fdG8wIgpmbGFzaElDOidBY3Rpb25Db25O
  %OAcm9sbGVyOjpFbGFzaDo6Rmxhc2hIYXNoewAGOgpAdXNlZHsA--2f1d03dee418f4c9751925da42
  1ae4730f9b55dd Parameters: {"period"=>"01/19/2009", "commit"=>"Select",
  "action"=>"call_in_sheet", "controller"=>"manager"}


NameError (undefined local variable or method 'lunch' for
  #<CallInAggregator:0x2589240>):
    /lib/reports.rb:368:in 'employee_record'
    /lib/reports.rb:306:in 'to_grouping'
    /lib/reports.rb:305:in 'each'
    /lib/reports.rb:305:in 'to_grouping'
    /usr/local/lib/ruby/gems/1.8/gems/ruport-1.4.0/lib/ruport/data/table.rb:169:in
        'initialize'
    /usr/local/lib/ruby/gems/1.8/gems/ruport-1.4.0/lib/ruport/data/table.rb:809:in
        'new'
    /usr/local/lib/ruby/gems/1.8/gems/ruport-1.4.0/lib/ruport/data/table.rb:809:in
        'Table'
    /lib/reports.rb:304:in 'to_grouping'
    /lib/reports.rb:170:in 'CallInAggregator'
    /lib/reports.rb:129:in 'setup'
    /usr/local/lib/ruby/gems/1.8/gems/ruport-1.4.0/lib/ruport/renderer.rb:337:in
        'render'
    /usr/local/lib/ruby/gems/1.8/gems/ruport-1.4.0/lib/ruport/renderer.rb:379:in
        'build'
    /usr/local/lib/ruby/gems/1.8/gems/ruport-1.4.0/lib/ruport/renderer.rb:335:in
        'render'
    /usr/local/lib/ruby/gems/1.8/gems/ruport-1.4.0/lib/ruport/renderer.rb:451:in
        'method_missing'
    /app/controllers/manager_controller.rb:111:in 'call_in_sheet'
    /app/controllers/application.rb:62:in 'on'
    /app/controllers/manager_controller.rb:110:in 'call_in_sheet'
    /vendor/rails/actionpack/lib/action_controller/base.rb:1104:in 'send'
    /vendor/rails/actionpack/lib/action_controller/base.rb:1104:in
        'perform_action_wit
```

Although the production application would display a rather boring "We're sorry, something went wrong" message upon triggering an error, our backend logs tell us exactly what request triggered the error and when it occurred. It also gives us information about the actual request, to aid in debugging. Though this particular bug is fairly boring, as it looks like it was just a typo that snuck through the cracks, logging each error that occurs along with its full stack trace provides essentially the same information that you'd get if you were running a script locally and ran into an error.

It's nice that some libraries and frameworks have logging built in, but sometimes we'll need to roll our own. To demonstrate this, we'll be walking through a `TCPServer` that does simple arithmetic operations in prefix notation. We'll start by taking a look at it without any logging or error-handling support:

```ruby
require "socket"

class Server

  def initialize
    @server    = TCPServer.new('localhost',port=3333)
  end

  def *(x, y)
    "#{Float(x) * Float(y)}"
  end

  def /(x, y)
    "#{Float(x) / Float(y)}"
  end

  def handle_request(session)
    action, *args = session.gets.split(/\s/)
    if ["*", "/"].include?(action)
      session.puts(send(action, *args))
    else
      session.puts("Invalid command")
    end
  end

  def run
    while session = @server.accept
      handle_request(session)
    end
  end
end
```

We can use the following fairly generic client to interact with the server, which is similar to the one we used in Chapter 2, *Designing Beautiful APIs*:

```ruby
require "socket"

class Client

  def initialize(ip="localhost",port=3333)
    @ip, @port = ip, port
  end

  def send_message(msg)
    socket = TCPSocket.new(@ip,@port)
    socket.puts(msg)
    response = socket.gets
    socket.close
    return response
  end
```

```
def receive_message
  socket = TCPSocket.new(@ip,@port)
  response = socket.read
  socket.close
  return response
end

end
```

Without any error handling, we end up with something like this on the client side:

```
client = Client.new

response = client.send_message("* 5 10")
puts response

response = client.send_message("/ 4 3")
puts response

response = client.send_message("/ 3 foo")
puts response

response = client.send_message("* 5 7.2")
puts response

## OUTPUTS ##

50.0
1.33333333333333
nil
client.rb:8:in 'initialize': Connection refused - connect(2) (Errno::ECONNREFUSED)
        from client.rb:8:in 'new'
        from client.rb:8:in 'send_message'
        from client.rb:35
```

When we send the erroneous third message, the server never responds, resulting in a `nil` response. But when we try to send a fourth message, which would ordinarily be valid, we see that our connection was refused. If we take a look server-side, we see that a single uncaught exception caused it to crash immediately:

```
server_logging_initial.rb:15:in 'Float':
invalid value for Float(): "foo" (ArgumentError)
        from server_logging_initial.rb:15:in '/'
        from server_logging_initial.rb:20:in 'send'
        from server_logging_initial.rb:20:in 'handle_request'
        from server_logging_initial.rb:25:in 'run'
        from server_logging_initial.rb:31
```

Though this does give us a sense of what happened, it doesn't give us much insight into when and why. It also seems just a bit fragile to have a whole server come crashing down on the account of a single bad request. With a little more effort, we can add logging and error handling and make things behave much better:

```ruby
require "socket"
require "logger"

class StandardError
  def report
    %{#{self.class}: #{message}\n#{backtrace.join("\n")}}
  end
end

class Server

  def initialize(logger)
    @logger   = logger
    @server   = TCPServer.new('localhost',port=3333)
  end

  def *(x, y)
    "#{Float(x) * Float(y)}"
  end

  def /(x, y)
    "#{Float(x) / Float(y)}"
  end

  def handle_request(session)
    action, *args = session.gets.split(/\s/)
    if ["*", "/"].include?(action)
      @logger.info "executing: '#{action}' with #{args.inspect}"
      session.puts(send(action, *args))
    else
      session.puts("Invalid command")
    end
  rescue StandardError => e
    @logger.error(e.report)
    session.puts "Sorry, something went wrong."
  end

  def run
    while session = @server.accept
      handle_request(session)
    end
  end
end

begin
  logger = Logger.new("development.log")
  host   = Server.new(logger)

  host.run
rescue StandardError => e
  logger.fatal(e.report)
  puts "Something seriously bad just happened, exiting"
end
```

We'll go over the details in just a minute, but first, let's take a look at the output on the client side running the identical code from earlier:

```
client = Client.new

response = client.send_message("* 5 10")
puts response

response = client.send_message("/ 4 3")
puts response

response = client.send_message("/ 3 foo")
puts response

response = client.send_message("* 5 7.2")
puts response

## OUTPUTS ##

50.0
1.33333333333333
Sorry, something went wrong.
36.0
```

We see that the third message is caught as an error and an apology is promptly sent to the client. But the interesting bit is that the fourth example continues to run normally, indicating that the server did not crash this time around.

Of course, if we swallowed all errors and just returned "We're sorry" every time something happened without creating a proper paper trail for debugging, that'd be a terrible idea. Upon inspecting the server logs, we can see that we haven't forgotten to keep ourselves covered:

```
# Logfile created on Sat Feb 21 07:07:49 -0500 2009 by /
I, [2009-02-21T07:08:54.335294 #39662]  INFO -- : executing: '*' with ["5", "10"]
I, [2009-02-21T07:08:54.335797 #39662]  INFO -- : executing: '/' with ["4", "3"]
I, [2009-02-21T07:08:54.336163 #39662]  INFO -- : executing: '/' with ["3", "foo"]
E, [2009-02-21T07:08:54.336243 #39662] ERROR -- :
ArgumentError: invalid value for Float(): "foo"
server_logging.rb:22:in 'Float'
server_logging.rb:22:in '/'
server_logging.rb:28:in 'send'
server_logging.rb:28:in 'handle_request'
server_logging.rb:36:in 'run'
server_logging.rb:45
I, [2009-02-21T07:08:54.336573 #39662]  INFO -- : executing: '*' with ["5", "7.2"]
```

Here we see two different levels of logging going on, INFO and ERROR. The purpose of our INFO logs is simply to document requests as parsed by our server. This is to ensure that the messages and their parameters are being processed as we expect. Our ERROR logs document the actual errors we run into while processing things, and you can see in this example that the stack trace written to the logfile is nearly identical to the one that was produced when our more fragile version of the server crashed.

Although the format is a little different, like the Rails logs, this provides us with everything we need for debugging. A time and date of the issue, a record of the actual request, and a trace that shows where the error originated. Now that we've seen it in action, let's take a look at how it all comes together.

We'll start with the small extension to `StandardError`:

```
class StandardError
  def report
    %{#{self.class}: #{message}\n#{backtrace.join("\n")}}
  end
end
```

This convenience method allows us to produce error reports that look similar to the ones you'll find on the command line when an exception is raised. Although `StandardError` objects provide all the same information, they do not have a single public method that provides the same report data that Ruby does, so we need to assemble it on our own.

We can see how this error report is used in the main `handle_request` method. Notice that the server is passed a `Logger` instance, which is used as `@logger` in the following code:

```
def handle_request(session)
  action, *args = session.gets.split(/\s/)
  if ["*", "/"].include?(action)
    @logger.info "executing: '#{action}' with #{args.inspect}"
    session.puts(send(action, *args))
  else
    session.puts("Invalid command")
  end
rescue StandardError => e
  @logger.error(e.report)
  session.puts "Sorry, something went wrong."
end
```

Here, we see where the messages in our logfile actually came from. Before the server attempts to actually execute a command, it records what it has parsed out using `@logger.info`. Then, it attempts to send the message along with its parameters to the object itself, printing its return value to the client end of the socket. If this fails for any reason, the relevant error is captured into `e` through `rescue`. This will catch all descendants of `StandardError`, which includes virtually all exceptions Ruby can throw. Once it is captured, we utilize the custom `StandardError#report` extension to generate an error report string, which is then logged as an error in the logfile. The apology is sent along to the client, thus completing the cycle.

That covers what we've seen in the logfile so far, but there is an additional measure for error handling in this application. We see this in the code that actually gets everything up and running:

```
begin
  logger = Logger.new("development.log")
  host   = Server.new(logger)

  host.run
rescue StandardError => e
  logger.fatal(e.report)
  puts "Something seriously bad just happened, exiting"
end
```

Although our response-handling code is pretty well insulated from errors, we still want to track in our logfile any server crashes that may happen. Rather than using ERROR as our designation, we instead use FATAL, indicating that our server has no intention of recovering from errors that bubble up to this level. I'll leave it up to you to figure out how to crash the server once it is running, but this technique also allows us to log things such as misspelled variable and method names among other issues within the Server class. To illustrate this, replace the run method with the following code:

```
def run
  while session = @server.accept
    handle_request(sessions)
  end
end
```

You'll end up crashing the server and producing the following log message:

```
F, [2009-02-21T07:39:40.592569 #39789] FATAL -- : NameError: undefined local
variable or method 'sessions' for #<Server:0x20c970>
server_logging.rb:36:in 'run'
server_logging.rb:45
```

This can be helpful if you're deploying code remotely and have some code that runs locally but not on the remote host, among other things.

Although we have not covered Logger in depth by any means, we've walked through an example that can be used as a template for more general needs. Most of the time, logging makes the most sense when you don't have easy, immediate access to the running code, and can be overkill in other places. If you're considering adding logging code to your applications, there are a few things to keep in mind:

- Error logging is essential for long-running server processes, during which you may not physically be watching the application moment by moment.
- If you are working in a multiprocessing environment, be sure to use a separate logfile for each process, as otherwise there will be clashes.
- Logger is powerful and includes a ton of features not covered here, including built-in logfile rotation.
- See the template for StandardError#report if you want to include error reports in your logs that look similar to the ones that Ruby generates on the command line.
- When it comes to logging error messages, FATAL should represent a bug from which your code has no intention of recovering; ERROR is more open-ended.

Depending on the kind of work you do, you may end up using Logger every day or not at all. If it's the former case, be sure to check out the API documentation for many of the features not covered here.

And with that, we've reached the end of another chapter. I'll just wrap up with some closing remarks, and then we can move on to more upbeat topics.

Conclusions

Dealing with defective code is something we all need to do from time to time. If we approach these issues in a relatively disciplined way, we can methodically corner and squash pretty much any bug that can be imagined. Debugging Ruby code tends to be a fluid process, starting with a good specification of how things should actually work, and then exercising various investigative tactics until a fix can be found. We don't necessarily need a debugger to track down issues in our code, but we do need to use Ruby's introspective features as much as possible, as they have the power to reveal to us exactly what is going on under the hood.

Once you get into a comfortable workflow for resolving issues in your Ruby code, it becomes more and more straightforward. If you find yourself lost while hunting down some bug, take the time to slow down and utilize the strategies we've gone over in this chapter. Once you get the hang of them, the tighter feedback loop will kick in and make your job much easier.

## CHAPTER 7

Reducing Cultural Barriers

Ten years ago, a book on best practices for any given programming language would seem perfectly complete without a chapter on multilingualization (m17n) and localization (L10n). In 2009, the story is just a little bit different.

Now that we've created a network of applications and infrastructure designed not simply to be used by hackers and researchers, but by nontechnical folks as part of their day-to-day lives, we are living in a very different world. With most software serving first and foremost as a communication medium, it is unrealistic to think that all conversations should be conducted in English or require the use of specialized tools otherwise. This presents a challenge to those who implement software that needs to be accessible to a global user base.

Although some may argue that it took too long to materialize, Ruby 1.9 provides a robust and elegant solution to the m17n problem. Rather than binding its users to a particular internal encoding and requiring complex manual manipulation of text into that format, Ruby 1.9 provides facilities that make it easy to transcode text from one encoding to another. This system is well integrated so that things like pattern matching and I/O operations can be carried out in all of the encodings Ruby supports, which provides a great deal of flexibility for those who need to do encoding-specific operations. Of course, because painless transcoding is possible, you can also write code that accepts and produces text in a wide variety of encodings, but uses a single encoding throughout its internals, improving the consistency and simplicity of the underlying implementation.

In this chapter, we're going to look at both of these approaches in some detail. We'll also look at some of the shortcuts Ruby offers when it comes to day-to-day scripting needs. In these cases, you may not need full-fledged support for arbitrarily encoded text, so there are ways to skip some steps if you know exactly what you'll be dealing with. By the time we wrap up with our discussion of m17n, you'll have a few solid strategies that can be adapted to fit your needs.

Once you are comfortable with how to store, manipulate, and produce internationalized text in various character encodings, you may want to know about how to customize your software so that its interface is adapted to whatever the native language and dialogue of its users might be. Although multilingualization and localization requirements don't necessarily come in pairs, they often do, so I'll wrap up this chapter with a brief demonstration of how to localize a simple Ruby application without excess duplication of effort.

Though we'll be talking about both topics, it's fair to say that technologically speaking, L10n is pretty easy, and m17n is fairly involved. This chapter won't necessarily teach you about either, but you should certainly review the basics of character encodings and have a working understanding of Ruby's m17n system before moving on. If you don't, go ahead and look over your favorite Ruby reference book before moving on, and maybe check out Joel Spolsky's classic article (*http://www.joelonsoftware.com/articles/Unicode .html*) on Unicode and character sets, which is the best I've seen as an introduction.

Once you're up to speed, we can move on to a practical example of m17n as seen in one of Ruby's standard libraries.

As always, we'll start with the deep dive and then go over some of the specifics later in the chapter. However, in this chapter in particular, I'm hoping that you don't skip the initial real-world example. Even if you don't fully grasp what's going on, the concepts it introduces are essential for understanding the rest of the content in this chapter. It also happens to be some of the coolest code in the book, so let's jump right in so you can see how it works.

m17n by Example: A Look at Ruby's CSV Standard Library

In a few other places in the book, I mentioned that Ruby's standard library is a good place to look for quality code that best practices can be gleaned from. When it comes to m17n, the place to look is the CSV library. This library is used for reading and writing files in the popular comma-separated-value tabular data format. We won't be talking much about the details of how this library is actually used here, but will instead be investigating a particular aspect of how it is implemented.

What we're interested in is how CSV manages to parse data that is in any of the character encodings that Ruby supports without transcoding the source text. To clarify the challenge, we can notice that generally speaking, character encodings are not necessarily compatible with one another:[*]

```
# coding: UTF-8

utf8_string = "foo — bar"
sjis_string = utf8_string.encode("Shift_JIS")

p utf8_string == sjis_string #=> false
```

---

[*] Throughout this chapter, note that — is the Japanese character for 1, not a double dash.

This issue is propagated well beyond `String` equality, and can cause more noisy problems in things like pattern matching or string manipulation:

```
sjis_string =~ /(\w+)\s —\s(\w+)/
encoding_test.rb:6:in '<main>': incompatible encoding regexp match
(UTF-8 regexp with Shift_JIS string) (Encoding::CompatibilityError)

utf8_string << sjis_string # RAISES
encoding_test.rb:6:in '<main>': incompatible character encodings:
UTF-8 and Shift_JIS (Encoding::CompatibilityError)
```

So the fact remains that some transcoding needs to be done. But imagine that in this example `sjis_string` represents some preloaded data that has not been converted yet. If our source encoding is set to use UTF-8, we could of course transcode the `sjis_string` to UTF-8 before operating on it. However, this could potentially be costly if our source text was large. To work around this, CSV converts its parsing patterns instead. We'll look at that in much greater detail in just a moment, but just to get a feel for it, let's look at an oversimplified example of how that might work:

```
def sjis_re(str)
  Regexp.new(str.encode("Shift_JIS"))
end

sjis_string =~ sjis_re("(\w+)\s —\s(\w+)")
p [$1, $2] #=> ["foo", "bar"]
```

Here, we use a UTF-8 string literal to build up a regular expression, but before it is constructed, the string is transcoded to Shift-JIS. As a result, the pattern it creates is capable of matching against Shift-JIS strings.

Although a bit more work than using `Regexp` literals, this presents a fairly natural way of defining regular expressions to match text that is in a different encoding from the source encoding. If we build on this concept a little bit, you can get a sense of how CSV's parser works.

Let's look at the CSV implementation from the bottom up. The end goal is to generate a parser in the encoding of the original data source that can extract cells from a tabular data format. To do this, CSV needs to be able to transcode some special characters into the encoding of the source text. These include the column separator, row separator, and literal quote character. As these can all be customized when a CSV is loaded, some general helpers for encoding strings and regular expressions come in handy:

```
# Builds a regular expression in <tt>@encoding</tt>.  All +chunks+ will be
# transcoded to that encoding.
#
def encode_re(*chunks)
  Regexp.new(encode_str(*chunks))
end

# Builds a String in <tt>@encoding</tt>.  All +chunks+ will be transcoded to
# that encoding.
#
```

```
def encode_str(*chunks)
  chunks.map { |chunk| chunk.encode(@encoding.name) }.join
end
```

In this code, `@encoding` refers to the `Encoding` object pulled from the underlying CSV string. For example, you might be trying to load a CSV file encoded in Shift-JIS:

```
# coding: UTF-8

require "csv"

CSV.read("data.csv", encoding: "Shift_JIS")
```

In essence, these two helper methods provide the same functionality as our `sjis_re` function that we built earlier. The main difference is that here, we have gleaned the necessary information from an `Encoding` object stored in the CSV instance rather than hardcoded a particular encoding to use. This makes perfect sense in the context of CSV, and hopefully is relatively easy to understand.

In addition to encoding regular expressions, because CSV accepts user-entered values that modify its core parser, it needs to escape them. Although the built-in `Regexp.escape()` method works with most of the encodings Ruby supports, at the time of the Ruby 1.9.1 release, it had some issues with a handful of them. To work around this, CSV rolls its own escape method:

```
# This method is an encoding safe version of Regexp.escape().  It will escape
# any characters that would change the meaning of a regular expression in the
# encoding of +str+.  Regular expression characters that cannot be transcoded
# to the target encoding will be skipped and no escaping will be performed if
# a backslash cannot be transcoded.
#
def escape_re(str)
  str.chars.map { |c| @re_chars.include?(c) ? @re_esc + c : c }.join
end
```

This means that once things like the column separator, row separator, and quote character have been specified by the user and converted into the specified encoding, this code can check to see whether the transcoded characters need to be escaped. To make things clearer, we can see that `@re_chars` is set in the `CSV` constructor as simply a list of regular expression reserved characters transcoded to the specified `@encoding`:

```
@re_chars =   %w[ \\ . [ ] - ^ $ ?
                  * + { } ( ) | #
                  \ \r \n \t \f \v ].
              map { |s| s.encode(@encoding) rescue nil }.compact
```

When we put these helpers together, we can see the big picture materialize within CSV's core parsers. Although the next code sample may look long at first, if you read through it, you'll see it's basically just a handful of regular expressions each doing a particular part of the CSV parsing job:

```
# Pre-compiles parsers and stores them by name for access during reads.
def init_parsers(options)
```

```ruby
    # store the parser behaviors
    @skip_blanks      = options.delete(:skip_blanks)
    @field_size_limit = options.delete(:field_size_limit)

    # prebuild Regexps for faster parsing
    esc_col_sep = escape_re(@col_sep)
    esc_row_sep = escape_re(@row_sep)
    esc_quote   = escape_re(@quote_char)
    @parsers = {
      # for empty leading fields
      leading_fields: encode_re("\\A(?:", esc_col_sep, ")+"),
      # The Primary Parser
      csv_row:        encode_re(
        "\\G(?:\\A|", esc_col_sep, ")",            # anchor the match
        "(?:", esc_quote,                          # find quoted fields
               "((?>[^", esc_quote, "]*)",         # "unrolling the loop"
               "(?>", esc_quote * 2,               # double for escaping
               "[^", esc_quote, "]*)*)",
               esc_quote,
               "|",                                # ... or ...
               "([^", esc_quote, esc_col_sep, "]*))",  # unquoted fields
        "(?=", esc_col_sep, "|\\z)"                # ensure field is ended
      ),
      # a test for unescaped quotes
      bad_field:      encode_re(
        "\\A", esc_col_sep, "?",                   # an optional comma
        "(?:", esc_quote,                          # a quoted field
               "(?>[^", esc_quote, "]*)",          # "unrolling the loop"
               "(?>", esc_quote * 2,               # double for escaping
               "[^", esc_quote, "]*)*",
               esc_quote,                          # the closing quote
               "[^", esc_quote, "]",               # an extra character
               "|",                                # ... or ...
               "[^", esc_quote, esc_col_sep, "]+", # an unquoted field
               esc_quote, ")"                      # an extra quote
      ),
      # safer than chomp!()
      line_end:       encode_re(esc_row_sep, "\\z"),
      # illegal unquoted characters
      return_newline: encode_str("\r\n")
    }
  end
```

By default, the `@col_sep` will be a comma, and the `@quote_char` will be a double-quote. The default `@row_sep` can vary depending on what sort of line endings are used in the file. These options can also be overridden when data is loaded. For example, if you for some reason had data columns separated by the Japanese character for 2, you could split things up that way:

```ruby
# coding: UTF-8

require "csv"

CSV.read("data.csv", encoding: "Shift_JIS", col_sep: "二")
```

All of these options get automatically transcoded to the specified `encoding`, which means you don't need to do the UTF-8 → Shift-JIS conversion manually here. This, combined with some of the other conveniences we've gone over, makes it clear that despite the fact that CSV manages to support every encoding Ruby does, it minimizes the amount an end user needs to know about the underlying grunt work. As long as the proper encoding is specified, CSV handles all the rest, and can even do things like auto-transcoding on load if you ask it to.

When it boils down to it, there isn't a whole lot of complexity here. By working with strings and regular expressions indirectly through encoding helpers, we can be sure that any pattern matching or text manipulation gets done in a compatible way. By translating the parser rather than the source data, we incur a fixed cost rather than one that varies in relation to the size of the data source. For a need like CSV processing, this is very important, as the format is often used for large data dumps.

The downside of this approach is of course that you need to be extra careful about how you work with your source text. It is not a big deal here because CSV processing is a well-specified task that has limited feature requirements. Constantly having to remember to encode every string and regular expression you use in your project could quickly become overwhelming if you are working on a more multifaceted problem.

In the next section, we'll cover an alternative m17n solution that isn't quite as pure as the approach CSV takes, but is generally less work to implement and still works fairly well for most needs.

Portable m17n Through UTF-8 Transcoding

Although it's nice to be able to support each character encoding natively, it can be quite difficult to maintain a complex system that works that way. The easy way out is to standardize on a single, fairly universal character encoding to write your code against. Then, all that remains to be done is to transcode any string that comes in, and possibly transcode again on the way out. The character set of choice for use in code that needs to be portable from one system to another is UTF-8.

Many Ruby libraries consume UTF-8 and UTF-8 only. The choice is a reasonable one, as UTF-8 is a proper superset of ASCII, meaning that code that pays no attention to specialized character encodings is likely to work without modification. UTF-8 also is capable of representing the myriad character sets that make up Unicode, which means it can represent nearly any glyph you might imagine in any other character encoding. As a variable-length character encoding, it does this fairly efficiently, so that users who do not need extra bytes to represent large character sets do not incur a significant memory penalty.

We're now going to walk through the general process of writing a UTF-8-enabled Ruby library. Along the way, we'll occasionally look at some examples from Prawn, to give a sense of what these techniques look like when they're applied in an actual project.

Source Encodings

A key aspect of any m17n-capable Ruby projects is to properly set the source encodings of its files. This is done via the magic comments that we have already seen in some of the earlier examples in this chapter. When it comes to Prawn, you'll see that each and every source file that makes up the library starts with a line like this:

```
# coding: UTF-8
```

In order for Ruby to pick it up, this comment must be the first line in the file, unless a shebang is present, such as in the following example:

```
#!/usr/bin/env ruby
# coding: UTF-8
```

In this case, the magic comment can appear on the second line. However, in all other situations, nothing else should come before it. Although Ruby is very strict about where you place the comment, it's fairly loose about the way you write it. Case does not matter as long as it's in the form of `coding: some_encoding`, and extra text may appear before or after it. This is used primarily for editor support, allowing things such as Emacs-style strings:

```
# -*- coding: utf-8 -*-
```

However you choose to format your magic comments, actually including them is important. Their purpose is to tell Ruby what encoding your regex and string literals are in. Forgetting to explicitly set the source encoding in this manner can cause all sorts of nasty problems, as it will force Ruby to fall back to US-ASCII, breaking virtually all internationalized text.

Once you set the source encoding to UTF-8 in all your files, if your editor is producing UTF-8 output, you can be sure of the encoding of your literals. That's the first step.

Working with Files

By default, Ruby uses your locale settings to determine the default external character encoding for files. You can check what yours is set to by running this code:

```
$ ruby -e "p Encoding.default_external"
```

On my system, this prints out `#<Encoding:UTF-8>`, but yours might be different. If your locale information isn't set, Ruby assumes that there is no suitable default encoding, reverting to `ASCII-8BIT` to interpret external files as sequences of untranslated bytes.

The actual value your `default_external` is set to doesn't really matter when you're developing code that needs to run on systems that you do not control. Because most libraries fall under this category, it means that you simply cannot rely on `File.open()` or `File.read()` to work without explicitly specifying an encoding.

This means that if you want to open a file that is in Latin-1 (ISO-8859-1), but process it within your UTF-8-based library, you need to write code something like this:

```
data = File.read("foo.txt", encoding:"ISO-8859-1:UTF-8")
```

Here, we've indicated that the file we are reading is encoded in ISO-8859-1, but that we want to transcode it to UTF-8 immediately so that the string we end up with in our program is already converted for us. Unless you need to retain the original encoding of the text for some reason, this is generally a good idea when processing files within a UTF-8 based library.

Writing back to file works in a similar fashion. Here's what it looks like to automatically transcode text back to Latin-1 from a UTF-8 source string:

```
File.open("foo.txt", "w:ISO-8859-1:UTF-8") { |f| f << data + "Some extra text" }
```

Although the syntax is slightly different here, the idea is the same. We specify first the external character encoding that is used for the file and second the internal encoding we are working with. So with this in mind, in a UTF-8-based library, you will need to supply an encoding string of the form external_format:UTF-8 whenever you're working with text files. Of course, if the external format happens to be UTF-8, you would just write something like this:

```
data = File.read("foo.txt", encoding: "UTF-8")
File.open("foo.txt", "w:UTF-8") { |f| f << data + "Some extra text"
```

The underlying point here is that if you want to work with files in a portable way, you need to be explicit about their character encodings. Without doing this, you cannot be sure that your code will work consistently from machine to machine. Also, if you want to make it so all of the internals of your system operate in a single encoding, you need to explicitly make sure the loaded files get translated to UTF-8 before you process the text in them. If you take care of these two things, you can mostly forget about the details, as all of the actual work will end up getting done on UTF-8 strings.

There is one notable exception to this rule, which is dealing with binary files. It used to be the case that at least on *nix, you could get away with code like this on Ruby 1.8:

```
img_data = File.read("foo.png")
```

Reading binary files this way was never a good idea, because it would cause data corruptions on Windows due to the fact that it does automatic conversions to the line endings of the files. However, there is now a reason not to write code like this, regardless of what platform you are on.

As we had mentioned before, Ruby looks to your default_external encoding when one is not explicitly specified. Because this is set by your locale, it can be any number of things. On my system, as my locale is set to UTF-8, Ruby thinks I'm trying to load a UTF-8 based file and interprets my binary as such. This promptly breaks things in all sorts of unpleasant ways, so it is something to be avoided. Luckily, if we simply use File.binread(), all these problems go away:

```
img_data = File.binread("foo.png")
img_data.encoding #=> #<Encoding:ASCII-8BIT>
```

For more complex needs, or for when you need to write a binary file, Ruby 1.9 has also changed the meaning of `"rb"` and `"wb"` in `File.open()`. Rather than simply disabling line-ending conversion, using these file modes will now set the external encoding to `ASCII-8BIT` by default. You can see this being used in Prawn's `Document#render_file` method, which simply takes the raw PDF string written by `Document#render` and outputs a binary file:

```
class Prawn::Document

  # ...

  def render_file(filename)
    File.open(filename,"wb") { |f| f << render }
  end

end
```

This approach may already seem familiar to those who have needed to deploy code that runs on Windows machines. However, this section is meant to remind folks who may not have previously needed to worry about this that they need to be careful as well.

There really isn't a whole lot to worry about when working with files using this m17n strategy, but the few things that you do need to do are important to remember. Unless you're working with binaries, be sure to explicitly specify the external encoding of your files, and transcode them to UTF-8 upon read or write. If you are working with binaries, be sure to use `File.binread()` or `File.open()` with the proper flags to make sure that your text is not accidentally encoded into the character set specified by your locale. This one can produce subtle bugs that you might not encounter until you run your code on another machine, so it's important to try to avoid in the first place.

Now that we've talked about source encodings and files, the main thing that's left to discuss is how to transcode input from users in a fairly organized way, and produce output in the formats you need. Though this is not complicated, it's worth looking at some real code to see how this is handled.

Transcoding User Input in an Organized Fashion

When dealing with user input, you need to make a decision regarding what should be transcoded and where. In the case of Prawn, we take a very minimalist approach to this. While we expect the end user to provide us with UTF-8-encoded strings, many of the features that involve simple comparisons work without the need for transcoding.

As it turns out, Ruby does a lot of special casing when it comes to strings containing only ASCII characters. Although strings that have different character encodings from one another are generally not comparable and cannot be combined through manipulations, these rules do not apply if each of them consists of only ASCII characters.

It turns out that in practice, you don't really need to worry about transcoding whenever you are comparing user input to a finite set of possible ASCII values.

Here's an example of a case where transcoding is not necessary:

```
# coding: iso-8859-1

require "prawn"

Prawn::Document.generate("output.pdf", :page_size => "LEGAL") do
  stroke_line [100,100], [200,200]
end
```

In this case, neither the filename nor the page size are transcoded within Prawn. Although we passed Latin-1 strings in, Prawn didn't bother to translate them to UTF-8, because it didn't need to. The filename is eventually passed straight through to `File.open()`, so no manipulations or comparisons are ever done on it. However, `:page_size` is used to look up page dimensions in a hash that looks something like this:

```
SIZES = {     "A4" => [595.28, 841.89 ],
           "FOLIO" => [612.00, 936.00 ],
           "LEGAL" => [612.00, 1008.00],
          "LETTER" => [612.00, 792.00 ]  }
```

Although the whole of Prawn's source is using UTF-8 literals, and the example we showed earlier is using Latin-1, the proper page size ends up getting looked up in the hash. As it turns out, the laziness of Ruby's m17n system really comes in handy.

When dealing with strings in which `String#ascii_only?` returns `true`, the object acts for all intents and purposes as if it were an ASCII string. It will play nice with strings of other encodings as long as they too consist entirely of ASCII characters.

This gives you a good criteria for what needs to be transcoded and what doesn't. If you can be sure that you never manipulate or compare a string, it can be safely ignored in most cases. In cases in which you do manipulation or comparison, if the input strings will consist of nothing more than ASCII characters in all cases, you do not need to transcode them. All other strings need to be transcoded to UTF-8 within your library unless you expect users to do the conversions themselves.

After combing your API, depending on your needs, the number of parameters that need to be converted may be a lot or a little. In the case of Prawn, even though it is a relatively complex system, it turned out to be a very small task to make the library work fairly well with the arbitrary strings that users pass in to our methods.

Essentially the only time we needed to normalize encodings of strings was when dealing with text that ends up getting displayed within the PDFs. Because our system essentially works by mapping Unicode code points to the actual outlines of characters (glyphs) that end up getting rendered to the document, we cannot simply deal with any text the user provides us. It needs to be transcoded.

If we look at the core `text()` method, we can see where this actually occurs in Prawn:

```
def text(text,options={})
  # we'll be messing with the strings encoding, don't change the users
```

```
    # original string
    text = text.to_s.dup    ## A ##

    save_font do
      options = text_options.merge(options)
      process_text_options(options)

      font.normalize_encoding(text) unless @skip_encoding  ## B ##

      # ... remainder of method is not important
    end
  end
```

On the line marked *A*, we see that the `text()` method makes a copy of the string, because we will change its encoding later. The few lines that follow it are not of interest, until we reach the line marked *B*. This line calls `Prawn::Font#normalize_encoding` with the text that is to be rendered, and that method is responsible for doing the transcoding. This method is actually implemented by subclasses of `Prawn::Font`, because different font systems require different encodings. In the interest of simplicity, we'll look at TTF fonts, where UTF-8 text is used:

```
module Prawn
  class Font
    class TTF < Font

      def normalize_encoding(text)
        text.encode!("UTF-8")
      end

    end
  end
end
```

Here we can see that the code for `Prawn::Font::TTF#normalize_encoding()` is just a thin wrapper on `String#encode!()`, which is used to modify the encoding of a string in place. The reason it exists at all is because different font systems have different requirements; for example, `Prawn::Font::AFM` uses Windows-1252 under the hood.

The underlying idea here is simple, though. You can clean up your code significantly by identifying the points where encodings matter in your code. Oftentimes, there will be a handful of low-level functions that are at the core of your system, and they are the places where transcoding needs to be done. In the case of Prawn, even with things like formatted text boxes and tables and other fancy means of putting content on the page, the core method that is used by all of those features is the single `text()` method. At this point, we call a `normalize_encoding` method that abstracts away the actual encoding that gets used. In the case of Prawn, this is especially important—although the core library works in UTF-8, depending on which font you use, text strings entered from the user may end up being transcoded into various different encodings.

Although some libraries may be more complex than others to implement in this manner, for a wide variety of purposes, this works fairly well. The main reason for using

UTF-8 is that it provides a good base encoding that most other encodings can be transcoded into. If you take advantage of Ruby's shortcuts when it comes to ASCII strings, you can safely ignore a lot of the finer points about whether two different encodings play nice together.

Though a library implemented in this way isn't truly set up to deal with arbitrary character encodings in the way that something like CSV implements its m17n support, it provides an easy solution that may work in most cases. Although the looseness of such a system does have some drawbacks, the advantages are often worth it.

Roughly, the process of building a UTF-8 based system goes like this:

- Be sure to set the source encoding of every file in your project to UTF-8 using magic comments.

- Use the `external:internal` encoding string when opening any I/O stream, specifying the internal encoding as UTF-8. This will automatically transcode files to UTF-8 upon read, and automatically transcode from UTF-8 to the external encoding on write.

- Make sure to either use `File.binread()` or include the `"b"` flag when dealing with binary files. Otherwise, your files may be incorrectly interpreted based on your locale, rather than being treated as a stream of unencoded bytes.

- When dealing with user-entered strings, only transcode those that need to be manipulated or compared to non-ASCII strings. All others can be left in their native encoding as long as they consist of ASCII characters only or they are not manipulated by your code.

- Do not rely on `default_external` or `default_internal`, and be sure to set your source encodings properly. This ensures that your code will not depend on environmental conditions to run.

- If you need to do a ton of text processing on user-entered strings that may use many different character mappings, it might not be a great idea to use this approach.

Although you may run into some other challenges depending on what your actual project is like, the tips above should get you most of the way to a working solution.

Each approach we've discussed so far illustrates a trade-off between high compatibility and simplicity of implementation. While UTF-8-based systems with limited automatic transcoding support represent a middle-of-the-road approach, we'll now look at how to use every possible shortcut to quickly get your job done at the expense of portability.

m17n in Standalone Scripts

Ruby is a scripting language at heart. Although the earlier m17n represents an elegant and highly flexible system, it would be tedious to think about all of its details when you just want to process some datafiles or run a quick one-liner on the command line.

Although we won't spend much time going over the minute details, I want to make sure that you get a chance to see how Ruby lets the m17n system get out of your way a bit when it comes to day-to-day scripting needs.

Inferring Encodings from Locale

The key things that Ruby's m17n system can modify when it comes to encodings are the source encoding, the default external encoding of files, and the default internal encoding that loaded files should be transcoded to. The following simple script inspects each of these values to see how they relate to your system's locale:

```
puts "Source encoding: #{__ENCODING__.inspect}"
puts "Default external: #{Encoding.default_external.inspect}"
puts "Default internal: #{Encoding.default_internal.inspect}"
puts "Locale charmap: #{ Encoding.locale_charmap.inspect}"
puts "LANG environment variable: #{ENV['LANG'].inspect}"
```

When we run this code without a magic comment, I get the following output on my system. Your exact values may vary, as I'll explain in a moment:

```
$ ruby encoding_checker.rb

Source encoding: #<Encoding:US-ASCII>
Default external: #<Encoding:UTF-8>
Default internal: nil
Locale charmap: "UTF-8"
LANG environment variable: "en_US.UTF-8"
```

Here, we see that the source encoding has fallen back to US-ASCII because none was explicitly set. However, the default external matches our locale charmap, which is inferred from the LANG environment variable. Although your locale may not be set to UTF-8, you should see that these values match each other on your system, as long as LANG is set to one of the encodings Ruby supports. A default internal encoding of nil tells us that text should not be transcoded automatically while reading and writing files, but be kept in the same encoding as the locale.

To see how these values can be influenced, we can change our locale via the LANG environment variable, and check what happens:

```
$ LANG="en_US.ISO8859-1" ruby encoding_checker.rb

Source encoding: #<Encoding:US-ASCII>
Default external: #<Encoding:ISO-8859-1>
Default internal: nil
Locale charmap: "ISO8859-1"
LANG environment variable: "en_US.ISO8859-1"
```

Here we see that rather than UTF-8, Latin-1 is used as the default external now. This means that if you modify this environment variable globally, Ruby will use it to determine what fallback encoding to use when dealing with I/O operations.

So on my system, where UTF-8 is the default external encoding, I can open files knowing that if I don't specify any particular character mapping, they will load in as UTF-8:

```
>> File.read("hello.txt")
=> "Hello, world\n"
>> File.read("hello.txt").encoding
=> #<Encoding:UTF-8>
```

On your system, your locale charmap will determine this. As long as your operating system is properly configured, Ruby should have a sensible default encoding for use in I/O operations.

Although this is very handy, one thing to keep in mind is that the locale settings on your system do not affect the default source encoding. This means that for all the source files you create, you need to set the actual source encoding via magic comment. This restriction is actually a good thing, as it makes it hard to make your Ruby programs so fragile that a change to LANG can break them. However, there is an exception in which allowing the locale to influence the source can be a good thing, and that's for quick one-liners.

Whenever we use ruby -e, the purpose is to do some sort of quick, one-off task. Those who use this technique often might have already found that there are all sorts of short-cuts that can be used when running in this mode. As it turns out, this applies to m17n as well:

```
$ ruby -e "p __ENCODING__"
#<Encoding:UTF-8>
```

Rather than falling back to ASCII, we can see that it infers the source encoding from the locale. To further illustrate that, we can reset LANG to Latin-1 again:

```
$ LANG="en_US.ISO8859-1" ruby -e "p __ENCODING__"
#<Encoding:ISO-8859-1>
```

As we can see, the source encoding is taken to be whatever our system is using for its locale, rather than requiring an explicit setting. This makes a lot of sense, because when we write one-liners, we typically want to use whatever our terminal is using as an encoding. It would also seem quite strange to embed a magic comment into a one-line script.

Because ruby -e will also infer the default external encoding in the same way that we've shown before when dealing with actual scripts, we end up with a powerful tool on our hands.

As you can see, Ruby's locale-based fallbacks make it possible in some cases to just ignore the details of the m17n system, or if necessary, to set an environment variable once and forget about it. The fact that ruby -e uses a locale-based source encoding means that you can also continue using Ruby as a command-line tool without too much friction. But now that we've looked at how Ruby's character mappings can be influenced by external means, we should take a look at how we can get a bit more fine-grained control over these things at the Ruby level.

Customizing Encoding Defaults

If we want to be explicit about our default external encoding, we can set it within our files via a simple accessor. In this example, we're indicating that the files we work with should be treated as Latin-1 by default, even though our script is encoded in UTF-8:

```
# coding: UTF-8
Encoding.default_external = Encoding.find("ISO-8859-1")

data = File.read("hello.txt")
p data.encoding #=> #<Encoding:ISO-8859-1>
```

If we plan to transcode our data upon load, we can also set the `default_internal` encoding. In the following example, we specify that I/O operations should by default be transcoded using the source encoding:

```
# coding: UTF-8
Encoding.default_external = Encoding.find("ISO-8859-1")
Encoding.default_internal = __ENCODING__

data = File.read("hello.txt")
p data.encoding #=> #<Encoding:UTF-8>
```

Here we see that the text loaded from the file ends up encoded in UTF-8. However, this is done in a safe way. The file is first loaded in using the `default_internal` encoding and then translated to the `default_external` encoding. To illustrate this further, the previous example is functionally equivalent to this more explicit one:

```
# coding: UTF-8

data = File.read("hello.txt", encoding: "ISO-8859-1:UTF-8")
p data.encoding #=> #<Encoding:UTF-8>
```

The difference is that when you set `default_external` and `default_internal`, the changes apply globally. Because this is a somewhat invasive change to make, you can see that messing with the internal and external encodings is reasonable to do only in scripting applications, since it does not apply well to code that needs to be portable.

However, in cases where it is reasonable to make this change globally, it can be used to avoid repeating encodings incessantly every time you do I/O operations. You can even specify these options on the command line, to allow them to be specified at the time the script is run:

```
$ ruby -E iso-8859-1:utf-8 hello.rb
#<Encoding:UTF-8>
```

Now our script is almost entirely devoid of explicit m17n details:

```
# coding: UTF-8

data = File.read("hello.txt")
p data.encoding #=> #<Encoding:UTF-8>
```

This is about as far as we'll want to take it in most cases, but there is one more example worth sharing before we move on.

As you may know, Ruby 1.8 did not have a comprehensive m17n system like Ruby 1.9 does. However, it did ship with an ability to enable a sort of UTF-8 mode, which would tell the interpreter that the strings it was working with as well the data pulled in from external files should be interpreted as UTF-8 text. This was provided by the *kcode* system, and specified via the -Ku flag. As it turns out, this works on Ruby 1.9.1 and even allows you to modify the source encoding of your files.

If we run the encoding_checker.rb file from before using -Ku, here's what you can expect to see:

```
$ ruby -Ku encoding_checker.rb
Source encoding: #<Encoding:UTF-8>
Default external: #<Encoding:UTF-8>
Default internal: nil
Locale charmap: "UTF-8"
LANG environment variable: "en_US.UTF-8"
```

Your locale settings may be different, but you should see that the source encoding and default external encoding have been set to UTF-8. Although this feature is primarily for backward compatibility, it is worth knowing about for a good "set it and forget it" default if you plan to work exclusively with UTF-8 in your scripts. Of course, if you have to work in most other encodings, you'll need to use some combination of the techniques we've covered earlier in this section, so this is far from a magic bullet.

Now that we've covered a few different ways to simplify your scripts to get some of the m17n roadblocks out of the way, here's a recap of the most important details to remember before we move on:

- The LANG environment variable that specifies your system locale is used by Ruby to determine the default external encoding of files. A properly set locale can allow Ruby to automatically load files in their native encodings without explicitly stating what character mapping they use.

- Although magic comments are typically required in files to set the source encoding, an exception is made for ruby -e-based command-line scripts. The source encoding for these one-liners is determined by locale. In most cases, this is what you will want.

- You can specify a default internal encoding that Ruby will automatically transcode loaded files into when no explicit internal encoding is specified. It is often reasonable to set this to match the source encoding in your scripts.

- You can set default external/internal encodings via the command-line switch -Eexternal:internal if you do not want to explicitly set them in your scripts.

- The -Ku flag still works for putting Ruby into "UTF-8" mode, which is useful for backward compatibility with Ruby 1.8.

- All of the techniques described in this section are suitable mostly for scripts or private use code. It is a bad idea to rely on locale data or manually set external and internal encodings in complex systems or code that needs to run on machines you do not have control over.

We've covered a lot of ground so far, and we'll be wrapping up with m17n to move on to L10n in just a short while. However, before we do, I'd like to cover just a couple short notes on how Ruby's new m17n system impacts lower-level code, and how to get around the issues it creates.

m17n-Safe Low-Level Text Processing

In previous versions of Ruby, strings were pretty much sequences of bytes rather than characters. This meant the following code seldom caused anyone to bat an eyelash:

```
File.open("hello.txt") { |f|
  loop do
    break if f.eof?
    chunk = "CHUNK: #{f.read(5)}"
    puts chunk unless chunk.empty?
  end
}
```

The purpose of the previous example is to print out the contents of the file in chunks of five bytes, which, when it comes to ASCII, means five characters. However, multibyte character encodings, especially variable-length ones such as UTF-8, cannot be processed using this approach. The reason is fairly simple.

Imagine this code running against a two-character, six-byte string in UTF-8 such as "吴佳". If we read five bytes of this string, we end up breaking the second character's byte sequence, resulting in the mangled string "吴\xE4\xBD". Of course, whether this is a problem depends on your reason for reading a file in chunks.

If we are processing binary data, we probably don't need to worry about character encodings or anything like that. Instead, just we read a fixed amount of data according to our needs, processing it however we'd like. But many times, the reason why we read data in chunks is not to process it at the byte level, but instead, to break it up into small parts as we work on it.

A perfect example of this, and a source of a good solution to the problem, is found within the CSV standard library. As we've seen before, this library is fully m17n-capable and takes great care to process files in a encoding-agnostic way. However, it also tries to be clever about certain things, which makes m17n support a bit more challenging.

Rather than assume \n is the default line ending to separate rows within a CSV, the library tries to determine what the line endings of a file are from a list of possibilities by examining a file in chunks. It cannot accomplish this task by reading in a single line of text, because it does not know the line endings yet. It would be highly inefficient to try to read in the whole file to determine the endings, because CSV data can become huge. Therefore, what is needed is a way to process the data in chunks while searching for a line ending that does not break multibyte characters.

The solution is actually relatively simple, so we'll take a look at the whole thing first and then discuss it in a little more detail:

```
def read_to_char(bytes)
  return "" if @io.eof?
  data = @io.read(bytes)
  begin
    encoded = encode_str(data)
    raise unless encoded.valid_encoding?
    return encoded
  rescue  # encoding error or my invalid data raise
    if @io.eof? or data.size >= bytes + 10
      return data
    else
      data += @io.read(1)
      retry
    end
  end
end
```

Here, `@io` is an `IO` object of some sort, typically a `File`, and the `encode_str()` method is the same function we covered toward the beginning of this chapter, which is a thin wrapper over `String#encode()`. If we walk through this step by step, we see that an empty string is returned if the stream is already at `eof?`. Assuming that it is not, a specified number of `bytes` is read.

Then, the string is encoded, and it is checked to see whether the character mapping is valid. To clarify what `valid_encoding?` does, we can look at this simple example:

```
p "吴佳".valid_encoding?       #=> true
p "吴\xE4\xBD".valid_encoding? #=> false
```

When the encoding is valid, `read_to_char` returns the chunk, assuming that the string was broken up properly. Otherwise, it raises an error, causing the `rescue` block to be executed. Here, we see that the core fix relies on buffering the data slightly to try to read a complete character. What actually happens here is that the method gets retried repeatedly, adding one extra byte to the `data` until it either reaches a total of 10 bytes over the specified chunk size, or hits the end of the file.

The reason why this works is that every encoding Ruby supports has a character size of less than 10 bytes. This is in fact a conservative estimate, but is sufficiently small to still be reasonable. Using this method, it is possible to process data in chunks in an encoding-safe way.

The code that we looked at here was pulled directly from the *csv* library, but it would be easy to tweak for your individual needs. The main idea is basically that we need to consume some extra bytes to complete a character sometimes, and we can determine whether this is necessary based on either an error from `String#encode()` or the state of

`String#valid_encoding?`. I'll leave the generalization of `read_to_char` as an exercise for you, as its implementation will likely depend on the context, but this code from CSV is a solid conceptual base to start from.

I'd like to wrap up this section by pointing out one other thing to remember about low-level operations on strings when it comes to m17n. If you're used to thinking of bytes as character codes, you'll need to rethink the way you are doing things. You might be used to getting character codes via `String#unpack`:

```
>> "Hello world".unpack("C*")
=> [72, 101, 108, 108, 111, 32, 119, 111, 114, 108, 100]
```

Though this can be made to work for a handful of encodings, if you need to keep your code character-mapping-agnostic, you'll want to actually use `String#ord` instead here:

```
>> "Hello world".chars.map(&:ord)
=> [72, 101, 108, 108, 111, 32, 119, 111, 114, 108, 100]
```

This will work fine with any encoding you work with, giving back the ordinal value based on the actual encoding rather than the byte value:

```
>> utf8_string
=> "吴佳"
>> utf8_string.chars.map(&:ord)
=> [21556, 20339]
```

There is more we could talk about here, but I'd rather not go through the gory details exhaustively. The underlying theme of working with low-level text operations in an m17n-safe way is that characters are not necessarily equivalent to bytes. If you remember that simple idea, most of the rest of the core ideas will fall into place.

Now that we've talked quite a bit about how to actually process text in a wide variety of character mappings, we'll discuss a slightly higher-level topic. If you are going to support multiple languages in your application, you'll want a clean and organized way to do it. The next section will give you some tips on how to accomplish that without too much of a hassle.

Localizing Your Code

To make an application truly multilingual, we need to do more than just be able to process and produce text in different languages. We also need to provide a way for the user interface to be translated into the natural languages we wish to support. If you wanted to support even a small handful of languages, neither building multiple versions of your application nor writing tons of special casing wherever text is displayed will be a maintainable solution. Instead, what is needed is a way to mark the relevant sections of text with meaningful tags that can then be altered by external translation files. This is the process of localization (L10n).

We're going to be looking at a tiny L10n package I put together when I realized there weren't any Ruby 1.9-based tools available that worked outside of Rails. It is called

`Gibberish::Simple`, and is a fork of the very cool `Gibberish` plug-in by Chris Wanstrath. The main modifications I made were to port the library to Ruby 1.9.1, remove all dependencies including the Rails integration, and change the system a bit so that it does not depend on core extensions. Other than that, all of the hard work was done by Chris and he deserves all the credit for the actual system, which, as you'll see in a minute, is quite easy to use.

We're going to first look at a very trivial web application using the Sinatra web framework. It implements the children's game "Rock, Paper, Scissors."[†] We'll look at it both before and after localization, to give you a feel for the actual process of localizing your text.

The entire application is dirt-simple, with only two screens. The first lets you choose from "Rock," "Paper," and "Scissors" for your weapon (Figure 7-1).

Figure 7-1. Choosing a weapon

The ERB template used to generate this view is trivial, as you might expect:

```
<html>
<head>
  <meta http-equiv="Content-Type" content="text/html; charset=UTF-8">
</head>
<body>
  <form method="post">
    <% ["Rock", "Paper", "Scissors"].each do |weapon| %>
      <input type="radio" name="weapon" value="<%= weapon %>">
        <%= weapon %>
      </input>
    <% end %>
    <input type="submit" value="Shoot">
  </form>
</body>
</html>
```

Here we're just doing some simple dynamic form generation, and even a basic understanding of HTML should be sufficient to understand what's going on, so I won't go into details.

After submitting this form data, the game logic is done behind the scenes and the opponent's choice is revealed (Figure 7-2).

[†] See *http://en.wikipedia.org/wiki/Rock-paper-scissors*.

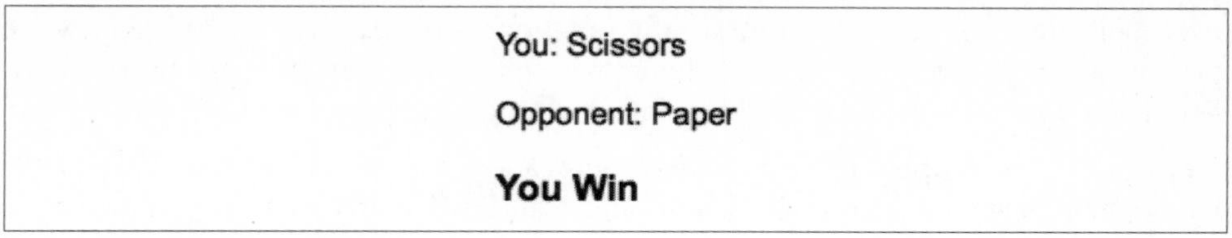

```
You: Scissors

Opponent: Paper

You Win
```

Figure 7-2. Announcing the winner

This ERB template is even more simple than the last one, as it just displays some pre-generated data:

```
<html>
<head>
  <meta http-equiv="Content-Type" content="text/html; charset=UTF-8">
</head>
<body>
  <p> You: <%= @player_weapon %></p>
  <p> Opponent: <%= @opponent_weapon %></p>
  <h3><%= end_game_message %></h3>
</body>
</html>
```

Tying the whole application together is the actual Sinatra application. It handles the game logic and generates the appropriate messages, but is not in any way complex. Here's the whole thing, which consists of nothing more than two URI handlers and a helper function that determines who won:

```
require "sinatra"

get '/rps' do
  erb :rps_start
end

post '/rps' do
  @player_weapon    = params[:weapon]
  @opponent_weapon  = %w[Rock Paper Scissors].sample
  erb :rps_end
end

helpers do
  def end_game_message
    return "It's a tie" if @player_weapon == @opponent_weapon

    winning_combos = [["Paper","Rock"],["Rock","Scissor"],["Scissors","Paper"]]
    if winning_combos.include?([@player_weapon, @opponent_weapon])
      "You Win"
    else
      "You Lose"
    end
  end
end
```

Although tiny, this does represent a fully functional application. The fact that we're presenting an interface for users to interact with means that interface can be localized. We'll now look at how to go about adding two languages, French and Chinese.

One option would be to code up separate views and some specialized translation logic for each language, but that approach doesn't scale particularly well. Instead, what we can do is come up with unique identifiers for each text segment in our application, and then create translation files that fill in the appropriate values depending on what language is selected. Ignoring how we actually integrate these translation files into our application for the moment, we can look at a couple of them to get a feel for how they look.

The following simple YAML file covers all the necessary Chinese translations for this application:

```
win: 你赢了
lose: 你输了
tie: 平局

rock: 石头
paper: 布
scissors: 剪刀

shoot: 开
you: 你
opponent: 对手
```

As you can see, these are direct mappings between English identifiers for text that appears in our application and their Chinese translations. Because all of the translation files will follow this same basic structure, you'll notice that the French translation file looks pretty much the same:

```
win: Tu gagnes
lose: Tu perds
tie: Egalité

rock: Caillou
paper: Feuille
scissors: Ciseaux

shoot: On y va !
you: Toi
opponent: Adversaire
```

With some translation files in hand, we can work on integrating `Gibberish::Simple` into our application. Before we do that, we'll look at a simple script that shows the basic mechanics of how things work. In the following example, it is assumed that *lang/cn.yml* and *lang/fr.yml* exist and are populated with the values here:

```
# coding: UTF-8

require "gibberish/simple"
```

```
# Tell Gibberish that lang/ exists in the same root directory as this file
Gibberish::Simple.language_paths << File.dirname(__FILE__)

# Let us use the T() translation helper globally
include Gibberish::Simple

p T("You Win", :win) #=> "You Win"

Gibberish::Simple.use_language(:fr) do
  p T("You Win", :win) #=> "Tu gagnes."
end

Gibberish::Simple.use_language(:cn) do
  p T("You Win", :win) #=> "你赢了"
end

# Because there is no matching file, this falls back to the defaults

Gibberish::Simple.use_language(:en) do
  p T("You Win", :win) #=> "You Win"
end
```

Here we see that our text display calls are wrapped in a method call to T(), which stands for translate. When no language is specified, this code displays the default value that is specified by the first argument. When a language is specified via the use_language block, T() will look up the appropriate translation via the unique tag for it. If use_language is given a language that does not have a matching YAML file, the defaults are reverted to. As you can see, for these basic needs, there isn't a whole lot to it.

Now, we're ready to take a look at the localized version of "Rock, Paper, Scissors." We can start with the main application and work our way out to the views. Though some changes were necessary, you'll see that the code is still pretty easy to follow:

```
require "sinatra"
require "gibberish/simple"

Gibberish::Simple.language_paths << File.dirname(__FILE__)
include Gibberish::Simple

get '/rps' do
  redirect '/rps/en'
end

get '/rps/:lang' do
  erb :rps_start
end

post '/rps/:lang' do
  @player_weapon   = params[:weapon]
  @opponent_weapon = %w[Rock Paper Scissors].sample
  erb :rps_end
end

helpers do
```

```
def end_game_message
  return T("It's a tie", :tie) if @player_weapon == @opponent_weapon

  winning_combos = [["Paper","Rock"],["Rock","Scissor"],["Scissors","Paper"]]
  if winning_combos.include?([@player_weapon, @opponent_weapon])
    T("You Win", :win)
  else
    T("You Lose", :lose)
  end
end

def weapon_name(weapon)
  T(weapon, weapon.downcase.to_sym)
end

def translated(&block)
  Gibberish::Simple.use_language(params[:lang], &block)
end
end
```

The first thing to notice is that I've decided to embed the language choice into the URI. This is the code that does that:

```
get '/rps' do
  redirect '/rps/en'
end

get '/rps/:lang' do
  erb :rps_start
end
```

You can see that going to **/rps** actually redirects you to **/rps/en**, which represents the English version of the game. The need for this code is mainly a consequence of the fact that we're building something web-based without a database backend. In other applications, you could store the current language in whatever way makes the most sense for the individual solution. The key idea here is only that we need to be able to tell `Gibberish::Simple` what language we want to work in. You'll see how it's used in a moment, but this `:lang` parameter is used by our `translated` helper to set the current language from within a view:

```
def translated(&block)
  Gibberish::Simple.use_language(params[:lang], &block)
end
```

The rest of the remaining changes are simply wrapping anything that will eventually be displayed to the user in `T()` calls. Notice this does not affect the actual logic of our code, which still works in terms of comparing "Rock," "Paper," and "Scissors" regardless of the language we're displaying the UI in. This is an important aspect of localizing your code: you want to do it as late as possible so that your business logic is not affected by translations. The `weapon_name` helper serves exactly this purpose:

```
def weapon_name(weapon)
  T(weapon, weapon.downcase.to_sym)
end
```

Beyond the additions of a couple helpers and some calls to T(), much of the code is left unchanged. The more significant work involved with localizing this application is done at the view level. What follows is the template from the first screen, the weapon selection form:

```
<html>
<head>
  <meta http-equiv="Content-Type" content="text/html; charset=UTF-8">
</head>
<body>
  <form method="post">
    <% translated do %>
      <% ["Rock", "Paper", "Scissors"].each do |weapon| %>
        <input type="radio" name="weapon" value="<%= weapon %>">
          <%= weapon_name(weapon) %>
        </input>
      <% end %>
      <input type="submit" value="<%= T('Shoot!',:shoot) %>">
    <% end %>
  </form>
</body>
</html>
```

Here, we see our helpers from the main application in action. The `translated` block is just syntactic sugar that infers from the URI which language to pass to `Gibberish::Simple.use_langauge`. Within this block, every string displayed to the user must be directly or indirectly passed through T() to be translated. However, we explicitly leave the values of the actual parameters untranslated, allowing our basic game logic to remain unmodified.

The second view is a bit easier because, as mentioned before, it's strictly displaying information:

```
<html>
<head>
  <meta http-equiv="Content-Type" content="text/html; charset=UTF-8">
</head>
<body>
  <% translated do %>
    <p><%= T("You", :you) %>: <%= weapon_name(@player_weapon) %></p>
    <p><%= T("Opponent", :opponent) %>: <%= weapon_name(@opponent_weapon) %></p>
    <h3><%= end_game_message %></h3>
  <% end %>
</body>
</html>
```

Here, we're just looking up a few more tagged text segments, so there's nothing new to worry about. With these three files modified, heading to the **/rps/en** URI gives you the same screens shown at the beginning of the chapter.

When we hit **/rps/cn**, we get the screen for weapon selection (Figure 7-3).

Figure 7-3. Weapon selection (Chinese)

Pressing the button brings us to the results screen (Figure 7-4).

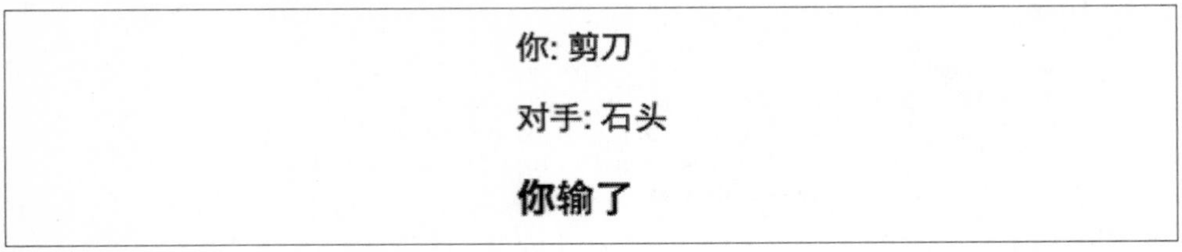

你: 剪刀

对手: 石头

你输了

Figure 7-4. Announcing the winner (Chinese)

When we switch to the /rps/fr URI, we get to pick our weapons in French (Figure 7-5).

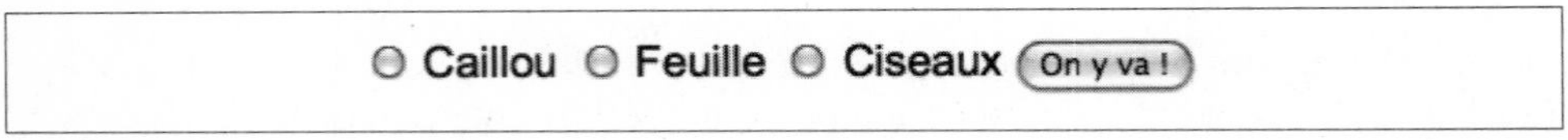

Figure 7-5. Weapon selection (French)

And, of course, we can see our final results as well (Figure 7-6).

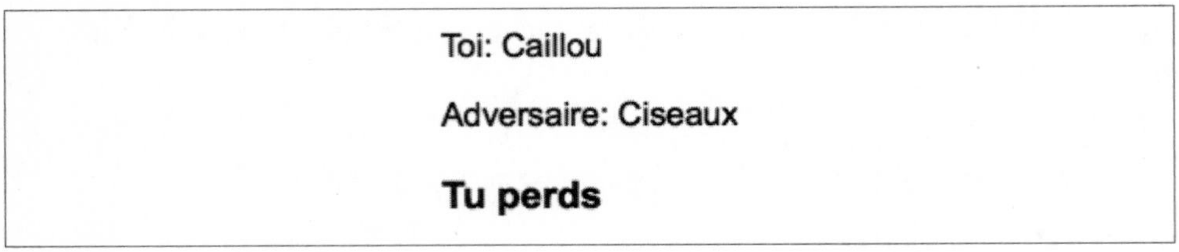

Toi: Caillou

Adversaire: Ciseaux

Tu perds

Figure 7-6. Announcing the winner (French)

At this point, we can take full advantage of the fact that the application has been localized. Adding new translations is as easy as dropping new YAML files into the lang directory. This is clear evidence of why it is better to offer general localization support than it is to offer a "Chinese Version" and "French Version" and however many other versions of your application you can imagine. This simple approach lets you easily customize the text used in your interface without much modification to your underlying business logic.

Of course, the example we've shown here is about as simple as you might imagine. In more complicated cases, you may have phrases where some text needs to be in a different order, depending on which language you are dealing with. This is especially common with things like names. To deal with things like this, you can create templates that allow for substitutions. We'll run through a simple example before wrapping things up here, just to give you an idea of how to work with situations like this.

In American English, names are typically represented as "Given Surname," such as "Gregory Brown." Here's how we'd express that as a default in `Gibberish::Simple`:

```
data = { given_name: "Gregory", surname: "Brown" }
p T("{given_name} {surname}", [:name, data]) #=> "Gregory Brown"
```

If we want to invert this order, we can easily do so in our templates. Here we've added a `:name` tag to the *lang/cn.yml* file that demonstrates how this is done:

```
name: "{surname}{given_name}"
```

Now, when we are dealing with a Chinese name, you can see that it gets composed with the last name first, and no space separating the last and first name:

```
data = { given_name: "佳", surname: "吴" }
Gibberish::Simple.use_language(:cn) do
  p T("{given_name} {surname}", [:name, data]) #=> "吴佳"
end
```

As you might imagine, this technique can be used to cover a lot of ground, providing substantial flexibility in how you display your text segments. Not only can each language have its own substitutions for text, but it can also control the order in which it is presented.

What we've covered so far should sufficiently cover most ordinary localization needs, so we'll use this as a convenient stopping point. Although I certainly recommend taking a look at `Gibberish::Simple`, most of the ideas we've covered here apply to any generalized L10n strategy you might implement. When it comes down to it, you need to remember only a few things:

- The first step in localizing an application is identifying the unique text segments that need to be translated.
- A generalized L10n system provides a way to keep all locale-specific content in translation files rather than tied up in the display code of your application.
- Every string that gets displayed to the user must be passed through a translation filter so that it can be customized based on the specified language. In `Gibberish::Simple`, we use `T()` for this; other systems may vary.
- Translation should be done at as late a stage as possible, so that L10n-related modifications to text do not interfere with the core business logic of your program.
- In many cases, you cannot simply interpolate strings in a predetermined order. `Gibberish::Simple` offers a simple templating mechanism that allows each translation file to specify how substrings should be interpolated into a text segment. If you roll your own system, be sure to keep this in consideration.

- Creating helper functions to simplify your translation code can come in handy when generating dynamic text output. For an example of this, go back and look at how weapon_name() was used in the simple Sinatra example discussed here.

- Because adding individual localization tags can be a bit tedious, it's often a good idea to wait until you have a fully fleshed-out application before integrating a general L10n system, if it is possible to do so.

If you keep these ideas in mind, you'll have no trouble integrating L10n support into your applications. Once a system is in place, it is quite cool to see how quickly translation files can change the overall interface to support different languages on the fly.

Conclusions

The process of multilingualization and localization is something that has been overlooked by programmers for far too long. This is mostly due to the fact that accomplishing any level of globalized support in software systems was until fairly recently a highly complex task. The demand for such functionality was also considerably lower before networked software dominated our ecosystem, due to the fact that software user bases typically were not globalized themselves.

In 2009, it is a whole different scene. If we want to write software that can be used comfortably by people all around the world, we need to rise to the occasion and make our code capable of speaking (or at least processing) the myriad collection languages that people are comfortable with. With Ruby 1.9, we have a powerful system for writing code that respects the cultural influences of our users, and we should take advantage of it whenever we can. The techniques shown in this chapter will help you make your software more accessible, whether it is open source or commercial. However, this chapter does not attempt to teach m17n, L10n in general, or the gritty details of how everything fits together in the context of Ruby. I strongly encourage you to read up on those topics before trying to apply any of the ideas you've gained here.

## CHAPTER 8

Skillful Project Maintenance

If you have done any significant amount of software development, you'll know that maintaining other people's code can be a nightmare. You may have noticed that even maintaining your own code can quickly become hellish if you are away from a project for more than a few months. On the surface, it may seem that any project that is not actively being worked on by its original developers is doomed to stagnate.

There are ways to fight back against software rot, many of which have little to do with the quality of the code itself. Instead, by following some conventions as to how you structure your project, you can make it easier to navigate. By using lightweight tools, you can simplify automatic generation of API documentation, manage dependencies and custom-built software packages, and automate your software build process in a number of ways.

When you combine the project management utilities Ruby provides (RDoc, Ruby-Gems, Rake, etc.) with some basic guidelines for how to lay things out, you end up with a powerful advantage. Rather than working around countless inconsistencies in overall project organization, you can reuse your knowledge from working on other projects to approach new codebases. Nowhere is this more valuable than in open source software, in which contributors may need to patch code that they have never worked with before.

For this reason, we're going to kick off this chapter with a look at the benefits that standards can offer us, through a brief review of the conventions used in the Haml project. As we explore its codebase, try to imagine yourself as the new maintainer of the project. In that way, we'll see how far our assumptions about the overall structure of a skillfully maintained Ruby project can get us.

Exploring a Well-Organized Ruby Project (Haml)

Haml is a clean and powerful XHTML templating engine for Ruby that is used by many as an alternative to ERB within web applications. It was originally developed by Hampton Catlin and is now actively maintained by Nathan Weizenbaum. Though the features of this library are certainly interesting in their own right, we'll primarily be focusing on the aspects of what makes Haml a maintainable project. To do this, we can pretend we have no idea what it actually does, and seek to discover a bit about these details by exploring the source code itself.

After grabbing the source,[*] we can start by looking for a file called *README* or something similar. We find one called *README.rdoc*, which gives us a nice description of why we might want to use Haml right at the top of the file:

```
Haml and Sass are templating engines for the two most common types of documents
on the web: HTML and CSS, respectively. They are designed to make it both easier
and more pleasant to code HTML and CSS documents, by eliminating redundancy,
reflecting the underlying structure that the document represents, and providing
elegant, easily understandable, and powerful syntax.
```

The rest of the file fills in other useful details, including how to install the library, some usage examples, a list of the executables it ships with, and some information on the authors. For a user, this might be enough to get up and running with the library. But from our "imaginary new maintainer" perspective, one line in the *README* caught my eye: *To use Haml and Sass programmatically, check out the RDocs for the Haml and Sass modules.*

This indicated to me that the project has autogenerated API documentation, which is as good a place as any to start when you're first getting to know the low-level details of a project. Noticing the project also has a *Rakefile*, we can check to see whether there is a task for generating the documentation:

```
sandal:haml $ rake --tasks
(in /Users/sandal/devel/haml)
rake benchmark                  # Benchmark haml against ERb.
rake clobber_package            # Remove package products
rake clobber_rcov               # Remove rcov products for rcov
rake clobber_rdoc               # Remove rdoc products
rake gem                        # Build the gem file haml-2.1.0.gem
rake install                    # Install Haml as a gem.
rake package                    # Build all the packages
rake profile                    # Run a profile of Haml.
rake rcov                       # Analyze code coverage with tests
rake rdoc                       # Build the rdoc HTML Files
rake release                    # Release a new Haml package to Rubyforge.
rake repackage                  # Force a rebuild of the package files
rake rerdoc                     # Force a rebuild of the RDOC files
rake test                       # Run tests / To run with an alternate versi...
rake test:rails_compatibility   # Test all supported versions of rails.
```

Sure enough, midway down the task list, we see `rake rdoc`. Running this command spits out a bunch of noisy output, and then eventually generates some HTML documentation in the *rdoc/* directory. If we open up *rdoc/index.html* in our browser, we can see a complete class listing of the project, along with the familiar *README* in HTML

---

[*] See *http://github.com/nex3/haml/tree/master*.

format. If we quickly scan the list of classes, `Haml::Engine` is among the most interesting, based on name. Pulling up the documentation, we see a brief summary of the object along with its methods and attributes (Figure 8-1).

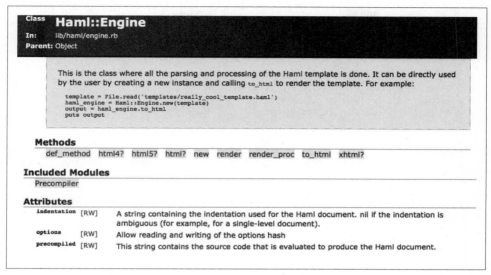

Figure 8-1. API documentation for Haml::Engine, generated by RDoc

Clicking on any of the methods in the list will bring us to their specific documentation, where we can even view their source, among other things. In the interest of peering under the hood, let's take a look at the source. We can see a hint from the RDoc that this library follows a common convention, with source files in *lib/module_name/ class_name.rb*, which in this case is *lib/haml/engine.rb*.

Looking at just the top of the file, we see that the RDoc is actually being generated directly from the source:

```
module Haml
  # This is the class where all the parsing and processing of the Haml
  # template is done. It can be directly used by the user by creating a
  # new instance and calling <tt>to_html</tt> to render the template. For example:
  #
  #   template = File.read('templates/really_cool_template.haml')
  #   haml_engine = Haml::Engine.new(template)
  #   output = haml_engine.to_html
  #   puts output
  class Engine
      #...
  end
end
```

We could read directly through the source now to see which functions are most important, but tests often provide a better road map to where the interesting parts are.

There are a few conventions for how to label test files, but the one Haml uses is straightforward and common. We find the relevant tests for `Haml::Engine` in *test/haml/engine.rb*.

Although we won't look through this file in great detail, you'll find that it provides comprehensive testing of the overall templating language that `Haml::Engine` processes. The top of the file starts with a couple helpers to keep the tests clean, including one that renders Haml to HTML:

```ruby
def render(text, options = {}, &block)
  scope = options.delete(:scope) || Object.new
  locals = options.delete(:locals) || {}
  engine(text, options).to_html(scope, locals, &block)
end
```

Already this gives us some hints as to how `Haml::Engine` works. We can see that this helper is further aided by another method that initializes the `Haml::Engine`, which is not particularly important for us to look at.

If we look just a little deeper in the file, we start to see how `render()` is being used to generate HTML for comparison to the expected values:

```ruby
def test_empty_render_should_remain_empty
  assert_equal('', render(''))
end

def test_attributes_should_render_correctly
  assert_equal("<div class='atlantis' style='ugly'></div>",
    render(".atlantis{:style => 'ugly'}").chomp)
end

def test_ruby_code_should_work_inside_attributes
  author = 'hcatlin'
  assert_equal("<p class='3'>foo</p>", render("%p{:class => 1+2} foo").chomp)
end
```

This is just a tiny sampling of what is covered in this test case, but it gives you a clear sense of how tests are very useful in describing how some code is meant to be used. If we wanted to dig around and make some changes to how the code worked, we would first need to verify that the tests actually complete successfully. We can use **rake** again for this. Though the output is a little messy, we can see that the whole suite is passing without errors upon running the **rake test** command:

```
sandal:haml $ rake test
(in /Users/sandal/devel/haml)
[ file list omitted ]
Started
.................................................................
.................................................................
....... merb couldn't be loaded, skipping a test...................
Finished in 5.031813 seconds.

232 tests, 1812 assertions, 0 failures, 0 errors
```

This tells us that Haml is working fine on our system, at least to the extent that the original developers have specified. It is impossible to know if tests are truly comprehensive, but by the looks of Haml's tests, which even include examples covering some regressions, you can be fairly confident that the tests will provide a decent safety net. By looking through these tests, we see that most of them hinge on the `Haml::Engine` constructor, as well as the `Haml::Engine#to_html` method.[†] Though we won't get into it here, this seems like a good entry point to study if you want to get more familiar with the core of Haml's implementation. Along the way, you will likely encounter new objects and methods that you aren't familiar with. When this happens, go back to the tests and API documentation as needed. Repeating this process is a surefire way to learn any well-tested library that follows common Ruby organizational conventions. But for now, let's revisit something we glossed over a bit earlier.

When we saw the `rake task` listing earlier, we saw all sorts of different tasks available to us. We covered the way to set up a test task in Chapter 1, *Driving Code Through Tests*—and we'll look at the RDoc generation task a little later on in this chapter—but one task that is particularly interesting is the `rake install` task, which will install Haml as a gem from the current sources. This can be very handy for testing your custom modifications locally, so let's take a look at how that works:

```
desc "Install Haml as a gem."
task :install => [:package] do
  sudo = RUBY_PLATFORM =~ /win32/ ? '' : 'sudo'
  gem  = RUBY_PLATFORM =~ /java/  ? 'jgem' : 'gem'
  sh %{#{sudo} #{gem} install --no-ri pkg/haml-#{File.read('VERSION').strip}}
end
```

Here, we see that Haml has provided a Rake task that will install a generated gem for you. It is smart about whether or not to use `sudo`, depending on whether you are running on Windows. It also has some provisions built in to check whether you're running on JRuby, where gems are installed via `jgem` instead of `gem`. Finally, it just executes a shell command in which it reads the current version from a file called *VERSION*. As you can see, the contents of this file are far from exciting:

```
sandal:haml $ cat VERSION
2.1.0
```

Using this approach, the Rakefile is kept independent of a particular version number, allowing a single place for updating version numbers. All of these tricks are done in the name of simplifying maintainability, making it easy to generate and install the library from source for testing.

Though I'll cover how to set up gem specs in detail later, we can take a quick look at the `:package` task that `:install` depends on. It is actually generated via a utility provided with Rake, called `Rake::GemPackageTask`:

---

† Which happens to be an alias to `Haml::Engine#render`, as indicated by the RDoc.

```
require 'rake/gempackagetask'
load    'haml.gemspec'

Rake::GemPackageTask.new(HAML_GEMSPEC) do |pkg|
  if Rake.application.top_level_tasks.include?('release')
    pkg.need_tar_gz  = true
    pkg.need_tar_bz2 = true
    pkg.need_zip     = true
  end
end
```

Here, we see that Haml customizes things a bit by generating zipped archives only when the :release task is executed. Otherwise, only a gem is produced. This is mainly because zipped archives are not necessary for a local gem install, and Haml uses its :package task both for preparing files for a release and for local builds.

Though we haven't dug down to actually fix anything in this code yet, or make any significant changes, we can see how much decent project organization comes into play when it comes to maintainability. Without any previous experience with the library, we were able to figure out what it is meant to do, saw a few examples of how it worked, generated documentation directly from the source that gave us some clues as to what the important objects were, and then found tests that described exactly how these objects should work.

We were able to run these tests to verify that the expectations set by the project maintainers were being upheld. We also saw how to build and install a package from source to be used system-wide via RubyGems. This provides us a way to try out our modifications locally before releasing the code in the wild, using the same packaging system that Ruby libraries are typically distributed through.

The important thing to remember here is that although Haml is a very good example of a Ruby library that is highly consistent with conventions, it didn't invent any of them. In fact, this entire section was written based on my previous assumptions on how a well-structured Ruby project should operate, based on my experiences working with many popular open source codebases. We'll now move from how this works in other people's code to how you can follow these conventions in your own projects. Once those basic ground rules are established, we can move on to specific details about how to use tools such as RDoc, RubyGems, and Rake effectively to make maintenance much easier.

Conventions to Know About

When we walked through Haml in the previous example, we could see that it had a high degree of discoverability baked in through the conventions it uses. Though Ruby is free-form in nature and allows you to structure your files in pretty much any way you want, it makes sense to standardize in most cases. Making your project easily accessible to your users so they can figure out some questions on their own is one of the easiest things you can do to make your project more maintainable. Though each of the tips in this section may seem a bit trivial, combining them can be very powerful.

What Goes in a README

A somewhat universal software development standard is to have a *README* file that provides a starting point to your software. Finding the right balance of information to include in this file can be a bit of a challenge.

Minimally speaking, a good *README* should include everything that is necessary to begin working with a project, and nothing more. For starters, you'll need a brief one- or two-paragraph description of what the project is for, and what problems it is meant to solve. Drawing from another good open source example, we can see that the *README* for James Gray's HighLine library opens in exactly this way:

```
== Description

Welcome to HighLine.

HighLine was designed to ease the tedious tasks of doing console input and
output with low-level methods like gets() and puts().  HighLine provides a
robust system for requesting data from a user, without needing to code all the
error checking and validation rules and without needing to convert the typed
Strings into what your program really needs.  Just tell HighLine what you're
after, and let it do all the work.
```

Next, it is generally a good idea to point out a couple of the core classes that make up the public API of your project. You don't need to be comprehensive here; you just need to point out where the good starting points might be for users who wish to browse the API documentation:

```
== Documentation

See HighLine and HighLine::Question for documentation.
```

Because sometimes raw API documentation isn't enough to get people started, it's often a good idea to include a brief synopsis of your project's capabilities through a few simple examples. You probably don't want to get into very complicated needs here, just something to help users get their feet wet:

```
== Examples

Basic usage:

  ask("Company?  ") { |q| q.default = "none" }

Validation:

  ask("Age?  ", Integer) { |q| q.in = 0..105 }
  ask("Name?  (last, first)  ") { |q| q.validate = /\A\w+, ?\w+\Z/ }

Type conversion for answers:
```

```
ask("Birthday?  ", Date)
ask("Interests?  (comma sep list)  ", lambda { |str| str.split(/,\s*/) })
```

Reading passwords:

```
ask("Enter your password:  ") { |q| q.echo = false }
ask("Enter your password:  ") { |q| q.echo = "x" }
```

ERb based output (with HighLine's ANSI color tools):

```
say("This should be <%= color('bold', BOLD) %>!")
```

Menus:

```
choose do |menu|
  menu.prompt = "Please choose your favorite programming language?  "

  menu.choice(:ruby) { say("Good choice!") }
  menu.choices(:python, :perl) { say("Not from around here, are you?") }
end
```

For more examples see the examples/ directory of this project.

If your install instructions are simple, you can just embed them in your *README* file directly. However, in the case of HighLine, several install methods are supported, and optional dependencies enable certain features. For this reason, the *README* simply contains a reference that tells the user to look in the *INSTALL* file. This is what that file looks like:

```
= Installing HighLine

RubyGems is the preferred easy install method for HighLine.  However, you can
install HighLine manually as described below.

== Installing the Gem

HighLine is intended to be installed via the
RubyGems[http://rubyforge.org/projects/rubygems/] system.  To get the latest
version, simply enter the following into your command prompt:

  $ sudo gem install highline

You must have RubyGems[http://rubyforge.org/projects/rubygems/] installed for
the above to work.

== Installing Manually

Download the latest version of HighLine from the
{RubyForge project page}[http://rubyforge.org/frs/?group_id=683].  Navigate to
the root project directory and enter:

  $ sudo ruby setup.rb

== Using termios
```

```
While not a requirement, HighLine will take advantage of the termios library if
installed (on Unix).  This slightly improves HighLine's character reading
capabilities and thus is recommended for all Unix users.

If using the HighLine gem, you should be able to add termios as easily as:

  $ sudo gem install termios

For manual installs, consult the termios documentation.
```

Finally, once you've told users what your project is, where to look for documentation, how it looks in brief, and how to get it installed, you'll want to let them know how to contact you in case something goes wrong:

```
== Questions and/or Comments

Feel free to email {James Edward Gray II}[mailto:james@grayproductions.net] or
{Gregory Brown}[mailto:gregory.t.brown@gmail.com] with any questions.
```

In the case of HighLine, we have a very minimal process because the library is small and simple. If you're working on a bigger project, this might be the right place to link to a mailing list or bug tracker.

This pretty much sums up everything you need to know to write a good *README*. Although this explanation is admittedly not Ruby-specific, it is a skill that helps make even in-house projects much more accessible. A decent *README* will instruct other developers about the bare minimum details, and get them launched in the right direction for working with your code.

Keep your *README* short and sweet so that it mainly points to information rather than containing a ton of information within itself. From a maintainability standpoint, this makes it much less likely that your *README* will become out-of-date or irrelevant.

Laying Out Your Library

Library files are generally kept in a *lib/* directory. Generally speaking, this directory should only have one file in it, and one subdirectory. Earlier when we looked at Haml, we saw that the structure was *lib/haml.rb* and *lib/haml/*. For HighLine, it is *lib/high line.rb* and *lib/highline/*.

The Ruby file in your *lib/* dir should bear the name of your project and act as a jumping-off point for loading dependencies as well as any necessary support libraries. The top of *lib/highline.rb* provides a good example of this:[‡]

```
#!/usr/local/bin/ruby -w

require "erb"
require "optparse"
```

[‡] Documentation omitted to simplify example.

```
require "stringio"
require "abbrev"

require "highline/compatibility"
require "highline/system_extensions"
require "highline/question"
require "highline/menu"
require "highline/color_scheme"

class HighLine
 # ...
end
```

Here we see some of the standard libraries HighLine needs to use, as well as the rest of the classes that make up the project. In HighLine's case, there are no deeply nested classes, so most of these map directly to class names, such as *"highline/question"* → HighLine::Question. This means that when you do a simple require "highline", all the necessary classes to use the library are loaded through this single file.

If you have deeply nested classes in your projects, you will typically repeat this process for each level of nesting. Here's a simple abstract example of how that might work:

```
# a.rb
require "a/b"

# a/b.rb

require "a/b/c"
require "a/b/d"

# a/b/c.rb

module A
  module B
    class C
       # ...
    end
  end
end

# a/b/d.rb

module A
  module B
    class D
       #...
    end
  end
end
```

With a file structure as indicated by the comments in the example code, and the necessary require statements in place, we end up being able to do this:

```
>> require "a"
=> true
```

```
>> A::B::C
=> A::B::C

>> A::B::D
=> A::B::D
```

Although this is much more important in large systems than small ones, it is a good habit to get into. Essentially, unless there is a good reason to deviate, files will often map to class names in Ruby. Nested classes that are large enough to deserve their own file should be loaded in the file that defines the class they are nested within. Using this approach allows the user a single entry point into your library, but also allows for running parts of the system in isolation.

Although these conventions will take you far, in certain cases it's fine to deviate from them. Filenames do not necessarily need to be representative of a class at all. For example, in HighLine, we have *lib/highline/import.rb*, which simply injects some of High-Line's functionality into `Kernel`. This code contains no class definitions to speak of. This is essentially organization by concept, and can work fine for certain needs. Prawn has a similar feature called *lib/prawn/measurement_extensions.rb*, which adds some methods to `Numeric` for simplified PDF point conversions. This is disabled by default, but once required, you end up with the following functionality:

```
>> require "prawn/measurement_extensions"
=> true
>> 1.in
=> 72
>> 1.mm
=> 2.83464566929134
```

In the more general case, you might have files that contain extensions to provide backward compatibility with Ruby 1.8, or ones that make minor changes to core Ruby classes. Decent names for these are *lib/myproject/compatibility.rb* and *lib/myproject/extensions.rb*, respectively. When things get complicated, you can of course nest these and work on individual classes one at a time. For example, the following extension might be called *lib/myproject/extensions/enumerable.rb*:

```
module Enumerable
  def injecting(x)
    inject(x){|a,i| yield(a,i); a }
  end
end
```

However you choose to organize your files, one thing is fairly well agreed upon: if you intend to modify core Ruby in any way, you should do it in files that are well marked as extension files, to help people hunt down changes that might conflict with other packages. Do not randomly go about opening core classes in your other library files, unless you want to frustrate your users.

Generally speaking, following sound naming conventions and setting up your `require`s in an organized fashion helps make it easier to remember where to find the various classes and modules that your project implements. Of course, this should be done in moderation, as relatively small projects might meaningfully fit all in one file. However, if and when you do decide to break things down, following this general approach should serve you well.

You'll notice that none of the kinds of files we've talked about so far are meant to be executed directly. Though scripts and applications that are meant to be run directly do not belong in *lib/*, they of course have a home and some basic guidelines to follow, so let's take a closer look at how to work with them.

Executables

Scripts and applications are usually placed in a *bin/* dir in Ruby projects. These are typically ordinary Ruby scripts that have been made executable via something like a combination of a shebang line and a `chmod +x` call. To make these appear more like ordinary command-line utilities, it is common to omit the file extension. As an example, we can take a look at the `haml` executable:

```
#!/usr/bin/env ruby
# The command line Haml parser.

$LOAD_PATH.unshift File.dirname(__FILE__) + '/../lib'
require 'haml'
require 'haml/exec'

opts = Haml::Exec::Haml.new(ARGV)
opts.parse!
```

Here we see most of the common conventions for working with Ruby scripts in action. You can see that the executable starts with a shebang line that indicates how to find the Ruby interpreter. This is followed by a line that adds the library to the loadpath by relative positioning. Finally, the remaining code simply requires the necessary library files and then delegates to an object that is responsible for handling command-line requests. Ideally speaking, most of your scripts in *bin/* will follow a similar approach.

Tests

There are a few common conventions for tests, depending on what your needs are. However, among the most straightforward is to simply place your tests in a */test* folder. For something like Prawn, we use the format *test/test_classname.rb*, but omit the namespace. So for `Prawn::Document`, we have *test/document_test.rb* rather than *test/ prawn_document_test.rb*. If you have a project that spans multiple namespaces, it's fine to organize your tests in a similar way to libraries. In the Haml library, a tool called Sass is also provided, so the test structure includes files like *test/haml/engine_test.rb* and *test/ sass/engine_test.rb*, which share the same basename but coexist peacefully due to the folder structure.

Consistency in naming of test files is important, because setting up files to run an automated test suite often involves matching a filename pattern. We'll get to this a bit later, but it is worth keeping in mind.

Ideally speaking, each individual test case should load a test helper file that does the grunt work of requiring all necessary libraries and providing supporting functionality as needed. This is done via a simple dynamic **require** relative to the position of the current test:

```
require File.dirname(__FILE__) + '/test_helper'
```

The purpose of a *test_helpers.rb* file is to DRY up configuration so that each test case does not begin with a chunk of boilerplate code that is repeated again and again. Individual test cases of course can have their own specific helpers within them, but those that are reused across many of the tests should end up here. Although we talk about this in much greater detail in Chapter 1, *Driving Code Through Tests*, here's a quick sample of a test helper file from Haml:

```
lib_dir = File.dirname(__FILE__) + '/../lib'
require File.dirname(__FILE__) + '/linked_rails'

require 'test/unit'
$:.unshift lib_dir unless $:.include?(lib_dir)
require 'haml'
require 'sass'

# required because of Sass::Plugin
unless defined? RAILS_ROOT
  RAILS_ROOT = '.'
  MERB_ENV = RAILS_ENV  = 'testing'
end

class Test::Unit::TestCase
  def munge_filename(opts)
    return if opts[:filename]
    test_name = caller[1].gsub(/^.*'(?:\w+ )*(\w+)'.*$/, '\1')
    opts[:filename] = "#{test_name}_inline.sass"
  end
end
```

Examples

In addition to tests, examples form a great way to discover how a system works, as well as an extra safety net for detecting regressions. Typically, these files will go in an *examples/* directory.

It is useful to organize these examples by concept, rather than class name. As an illustration, here's what HighLine's *examples/* directory looks like:

```
$ ls examples/
ansi_colors.rb      limit.rb    password.rb
asking_for_arrays.rb menus.rb    trapping_eof.rb
```

```
basic_usage.rb    overwrite.rb    using_readline.rb
color_scheme.rb   page_and_wrap.rb
```

Each of these names hint at what these examples will demonstrate, making it easy for users to find what they are interested in. If you have a more complex system, you can use folders to organize your examples into groups. Here's what that approach looks like in Prawn:

```
$ ls -R examples/
bounding_box            general      m17n
font_calculations.pdf   graphics     text

examples/bounding_box:
bounding_boxes.rb    russian_boxes.rb

examples/general:
background.rb    measurement_units.rb     page_geometry.rb
canvas.rb        multi_page_layout.rb

examples/graphics:
basic_images.rb    image_flow.rb        remote_images.rb
cmyk.rb            image_position.rb    ruport_style_helpers.rb
curves.rb          line.rb              stroke_bounds.rb
hexagon.rb         png_types.rb
image_fit.rb       polygons.rb

examples/m17n:
chinese_text_wrapping.rb    utf8.rb
euro.rb                     win_ansi_charset.rb
sjis.rb

examples/text:
alignment.rb             font_size.rb        span.rb
dfont.rb                 kerning.rb          text_box.rb
family_based_styling.rb  simple_text.rb      text_flow.rb
font_calculations.rb     simple_text_ttf.rb
```

However you choose to organize your examples, you'll want to use a similar trick to writing your binary files, in that your examples should modify the loadpath to include your library based on their relative positions. This is to prevent you from having to install your locally modified library before running your examples against it. Here's an example from Prawn to see what this looks like:

```
# encoding: utf-8
#
# Demonstrates how to enable absolute positioning in Prawn by temporarily
# removing the margin_box via Document#canvas()
#
$LOAD_PATH.unshift(File.join(File.dirname(__FILE__), '..', '..', 'lib'))
require "prawn"

Prawn::Document.generate("canvas.pdf") do
  canvas do
    text "This text should appear at the absolute top left"
```

```
    # stroke a line to show that the relative coordinates are the same as absolute
    stroke_line [bounds.left,bounds.bottom], [bounds.right,bounds.top]
  end
end
```

There might be some other conventions to be aware of, but the ones we've covered so far are the most common. Even if they seem a bit dull on their own, they really will help make your project maintainable. By writing your code in a conventional way, you spare yourself the need to write copious documentation about the overall organization of your project. Most of the tips here focus on discoverability, which is essential for making your project easier for others to maintain, or for when you get reassigned to some of your own old code a couple years down the line. Here are the key things to remember about the conventions we've discussed so far:

- Every project, large or small, deserves a README file. At a minimum, it should include a short description of what the project is useful for, a small sampling of code examples that illustrate some core features, and some pointers of where to dig deeper if the user is interested in learning more. It should also indicate whom to contact when something goes wrong, whether it be an individual developer or a team that's operating a mailing list or bug tracker.

- The key folders to remember are *lib/*, *bin/*, *examples/*, and *test/*. Each has its own conventions about what it should contain and how it should be organized, which is significant both for the sake of consistency and to satisfy various other software tools that depend on these conventions.

- One thing to remember about files in *lib/* is that you should be sure to explicitly separate out core extensions from your main library classes. Instead, keep them in a file such as *lib/projectname/extensions.rb*. If you have a lot of extensions, it might make sense to break them out class by class, such as *lib/projectname/extensions/ string.rb*.

- Well-organized tests and examples can go a long way to improving the understandability of a project, which, in turn, improves the maintainability.

- Whether you follow standard Ruby conventions or not in your project organization, you should strive to be consistent. The easier it is to navigate around a project, the more likely it is that you'll be able to understand it if you have to look at it again a few years down the line.

- If you plan to distribute your code publicly, be sure to include a *LICENSE* text file, possibly paired with a *COPYING* file if you are offering the GNU GPL as a licensing option.

API Documentation via RDoc

RDoc provides an easy and powerful way to document your Ruby APIs. By simply writing comments in your source code with some lightweight markup here and there, you can automatically generate comprehensive documentation. Of course, a documentation tool isn't going to be all that useful without some solid guidelines for how functions should actually be documented. We'll cover both RDoc and Ruby documentation best practices here, as they complement each other nicely.

Basic Documentation Techniques and Guidelines

Usually, you'll want to start off the documentation for any function with a short description of what it does. You can then follow up with a description of the accepted arguments and any defaults used. Finally, if it makes sense to do so, an example or two helps make things easier to follow. Figure 8-2 shows how we do this for the `Prawn::Document` constructor method.

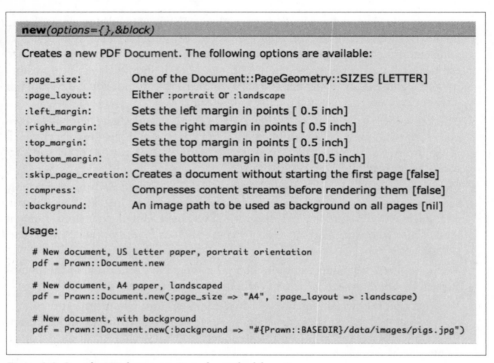

new(options={},&block)

Creates a new PDF Document. The following options are available:

`:page_size:`	One of the Document::PageGeometry::SIZES [LETTER]
`:page_layout:`	Either `:portrait` or `:landscape`
`:left_margin:`	Sets the left margin in points [0.5 inch]
`:right_margin:`	Sets the right margin in points [0.5 inch]
`:top_margin:`	Sets the top margin in points [0.5 inch]
`:bottom_margin:`	Sets the bottom margin in points [0.5 inch]
`:skip_page_creation:`	Creates a document without starting the first page [false]
`:compress:`	Compresses content streams before rendering them [false]
`:background:`	An image path to be used as background on all pages [nil]

Usage:

```
# New document, US Letter paper, portrait orientation
pdf = Prawn::Document.new

# New document, A4 paper, landscaped
pdf = Prawn::Document.new(:page_size => "A4", :page_layout => :landscape)

# New document, with background
pdf = Prawn::Document.new(:background => "#{Prawn::BASEDIR}/data/images/pigs.jpg")
```

Figure 8-2. Sample API documentation of a method from Prawn

Although the end result is nicely formatted, it doesn't take much extra work in the source comments to get this sort of output. Here's what the actual code comments that match Figure 8-2 look like:

```
class Prawn::Document

    # Creates a new PDF Document.  The following options are available:
    #
    # <tt>:page_size</tt>:: One of the Document::PageGeometry::SIZES [LETTER]
```

```
# <tt>:page_layout</tt>:: Either <tt>:portrait</tt> or <tt>:landscape</tt>
# <tt>:left_margin</tt>:: Sets the left margin in points [ 0.5 inch]
# <tt>:right_margin</tt>:: Sets the right margin in points [ 0.5 inch]
# <tt>:top_margin</tt>:: Sets the top margin in points [ 0.5 inch]
# <tt>:bottom_margin</tt>:: Sets the bottom margin in points [0.5 inch]
# <tt>:skip_page_creation</tt>:: Toggles manual page creation [false]
# <tt>:compress</tt>:: Compresses content streams before rendering them [false]
# <tt>:background</tt>:: An image path to be used as background on all pages [nil]
#
# Usage:
#
#    # New document, US Letter paper, portrait orientation
#    pdf = Prawn::Document.new
#
#    # New document, A4 paper, landscaped
#    pdf = Prawn::Document.new(:page_size => "A4", :page_layout => :landscape)
#
#    # New document, with background
#    img = "#{Prawn::BASEDIR}/data/images/pigs.jpg"
#    pdf = Prawn::Document.new(:background => img)
#
def initialize
    #...
end

end
```

As you can see here, we just use a little HTML-style formatting to indicate that the options text should be displayed in a fixed-width font, then use the :: syntax to indicate that this is a two-column table. The rest of the text is essentially just plain text. Code samples are automatically formatted, as long as they are indented a bit from the prose.

As another example, we can look at some of the API documentation from Ruby's *pstore* standard library. The one in Figure 8-3 uses a heading to make the example stand out, and it also includes a warning about when using the function is valid and the error you will encounter otherwise.

```
abort()

Ends the current PStore#transaction, discarding any changes to the data store.

Example:

require "pstore"

store = PStore.new("data_file.pstore")
store.transaction do   # begin transaction
  store[:one] = 1      # this change is not applied, see below...
  store[:two] = 2      # this change is not applied, see below...

  store.abort          # end transaction here, discard all changes

  store[:three] = 3    # this change is never reached
end

WARNING: This method is only valid in a PStore#transaction. It will raise PStore::Error if called at any other time.

[Source]
```

Figure 8-3. API documentation with a formatted heading

The comments used to generate this are simple, as you might expect:

```
# Ends the current PStore#transaction, discarding any changes to the data
# store.
#
# == Example:
#
#  require "pstore"
#
#  store = PStore.new("data_file.pstore")
#  store.transaction do  # begin transaction
#    store[:one] = 1     # this change is not applied, see below...
#    store[:two] = 2     # this change is not applied, see below...
#
#    store.abort         # end transaction here, discard all changes
#
#    store[:three] = 3   # this change is never reached
#  end
#
# *WARNING*:  This method is only valid in a PStore#transaction.  It will
# raise PStore::Error if called at any other time.
#
def abort
  # ...
end
```

You can see that through simple markup, you can generate nice HTML output without sacrificing the readability of the plain text. You might have also noticed that RDoc will link together documentation about classes or methods in your project without specifying any special syntax.

Although you can get very far with just the basic formatting in these two examples, there are times where finer-grained control is needed. We'll now go over a way to give the **rdoc** generator some hints as to how your code and comments should be processed.

Controlling Output with RDoc Directives

Even if your code is not commented, running RDoc against it will generate some useful content that clearly lays out the structure of your API. You can get a whole lot more out of it by generating your documentation from commented code that includes some light formatting syntax. In many cases, the default behaviors for documentation generation work well enough, and this is why many people never bother to learn about the directives you can use to customize things.

We'll cover just a few of the things you can do with RDoc directives, focusing mainly on the kinds of things I've found useful in my projects and have seen used effectively in other projects. If you want to know the full range of what is available, be sure to consult the RDoc website (*http://rdoc.rubyforge.org/RDoc.html*) for a complete listing.

We'll start with one of the most simple and common directives available, :nodoc:. Although RDoc is smart enough to hide private methods, it can't really make a

---

judgment call about whether a method belongs to the external or internal API of a project. Ideally speaking, we want to expose our users only to the functions we intend for them to use. By hiding everything that the typical user won't need to know about, we can really cut down on the noise in our documentation.

Using this directive is easy—just drop it in wherever you want to exclude some content from the generated documentation. The most simple case is doing this at the method level:

```
class Prawn::Document

  # Stores the current state of the named attributes, executes the block, and
  # then restores the original values after the block has executed.
  #
  def mask(*fields) # :nodoc:
    stored = {}
    fields.each { |f| stored[f] = send(f) }
    yield
    fields.each { |f| send("#{f}=", stored[f]) }
  end

end
```

Here we have a method that is part of the public interface of `Prawn::Document`, but is meant primarily for internal use. By adding a `:nodoc:` comment on the same line as the method signature, we can ensure that this method will not appear in the generated documentation. We can also use this directive at the class/module level:

```
# reference.rb : Implementation of PDF indirect objects

module Prawn

  class Reference #:nodoc:

    # seecrets

  end

end
```

End users of Prawn will likely never need to worry about how we implement what are essentially pointers to low-level PDF data structures, so we can safely hide this entire class from public view, as far as documentation is concerned. Because the syntax is identical to skipping the documentation for a function, it is easy to remember.

It may look like the `:nodoc:` directive operates at the block level, hiding everything nested inside a class or module. However, this is not the case by default. This means that if I had a module called `Prawn::Reference::Helpers`, it would still be documented unless explicitly marked otherwise with a subsequent `:nodoc:` comment. There is a way to hide everything nested within a class, using the `:nodoc: all` directive, but I would not recommend it, as it may accidentally hide worthwhile information.

It is important use :nodoc: with a bit of caution. If you expose too little documentation to your users, they may not find the features they need easily enough. Generally speaking, you should use :nodoc: only on features that are clearly a part of your project's internals, and not on features that might be a bit low-level but could still be potentially useful to others. If in doubt, keep your documentation public, putting a warning or two in the comments as needed.

Sometimes you don't need to outright hide a function's documentation, but rather, just modify it a bit. The following code is an example of where this feature comes in handy:

```
class Prawn::Document
  # :call-seq:
  #   bounding_box(point, options={}, &block)
  #
  # A bounding box serves two important purposes:
  # * Provide bounds for flowing text, starting at a given point
  # * Translate the origin (0,0) for graphics primitives, for the purposes
  # of simplifying coordinate math.
  #
  # (rest omitted, as this documentation is pretty lengthy)
  #
  def bounding_box(*args, &block)
    init_bounding_box(block) do
      translate!(args[0])
      @bounding_box = BoundingBox.new(self, *args)
    end
  end
end
```

Here, the :call-seq: hook is used to modify what will be displayed as the method signature in the documentation. The reason is that the function shown is nothing more than a simple wrapper around a constructor for another object. In cases like these, it's best to slurp up all the arguments and pass them along, because then the exact signature of the constructor does not need to be known.

However, since documentation involving anything(*args, &block) can be a little opaque, :call-seq gives us a way to give a better hint at the interface of our function. In the end result, the documentation is displayed as if the method had the signature specified in :call-seq:, so it is completely transparent in nature.

You can also use :call-seq: to provide hints at function return values, as you can see in this example from Jeremy Hinegardner's *hitimes* library:[§]

```
module Hitimes

  class Timer

    class << self

      #
```

[§] A high-resolution timer library: *http://copiousfreetime.rubyforge.org/hitimes*.

```
          # :call-seq:
          # Timer.now -> Timer
          #
          # Return a newly allocated Timer that has already been started
          #
          def now
            t = Timer.new
            t.start
            return t
          end

          #
          # :call-seq:
          # Timer.measure { ... } -> Float
          #
          # Return the number of seconds that a block of code took to
          # execute.
          #
          def measure( &block )
            Interval.measure { yield }
          end
        end

      # ...
    end
  end
```

The `:call-seq:` directive will completely replace the method signature with everything that comes after it continuing up until the next blank line. In this way, you can tell RDoc exactly how you want your method's signature to be represented. Although this feature is a must-have in certain cases, you can of course rely on the defaults in many cases, so your best bet is to try to see how things look without `:call-seq:` first and then tweak things as needed.

The last directive trick I'll show before we move on provides a simple way to group together sets of functions into distinct sections within your documentation. This provides a way for RDoc to generate a table of contents for navigating your module or class definition.

The following example shows this directive being used within `Prawn::Measurements`, which supports both imperial and metric conversions:

```
module Prawn
  module Measurements

    # -----------------------------------------------------------------
    # :section: Imperial Conversions
    # Convert several metric units to one another and to PDF points
    # -----------------------------------------------------------------

    def ft2in(ft)
      return ft * 12
    end
```

```
def in2pt(inch)
  return inch * 72
end

# ...

# -------------------------------------------------------------------
# :section: Metric Conversions
# Convert several metric units to one another and to PDF points
# -------------------------------------------------------------------

def cm2mm(cm)
  return cm*10
end

def mm2pt(mm)
  return mm*(72 / 25.4)
end

    # ...
  end
end
```

The `:section:` directive allows you to embed a description of the section that is displayed in the generated documentation. To get a sense of how this works, Figure 8-4 shows a screenshot of the "Imperial Conversions" section.

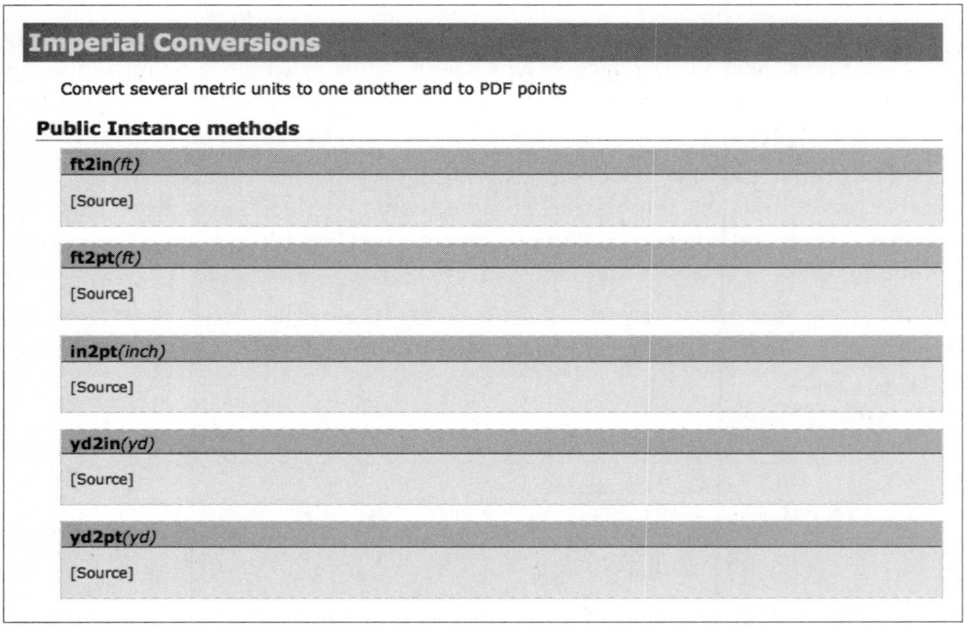

Figure 8-4. API documentation with section-based layout

Grouping by sections in RDoc is a majorly underused feature and goes a long way toward making your documentation easy to approach. Although not all classes and modules can be meaningfully split up this way, it is a really good idea to use this feature if it makes sense to do so. Section titles and descriptions can help your users or fellow developers pinpoint the parts of a class they are interested in.

Though we could go on to discuss even more RDoc directives, we've probably covered enough to get you started. When you put together the ideas in this section, you can easily see that Ruby provides a powerful documentation system that is easy to work with and use. I have not covered the specifics of how the actual `rdoc` command-line utility works, as this is something you can easily look up. However, we will cover how to build an RDoc generation task for Rake a little bit later in this chapter, so be sure to look out for that if you want an easy way to automate your documentation generation.

We're about to move on to other things, but before we do that, here are the key things to remember about RDoc and the process of documenting Ruby projects in general:

- Good documentation provides clear examples of how to use your code, clearly documents the interface of your functions, and provides enough contextual description to give you a sense of whether a given function is going to be useful to you.

- Although RDoc's formatting language is simple and does not greatly affect the readability of plain-text comments, it's worth remembering that without a little attention to markup, the RDoc generated from your source files may have some minor issues.

- Features that are part of the public interface of your project but are intended more for internal or specialized use can be hidden via the `:nodoc:` directive, either at the function or class/module level.

- The `:call-seq:` method can be used to create custom overrides of documented method signatures. This can be quite useful for documenting methods with dynamic argument processing. It is also useful for indicating what a method might return, which is not something RDoc does by default.

- Using the `:section:` directive, you can break up the documentation of a class or module into distinctly grouped segments, each with an optional description. This is a great organizational technique that is severely underused at this point in the Ruby community.

So far, we've been talking about nuts-and-bolts project maintenance techniques that make your project more accessible to others. Now, we'll focus on the task of actually making your code available to others, in the form of RubyGems.

The RubyGems Package Manager

When you run code locally, it is possible to take a lot of things for granted. You can use various tricks to hack Ruby's loadpath from the command line, count on certain packages being installed, and otherwise introduce dependencies on the particular configuration of your machine.

RubyGems provides a way to help mitigate all these concerns, in the form of a full-blown package management system. I assume that everyone who is reading this book is familiar with installing software from gems, but has not necessarily managed their own gems before. Knowing how to build your own packages can be useful, whether you're distributing open source code or just sharing packages within an organization, so we'll focus on that aspect here.

Writing a Gem::Specification

A gem specification (or gemspec) is essentially a project manifest with some special metadata that is used at package install time. The easiest way to describe how to build a gemspec is by working through a real example of one. As we've had good luck so far with looking at how Haml does things, we can turn to it yet again without being disappointed:

```ruby
require 'rubygems'
require 'rake'

HAML_GEMSPEC = Gem::Specification.new do |spec|
  spec.name = 'haml'
  spec.rubyforge_project = 'haml'
  spec.summary = "An elegant, structured XHTML/XML templating engine. " +
                 "Comes with Sass, a similar CSS templating engine."
  spec.version = File.read('VERSION').strip
  spec.authors = ['Nathan Weizenbaum', 'Hampton Catlin']
  spec.email = 'haml@googlegroups.com'
  spec.description = <<-END
    Haml (HTML Abstraction Markup Language) is a layer on top of XHTML or XML
    that's designed to express the structure of XHTML or XML documents
    in a non-repetitive, elegant, easy way,
    using indentation rather than closing tags
    and allowing Ruby to be embedded with ease.
    It was originally envisioned as a plugin for Ruby on Rails,
    but it can function as a stand-alone templating engine.
  END

  # We need the revision file to exist,
  # so we just create it if it doesn't.
  # It'll usually just get overwritten, though.
  File.open('REVISION', 'w') { |f| f.puts "(unknown)" } unless File.exist?('REVISION')
  readmes = FileList.new('*') do |list|
    list.exclude(/(^|[^.a-z])[a-z]+/)
    list.exclude('TODO')
    list.include('REVISION')
  end.to_a
  spec.files = FileList['rails/init.rb', 'lib/**/*', 'bin/*', 'test/**/*',
    'extra/**/*', 'Rakefile', 'init.rb'].to_a + readmes
  spec.executables = ['haml', 'html2haml', 'sass', 'css2sass']
  spec.homepage = 'http://haml.hamptoncatlin.com/'
```

```
    spec.has_rdoc = true
    spec.extra_rdoc_files = readmes
    spec.rdoc_options += [
      '--title', 'Haml',
      '--main', 'README.rdoc',
      '--exclude', 'lib/haml/buffer.rb',
      '--line-numbers',
      '--inline-source'
    ]
    spec.test_files = FileList['test/**/*_test.rb'].to_a
  end
```

Even if you haven't built a `Gem::Specification` before, you'll note that most of these attributes are just routine metadata that is associated with any ordinary Ruby project. So let's break things down and look at the more interesting aspects of the specification and what they do. We'll start with the code that indicates what files should be included in the gem:

```
File.open('REVISION', 'w') { |f| f.puts "(unknown)" } unless File.exist?('REVISION')
readmes = FileList.new('*') do |list|
  list.exclude(/(^|[^.a-z])[a-z]+/)
  list.exclude('TODO')
  list.include('REVISION')
end.to_a

spec.files = FileList['rails/init.rb', 'lib/**/*', 'bin/*', 'test/**/*',
    'extra/**/*', 'Rakefile', 'init.rb'].to_a + readmes
```

Here we see that Haml is filtering the project files to decide which text files it should include as part of the package. These include things like *README.rdoc*, *MIT-LICENSE*, *VERSION*, *FAQ*, and other common text files you'll find littering open source Ruby projects. Using a `FileList` to build up `readmes` allows files to be automatically included based on a naming convention rather than explicitly added to the list. After this is done, the `readmes` list is combined with another `FileList` that uses globs to pull in all of the necessary library, executable, and test files, among other things.

It is important to keep in mind that only files specified in this way will be included in a gem, and those that do not match these patterns and globs will not be included without modification. If you want to see exactly what files were included in any given gem you have installed, you can use the `gem unpack` command to dump its source into your working directory, which can be a useful way to debug issues with your gem specifications when it comes to this particular issue.

Making sure that your gem knows what files to use is the most important thing, but there are other configuration-related issues that are useful to deal with as well. If you follow the convention of putting your executables in *bin/*, you can let RubyGems know which ones should be accessible from your system path using the following bit of code:

```
spec.executables = ['haml', 'html2haml', 'sass', 'css2sass']
```

This code will properly install your executables in a system-independent way, allowing them to work even on the Windows command line. On Mac OS X, here's what I see after installing the Haml gem:

```
$ which haml
/usr/local/bin/haml

$ which html2haml
/usr/local/bin/html2haml
```

This is a great feature, because it means that you can easily package and distribute not just libraries as RubyGems, but scripts, utilities, and applications as well.

If you want to give your users the opportunity to run your tests automatically at install time, you can easily do that as well. We see that Haml does this via a simple `FileList` that describes the naming convention of its tests:

```
spec.test_files = FileList['test/**/*_test.rb'].to_a
```

This feature can be a little tricky to get right, and as it turns out `gem install haml --tests` does not work properly on my machine, due to some dependency-related issues. In order for this feature to work properly, you need to be very explicit about your dependencies and very disciplined about the assumptions you make regarding your current `$LOAD_PATH`. I include a mention of it here because it is a solid practice when done right—but with the warning that the vast majority of RubyGems do not handle this properly, whether or not they include this line in their gemspec.

The last interesting thing about this particular gem specification is that it provides some information about how its RDoc should be rendered. If you didn't already know about it, RubyGems ships with a gem hosting/documentation server that can list all of the API documentation for your installed gems. This is usually fired up via the **gem server** command, which will start a service that is accessible at *http://localhost:8808*. By specifying some details about whether and how this RDoc should be generated in your gemspec, you can control what your users will end up seeing. Here are the RDoc-related lines from the Haml gemspec:

```
spec.has_rdoc = true
spec.extra_rdoc_files = readmes
spec.rdoc_options += [
  '--title', 'Haml',
  '--main', 'README.rdoc',
  '--exclude', 'lib/haml/buffer.rb',
  '--line-numbers',
  '--inline-source'
]
```

The first line here indicates that the gem does ship with a meaningful RDoc, allowing it to be generated for viewing from the gem server. The next line indicates that there are some extra files that should be included; by default, only files in *lib/* will be processed. Finally, an array of raw options are specified to be passed along to the underlying rdoc executable on the user's system. I won't cover these in detail, but they should be fairly self-explanatory.

Now that we've covered most of the interesting aspects of a `Gem::Specification`, we can briefly mention how to build a gem. We showed earlier how to do this via a custom Rake task, but in case you want to build a standalone gem, here's a quick example:

```
$ gem build haml.gemspec
Successfully built RubyGem
Name: haml
Version: 2.1.0
File: haml-2.1.0.gem
```

Once you have a gem in hand, you can pass it around for direct installation from file, host it locally via **gem server** by simply installing it yourself, or upload it to a distributor such as RubyForge or GitHub for an open source release.

If your gem does not depend on other Ruby libraries, you're pretty much all set at this point. However, many times we build our libraries and applications on top of other, lower-level libraries. In those cases, we don't want to force our users to manually install all the dependencies they'll need. Luckily, RubyGems makes it easy to work around this.

Working with Dependencies

Manual dependency resolution can be hellish to deal with. However, if we configure things properly, end users should never need to think much about the dependencies of the gems they install. This is done through direct dependency mapping within a gem-spec. An interesting application of this is in the *prawn* gem, which is really nothing more than a stub that indicates which subpackages need to be installed to have a full Prawn installation up and running:

```ruby
Gem::Specification.new do |spec|
  spec.name = "prawn"
  spec.version = "0.5.0"
  spec.platform = Gem::Platform::RUBY
  spec.summary = "A fast and nimble PDF generator for Ruby"
  spec.add_dependency('prawn-core', '~> 0.5.0')
  spec.add_dependency('prawn-layout', '~> 0.2.0')
  spec.add_dependency('prawn-format', '~> 0.1.0')
  spec.author = "Gregory Brown"
  spec.email = "gregory.t.brown@gmail.com"
  spec.rubyforge_project = "prawn"
  spec.homepage = "http://prawn.majesticseacreature.com"
  spec.description = "Prawn is a fast, tiny, and nimble PDF generator for Ruby"
end
```

In this example, only three lines are of particular interest:

```ruby
spec.add_dependency('prawn-core', '~> 0.5.0')
spec.add_dependency('prawn-layout', '~> 0.2.0')
spec.add_dependency('prawn-format', '~> 0.1.0')
```

In this example, we are indicating that in order to install *prawn*, three other gems need to be installed: *prawn-core*, *prawn-layout*, and *prawn-format*. Here we are using what is called a pessimistic version constraint, to help ensure that the versions we install are compatible with one another.

The way it works is that when you use ~>, you are indicating that your gem will work with any version within a certain line of releases. We could actually rewrite the specification in a more explicit way:

```
spec.add_dependency('prawn-core',   '>= 0.5.0', '< 0.6.0')
spec.add_dependency('prawn-layout', '>= 0.2.0', '< 0.3.0')
spec.add_dependency('prawn-format', '>= 0.1.0', '< 0.2.0')
```

This would mean the same exact thing, but requires a lot more typing. So essentially, what this operator offers is a little flexibility in your last version number. You could actually be even more flexible with this, where ~> 1.0 means any 1.*x.y* version.

Because every project is maintained in a different way, the right string to use depends highly on individual release policies. In the case of Prawn, we guarantee that our officially supported gems will not change API at all from x.y.z to x.y.(z+1), but that API changes are possible when the middle version number changes. Therefore, our gem specifications are tailored to fit to that maintenance strategy.

In other situations, you may want to go to one extreme or another regarding versioning. For example, you can lock to an exact version of a gem:

```
spec.add_dependency('ruport', '=1.0.0')
```

If you have this in your gemspec, Ruport 1.0.0 will be installed specifically, and when your library is loaded or an executable is used, you can be sure that exact version of the dependency will be loaded as well. Although this is the best way to be absolutely sure your code will work the same on your system as it will on others, it is also quite constraining. RubyGems is not currently capable of activating more than one version of a library simultaneously, so this means that you may introduce some conflicts with other packages that rely on different versions of your dependencies. Generally speaking, unless there is a very good reason for specifying an exact dependency version, you should be a bit more lenient, allowing the user to lock down to a particular as necessary via the Kernel#gem method.

On the other end of the spectrum, it is also possible to specify a dependency without any version at all:

```
spec.add_dependency('highline')
```

When you do this, your gem will only check to make sure the dependency is installed, and will do absolutely no version checking. This means that if the installed version of a gem on a user's system is ancient or bleeding edge while yours is somewhere in between, some conflicts may arise. Of course, this does put the power back in the user's hands. The important thing to remember if you go this route is to clearly document which versions of your dependencies are required, but at that point, you might as well just go ahead and use either version ranges or pessimistic version constraints.

That having been said, this feature can be quite useful in alpha- or beta-level projects that have not yet solidified what exact versions of various libraries they will depend on, as it allows for the greatest level of control from the end user perspective.

A final note about developing gem specifications is that occasionally, some extra libraries are needed for development but not for actually running your software. Ruby-Gems allows you to specify development dependencies that can be installed alongside the runtime dependencies via the `gem install whatever --development` command. This can be useful for helping potential contributors get set up with all the necessary tools they'll need for building your project and running its tests.

At the time of writing this chapter, we haven't set this up yet in the *prawn* gem, but if we do, it'll end up looking something like this:

```
spec.add_runtime_dependency('prawn-core', '~> 0.5.0')
spec.add_runtime_dependency('prawn-layout', '~> 0.2.0')
spec.add_runtime_dependency('prawn-format', '~> 0.1.0')

spec.add_development_dependency('test-unit', '= 1.2.3')
spec.add_development_dependency('test-spec', '~> 0.9.0')
spec.add_development_dependency('mocha', '~> 0.9.0')
```

In this code, `add_runtime_dependency` is just an alias for `add_dependency`, but it provides a clearer indication of which dependencies are meant for runtime and which are solely for development. If we specified our gem in this way, *prawn-core*, *prawn-layout*, and *prawn-format* would always be installed, but *test-unit*, *test-spec*, and *mocha* would be installed only if the `--development` flag were used. Development dependencies are a great idea and are fairly new in RubyGems, so with a little luck, more projects will start using them in the future.

There is a ton more we could discuss about the RubyGems system, but my goal was to expose you only to the things you'll need to know to package your code up and start sharing it with others, whether between coworkers or with the Ruby community at large. I've tried to cover some of the features that first-time gem builders typically miss out on, in hopes that we can take better advantage of the full-blown package management system Ruby provides us. Here are the key things to remember:

- Gems do not automatically include certain files or folders within a project. Instead, it is necessary to list explicitly in your gemspec which files should be included. In most cases, a `FileList` is useful for aggregation here, which can be used by simply requiring the *rake* library.
- You can specify which scripts in your gem are executable, and RubyGems will take care of putting these executables in the right place on your system, setting up proper file modes regardless of what operating system you are on.

- If you enable RDoc generation, your gem will automatically generate its documentation upon install on a user's machine, viewable through a locally running `gem server`.

- A severely underused feature is `spec.test_files`, but special care must be given to both dependency specification and loadpath hackery to make it work properly.

- RubyGems provides a fairly robust solution for dependency resolution that provides a high degree of flexibility when it comes to deciding how strict to be about versioning for any library your package depends on.

- If your project has development-specific dependencies that are not needed at runtime, add them to your gemspec via `spec.add_development_dependency()`.

We've talked about organizing, documenting, and packaging your code. Now it's time to talk about how to manage these tasks all in one place.

Rake: Ruby's Built-in Build Utility

We already covered a bit about Rake in the very beginning of this chapter. I am also quite sure that anyone who would buy this book at least knows what a Rakefile is and has probably used one before. This toolkit was initially popular among project maintainers for simplifying package and documentation generation, but was popularized by Rails as a way to wrap pretty much any task into something that could be conveniently triggered on the command line. Although `rake` technically is little more than a Ruby replacement for `make`, the flexibility of configuring it via a general-purpose language such as Ruby has really made it a powerful tool.

We already covered some of the built-in features of Rake, including `Rake::GemPackage Task`, but let's take a look at another one. The following code is what Haml uses to provide a `rake rdoc` task:

```ruby
Rake::RDocTask.new do |rdoc|
  rdoc.title    = 'Haml/Sass'
  rdoc.options << '--line-numbers' << '--inline-source'
  rdoc.rdoc_files.include(*FileList.new('*') do |list|
                            list.exclude(/(^|[^.a-z])[a-z]+/)
                            list.exclude('TODO')
                          end.to_a)
  rdoc.rdoc_files.include('lib/**/*.rb')
  rdoc.rdoc_files.exclude('TODO')
  rdoc.rdoc_files.exclude('lib/haml/buffer.rb')
  rdoc.rdoc_files.exclude('lib/sass/tree/*')
  rdoc.rdoc_dir = 'rdoc'
  rdoc.main = 'README.rdoc'
end
```

Here we see that the options used are very similar to what we discussed in the previous section about RubyGems. However, once this is set up, you can simply type `rake rdoc` at any time to generate the API documentation directly from the current source code. This does not require installing the library or running a long string of command-line arguments, which are the two main reasons it is beneficial to us. When we used this command earlier, we didn't need to know a thing about it; we were able to just know what it did and execute it based on the `rake --tasks` listing for the project.

Rake provides a great way to increase the discoverability of your project, in that it allows users who do not necessarily understand the details about the underlying processes to do administrative tasks. Any shell scripts to maintain projects are ripe candidates for being wrapped with Rake.

To give you an example of how you'd use this for custom needs, I can show you what I use to generate a local copy of this book in PDF format. I have been writing it in AsciiDoc and generating DocBook XML. I then use `dblatex` to render a PDF for me. Rather than remember all the details of how to do this, I much prefer to type the following command whenever I want a new build of my book:

```
rake build
```

Here's the pair of tasks that makes it possible for me to do this:[||]

```
task :convert_all do
  FileList[File.join(File.dirname(__FILE__), 'manuscript', '*.txt')].each do |src|
    target = File.join target_dir, File.basename(src).sub(".txt", ".xml")
    chap = File.basename(target)
    sh "asciidoc -d book -b docbook -a sectids! -o ch_#{chap} -s #{src}"
  end
end

task :build => [:convert_all] do
  sh "dblatex book.xml"
  sh "open book.pdf"
end
```

These tasks yet again make gratuitous use of `FileList` for doing glob-based filtering of a directory. In `:convert_all`, we are taking all the *.txt* files in a manuscript/directory and running them through `asciidoc` to generate DocBook XML. Our `:build` task depends on `convert_all`, which ensures that new XML documents are generated from the text-based sources every time we end up building a PDF. The PDF is generated by `dblatex` and then displayed in OS X Preview via the `open` command.

This is just one example of a custom Rake task, but there are endless possibilities. Heading back to the Haml Rakefile, we can see that the developers even use Rake to manage pushing releases out to RubyForge using the `rubyforge` command-line utility:[#]

[||] The `convert_all` task was actually based on a contribution Rick DeNatale made to my build process for *The Ruport Book (http://ruportbook.com/)*.

[#] See *http://rubyforge.org/projects/codeforpeople*.

```ruby
  desc "Release a new Haml package to Rubyforge. Requires the NAME and VERSION flags."
  task :release => [:package] do
    name, version = ENV['NAME'], ENV['VERSION']
    package = "#{ENV['NAME']} (v#{ENV['VERSION']})"
    sh %{rubyforge login}
    sh %{rubyforge add_release haml haml "#{package})" pkg/haml-#{version}.gem}
    sh %{rubyforge add_file haml haml "#{package}" pkg/haml-#{version}.tar.gz}
    sh %{rubyforge add_file haml haml "#{package}" pkg/haml-#{version}.tar.bz2}
    sh %{rubyforge add_file haml haml "#{package}" pkg/haml-#{version}.zip}
  end
```

In HighLine, we also used Rake to upload our website and documentation for the project via scp:

```ruby
  desc "Upload current documentation to Rubyforge"
  task :upload_docs => [:rdoc] do
    sh "scp -r doc/html/* " +
       "bbazzarrakk@rubyforge.org:/var/www/gforge-projects/highline/doc/"
    sh "scp -r site/* " +
       "bbazzarrakk@rubyforge.org:/var/www/gforge-projects/highline/"
  end
```

As you can see, a well-tuned Rakefile is an asset to have in any project. If you want to use tasks from a number of sources, or have a large number of tasks that might end up causing name clashes, you can even use namespaces to segment things out. Though I'll leave the details for the reader to discover, the basic syntax looks like this:

```ruby
  namespace :site do
    task :generate do
      puts "Generating site"
    end
  end

  namespace :docs do
    task :generate do
      puts "Generating Documents"
    end
  end
```

Here's how you'd run each of these tasks on the command line:

```
  $ rake site:generate
  (in /Users/sandal)
  Generating site

  $ rake docs:generate
  (in /Users/sandal)
  Generating Documents
```

Of course, if you only have a few tasks that aren't very related to one another, there is no need to worry about namespacing. Unless you are managing a fairly large number of tasks, or redistributing tasks as part of a library, you can stick to the basics.

Rake is a very powerful tool that deserves its own chapter or even its own cookbook. There are a ton of useful recipes out there in the wild, so be sure to make the Rakefile one of your first stops in any new codebase you need to review. Understanding and using Rake effectively is key to successfully managing any moderately complex Ruby project, so be sure not to overlook its significance and practical utility.

If you want to make the most out of this tool, there are just a few things to keep in mind:

- Rake provides custom tasks for common needs such as generating RDoc, running unit tests and packaging up a project for distribution. Because these tasks are highly configurable, it is better to use them than to reinvent the wheel.

- Any other repetitive action that is necessary for maintaining your project can be wrapped in a task to simplify things. Typically, any lengthy command that needs to be run in the shell is fair game for this sort of simplification.

- Any task that has a preceding `desc()` call will be listed with a meaningful message in the `rake --tasks` output for your project.

- Rake's ability to define prerequisite tasks allows you to build dependency-based workflows that allow you to model multiple-step tasks as needed.

- Namespaces can be used to segment off tasks into their own subspaces, minimizing the risk of naming clashes.

I've tried to stick mainly to the easily overlooked aspects of Rake here, but there is a whole lot that we could have covered and didn't. Be sure to consult the Rake documentation if you're interested in finding out more.

Conclusions

Depending on what you were looking for, this chapter may have been a bit different from what you were expecting based on the title. However, what you will find is that the things we've discussed here will really take you far when it comes to improving the maintainability of your projects. Though far from glamorous, things like good documentation, well-organized folders and files, and a way to automate as much of the grunt work as possible does a whole lot for your projects.

Poorly maintained projects can be a huge drain on developer productivity and morale, yet nicely curated code can be downright enjoyable to work with, even if you're brand-new to a project. The tools and techniques we've discussed so far aren't going to make maintenance completely painless, but will still provide a solid foundation to work off of that will grow over time.

We've now reached the end of the last official chapter in this book. However, I hope that you will not stop here, as there are still three very useful appendixes left for your enjoyment. If you turn the page, you'll notice that these aren't simply tables of reference data for looking up, but instead, tightly packed bundles of bonus material that didn't quite fit into the main flow of the book. There is still a ton of real code left to walk through in the book, so if you put it down now, you'd be short-changing yourself.

Whether you continue to read on or not, I hope you have enjoyed what you have read so far, and that you can put it into practice in your day-to-day work.

Writing Backward-Compatible Code

Not everyone has the luxury of using the latest and greatest tools available. Though Ruby 1.9 may be gaining ground among developers, much legacy code still runs on Ruby 1.8. Many folks have a responsibility to keep their code running on Ruby 1.8, whether it is in-house, open source, or a commercial application. This appendix will show you how to maintain backward compatibility with Ruby 1.8.6 without preventing your code from running smoothly on Ruby 1.9.1.

I am assuming here that you are backporting code to Ruby 1.8, but this may also serve as a helpful guide as to how to upgrade your projects to 1.9.1. That task is somewhat more complicated however, so your mileage may vary.

The earlier you start considering backward compatibility in your project, the easier it will be to make things run smoothly. I'll start by showing you how to keep your compatibility code manageable from the start, and then go on to describe some of the issues you may run into when supporting Ruby 1.8 and 1.9 side by side.

Please note that when I mention 1.8 and 1.9 without further qualifications, I'm talking about Ruby 1.8.6 and its compatible implementations and Ruby 1.9.1 and its compatible implementations, respectively. We have skipped Ruby 1.8.7 and Ruby 1.9.0 because both are transitional bridges between 1.8.6 and 1.9.1 and aren't truly compatible with either.

Another thing to keep in mind is that this is definitely not intended to be a comprehensive guide to the differences between the versions of Ruby. Please consult your favorite reference after reviewing the tips you read here.

But now that you have been sufficiently warned, we can move on to talking about how to keep things clean.

Avoiding a Mess

It is very tempting to run your test suite on one version of Ruby, check to make sure everything passes, then run it on the other version you want to support and see what breaks. After seeing failures, it might seem easy enough to just drop in code such as the following to make things go green again:

```
def my_method(string)
  lines = if RUBY_VERSION < "1.9"
    string.to_a
  else
    string.lines
  end
  do_something_with(lines)
end
```

Resist this temptation! If you aren't careful, this will result in a giant mess that will be difficult to refactor, and will make your code less readable. Instead, we can approach this in a more organized fashion.

Selective Backporting

Before duplicating any effort, it's important to check and see whether there is another reasonable way to write your code that will allow it to run on both Ruby 1.8 and 1.9 natively. Even if this means writing code that's a little more verbose, it's generally worth the effort, as it prevents the codebase from diverging.

If this fails, however, it may make sense to simply backport the feature you need to Ruby 1.8. Because of Ruby's open classes, this is easy to do. We can even loosen up our changes so that they check for particular features rather than a specific version number, to improve our compatibility with other applications and Ruby implementations:

```
class String
  unless "".respond_to?(:lines)
    alias_method :lines, :to_a
  end
end
```

Doing this will allow you to rewrite your method so that it looks more natural:

```
def my_method(string)
  do_something_with(string.lines)
end
```

Although this implementation isn't exact, it is good enough for our needs and will work as expected in most cases. However, if we wanted to be pedantic, we'd be sure to return an Enumerator instead of an Array:

```
class String
  unless "".respond_to?(:lines)
    require "enumerator"

    def lines
      to_a.enum_for(:each)
    end
```

```
    end
  end
```

If you aren't redistributing your code, passing tests in your application and code that works as expected are a good enough indication that your backward-compatibility patches are working. However, in code that you plan to distribute, open source or otherwise, you need to be prepared to make things more robust when necessary. Any time you distribute code that modifies core Ruby, you have an implicit responsibility of not breaking third-party libraries or application code, so be sure to keep this in mind and clearly document exactly what you have changed.

In Prawn, we use a single file, *prawn/compatibility.rb*, to store all the core extensions used in the library that support backward compatibility. This helps make it easier for users to track down all the changes made by the library, which can help make subtle bugs that can arise from version incompatibilities easier to spot.

In general, this approach is a fairly solid way to keep your application code clean while supporting both Ruby 1.8 and 1.9. However, you should use it only to add new functionality to Ruby 1.8.6 that isn't present in 1.9.1, and not to modify existing behavior. Adding functions that don't exist in a standard version of Ruby is a relatively low-risk procedure, whereas changing core functionality is a far more controversial practice.

Version-Specific Code Blocks

If you run into a situation where you really need two different approaches between the two major versions of Ruby, you can use a trick to make this a bit more attractive in your code.

```ruby
if RUBY_VERSION < "1.9"
  def ruby_18
    yield
  end

  def ruby_19
    false
  end
else
  def ruby_18
    false
  end

  def ruby_19
    yield
  end
end
```

Here's an example of how you'd make use of these methods:

```ruby
def open_file(file)
  ruby_18 { File.open("foo.txt","r") } ||
    ruby_19 { File.open("foo.txt", "r:UTF-8") }
end
```

Of course, because this approach creates a divergent codebase, it should be used as sparingly as possible. However, this looks a little nicer than a conditional statement and provides a centralized place for changes to minor version numbers if needed, so it is a nice way to go when it is actually necessary.

Compatibility Shims for Common Operations

When you need to accomplish the same thing in two different ways, you can also consider adding a method to both versions of Ruby. Although Ruby 1.9.1 shipped with `File.binread()`, this method did not exist in the earlier developmental versions of Ruby 1.9.

Although a handful of `ruby_18` and `ruby_19` calls here and there aren't that bad, the need for opening binary files was pervasive, and it got tiring to see the following code popping up everywhere this feature was needed:

```
ruby_18 { File.open("foo.jpg", "rb") } ||
  ruby_19 { File.open("foo.jpg", "rb:BINARY") }
```

To simplify things, we put together a simple `File.read_binary` method that worked on both Ruby 1.8 and 1.9. You can see this is nothing particularly exciting or surprising:

```
if RUBY_VERSION < "1.9"
  class File
    def self.read_binary(file)
      File.open(file,"rb") { |f| f.read }
    end
  end
else
  class File
    def self.read_binary(file)
      File.open(file,"rb:BINARY") { |f| f.read }
    end
  end
end
```

This cleaned up the rest of our code greatly, and reduced the number of version checks significantly. Of course, when `File.binread()` came along in Ruby 1.9.1, we went and used the techniques discussed earlier to backport it to 1.8.6, but prior to that, this represented a nice way to attack the same problem in two different ways.

Now that we've discussed all the relevant techniques, I can show you what *prawn/ compatibility.rb* looks like. This file allows Prawn to run on both major versions of Ruby without any issues, and as you can see, it is quite compact:

```
class String  #:nodoc:
  unless "".respond_to?(:lines)
    alias_method :lines, :to_a
  end
end
```

```
unless File.respond_to?(:binread)
  def File.binread(file)
    File.open(file,"rb") { |f| f.read }
  end
end

if RUBY_VERSION < "1.9"

  def ruby_18
    yield
  end

  def ruby_19
    false
  end

else

  def ruby_18
    false
  end

  def ruby_19
    yield
  end

end
```

This code leaves Ruby 1.9.1 virtually untouched and adds only a couple of simple features to Ruby 1.8.6. These small modifications enable Prawn to have cross-compatibility between versions of Ruby without polluting its codebase with copious version checks and workarounds. Of course, there are a few areas that needed extra attention, and we'll about the talk sorts of issues to look out for in just a moment, but for the most part, this little compatibility file gets the job done.

Even if someone produced a Ruby 1.8/1.9 compatibility library that you could include into your projects, it might still be advisable to copy only what you need from it. The core philosophy here is that we want to do as much as we can to let each respective version of Ruby be what it is, to avoid confusing and painful debugging sessions. By taking a minimalist approach and making it as easy as possible to locate your platform-specific changes, we can help make things run more smoothly.

Before we move on to some more specific details on particular incompatibilities and how to work around them, let's recap the key points of this section:

- Try to support both Ruby 1.8 and 1.9 from the ground up. However, be sure to write your code against Ruby 1.9 first and then backport to 1.8 if you want prevent yourself from writing too much legacy code.

- Before writing any version-specific code or modifying core Ruby, attempt to find a way to write code that runs natively on both Ruby 1.8 and 1.9. Even if the solution turns out to be less beautiful than usual, it's better to have code that works without introducing redundant implementations or modifications to core Ruby.

- For features that don't have a straightforward solution that works on both versions, consider backporting the necessary functionality to Ruby 1.8 by adding new methods to existing core classes.

- If a feature is too complicated to backport or involves separate procedures across versions, consider adding a helper method that behaves the same on both versions.

- If you need to do inline version checks, consider using the `ruby_18` and `ruby_19` blocks shown in this appendix. These centralize your version-checking logic and provide room for refactoring and future extension.

With these thoughts in mind, let's check out some incompatibilities you just can't work around, and how to avoid them.

Nonportable Features in Ruby 1.9

There are some features in Ruby 1.9 that you simply cannot backport to 1.8 without modifying the interpreter itself. Here we'll talk about just a few of the more obvious ones, to serve as a reminder of what to avoid if you plan to have your code run on both versions of Ruby. In no particular order, here's a fun list of things that'll cause a backport to grind to a halt if you're not careful.

Pseudo-Keyword Hash Syntax

Ruby 1.9 adds a cool feature that lets you write things like:

```
foo(a: 1, b: 2)
```

But on Ruby 1.8, we're stuck using the old key => value syntax:

```
foo(:a => 1, :b => 2)
```

Multisplat Arguments

Ruby 1.9.1 offers a downright insane amount of ways to process arguments to methods. But even the more simple ones, such as multiple splats in an argument list, are not backward compatible. Here's an example of something you can do on Ruby 1.9 that you can't do on Ruby 1.8, which is something to be avoided in backward-compatible code:

```
def add(a,b,c,d,e)
  a + b + c + d + e
end

add(*[1,2], 3, *[4,5]) #=> 15
```

The closest thing we can get to this on Ruby 1.8 would be something like this:

```
add(*[[1,2], 3, [4,5]].flatten) #=> 15
```

Of course, this isn't nearly as appealing. It doesn't even handle the same edge cases that Ruby 1.9 does, as this would not work with any array arguments that are meant to be kept as an array. So it's best to just not rely on this kind of interface in code that needs to run on both 1.8 and 1.9.

Block-Local Variables

On Ruby 1.9, block variables will shadow outer local variables, resulting in the following behavior:

```
>> a = 1
=> 1
>> (1..10).each { |a| a }
=> 1..10
>> a
=> 1
```

This is not the case on Ruby 1.8, where the variable will be modified even if not explicitly set:

```
>> a = 1
=> 1
>> (1..10).each { |a| a }
=> 1..10
>> a
=> 10
```

This can be the source of a lot of subtle errors, so if you want to be safe on Ruby 1.8, be sure to use different names for your block-local variables so as to avoid accidentally overwriting outer local variables.

Block Arguments

In Ruby 1.9, blocks can accept block arguments, which is most commonly seen in define_method:

```
define_method(:answer) { |&b| b.call(42) }
```

However, this won't work on Ruby 1.8 without some very ugly workarounds, so it might be best to rethink things and see whether you can do them in a different way if you've been relying on this functionality.

New Proc Syntax

Both the stabby Proc and the .() call are new in 1.9, and aren't parseable by the Ruby 1.8 interpreter. This means that calls like this need to go:

```
>> ->(a) { a*3 }.(4)
=> 12
```

Instead, use the trusty `lambda` keyword and `Proc#call` or `Proc#[]`:

```
>> lambda { |a| a*3 }[4]
=> 12
```

Oniguruma

Although it is possible to build the Oniguruma regular expression engine into Ruby 1.8, it is not distributed by default, and thus should not be used in backward-compatible code. This means that if you're using named groups, you'll need to ditch them. The following code uses named groups:

```
>> "Gregory Brown".match(/(?<first_name>\w+) (?<last_name>\w+)/)
=> #<MatchData "Gregory Brown" first_name:"Gregory" last_name:"Brown">
```

We'd need to rewrite this as:

```
>> "Gregory Brown".match(/(\w+) (\w+)/)
=> #<MatchData "Gregory Brown" 1:"Gregory" 2:"Brown">
```

More advanced regular expressions, including those that make use of positive or negative look-behind, will need to be completely rewritten so that they work on both Ruby 1.8's regular expression engine and Oniguruma.

Most m17n Functionality

Though it may go without saying, Ruby 1.8 is not particularly well suited for working with character encodings. There are some workarounds for this, but things like magic comments that tell what encoding a file is in or `String` objects that are aware of their current encoding are completely missing from Ruby 1.8.

Although we could go on, I'll leave the rest of the incompatibilities for you to research. Keeping an eye on the issues mentioned in this section will help you avoid some of the most common problems, and that might be enough to make things run smoothly for you, depending on your needs.

So far we've focused on the things you can't work around, but there are lots of other issues that can be handled without too much effort, if you know how to approach them. We'll take a look at a few of those now.

Workarounds for Common Issues

Although we have seen that some functionality is simply not portable between Ruby 1.8 and 1.9, there are many more areas in which Ruby 1.9 just does things a little differently or more conveniently. In these cases, we can develop suitable workarounds that allow our code to run on both versions of Ruby. Let's take a look at a few of these issues and how we can deal with them.

Using Enumerator

In Ruby 1.9, you can get back an `Enumerator` for pretty much every method that iterates over a collection:

```
>> [1,2,3,4].map.with_index { |e,i| e + i }
=> [1, 3, 5, 7]
```

In Ruby 1.8, `Enumerator` is part of the standard library instead of core, and isn't quite as feature-packed. However, we can still accomplish the same goals by being a bit more verbose:

```
>> require "enumerator"
=> true
>> [1,2,3,4].enum_for(:each_with_index).map { |e,i| e + i }
=> [1, 3, 5, 7]
```

Because Ruby 1.9's implementation of `Enumerator` is mostly backward-compatible with Ruby 1.8, you can write your code in this legacy style without fear of breaking anything.

String Iterators

In Ruby 1.8, `Strings` are `Enumerable`, whereas in Ruby 1.9, they are not. Ruby 1.9 provides `String#lines`, `String#each_line`, `String#each_char`, and `String#each_byte`, all of which are not present in Ruby 1.8.

The best bet here is to backport the features you need to Ruby 1.8, and avoid treating a `String` as an `Enumerable` sequence of lines. When you need that functionality, use `String#lines` followed by whatever enumerable method you need.

The underlying point here is that it's better to stick with Ruby 1.9's functionality, because it'll be less likely to confuse others who might be reading your code.

Character Operations

In Ruby 1.9, strings are generally character-aware, which means that you can index into them and get back a single character, regardless of encoding:

```
>> "Foo"[0]
=> "F"
```

This is not the case in Ruby 1.8.6, as you can see:

```
>> "Foo"[0]
=> 70
```

If you need to do character-aware operations in Ruby 1.8 and 1.9, you'll need to process things using a regex trick that gets you back an array of characters. After setting

`$KCODE="U"`,[*] you'll need to do things like substitute calls to `String#reverse` with the following:

```
>> "résumé".scan(/./m).reverse.join
=> "émusér"
```

Or as another example, you'll replace `String#chop` with this:

```
>> r = "résumé".scan(/./m); r.pop; r.join
=> "résum"
```

Depending on how many of these manipulations you'll need to do, you might consider breaking out the Ruby 1.8-compatible code from the clearer Ruby 1.9 code using the techniques discussed earlier in this appendix. However, the thing to remember is that anywhere you've been enjoying Ruby 1.9's m17n support, you'll need to do some re-work. The good news is that many of the techniques used on Ruby 1.8 still work on Ruby 1.9, but the bad news is that they can appear quite convoluted to those who have gotten used to the way things work in newer versions of Ruby.

Encoding Conversions

Ruby 1.9 has built-in support for transcoding between various character encodings, whereas Ruby 1.8 is more limited. However, both versions support `Iconv`. If you know exactly what formats you want to translate between, you can simply replace your `string.encode("ISO-8859-1")` calls with something like this:

```
Iconv.conv("ISO-8859-1", "UTF-8", string)
```

However, if you want to let Ruby 1.9 stay smart about its transcoding while still providing backward compatibility, you will just need to write code for each version. Here's an example of how this was done in an early version of Prawn:

```
if "".respond_to?(:encode!)
  def normalize_builtin_encoding(text)
    text.encode!("ISO-8859-1")
  end
else
  require 'iconv'
  def normalize_builtin_encoding(text)
    text.replace Iconv.conv('ISO-8859-1//TRANSLIT', 'utf-8', text)
  end
end
```

Although there is duplication of effort here, the Ruby 1.9-based code does not assume UTF-8-based input, whereas the Ruby 1.8-based code is forced to make this assumption. In cases where you want to support many encodings on Ruby 1.9, this may be the right way to go.

---

[*] This is necessary to work with UTF-8 on Ruby 1.8, but it has no effect on 1.9.

Although we've just scratched the surface, this handful of tricks should cover most of the common issues you'll encounter. For everything else, consult your favorite language reference.

Conclusions

Depending on the nature of your project, getting things running on both Ruby 1.8 and 1.9 can be either trivial or a major undertaking. The more string processing you are doing, and the greater your need for multilingualization support, the more complicated a backward-compatible port of your software to Ruby 1.8 will be. Additionally, if you've been digging into some of the fancy new features that ship with Ruby 1.9, you might find yourself doing some serious rewriting when the time comes to support older versions of Ruby.

In light of all this, it's best to start (if you can afford to) by supporting both versions from the ground up. By writing your code in a fairly backward-compatible subset of Ruby 1.9, you'll minimize the amount of duplicated effort that is needed to support both versions. If you keep your compatibility hacks well organized and centralized, it'll be easier to spot any problems that might crop up.

If you find yourself writing the same workaround several times, think about extending the core with some helpers to make your code clearer. However, keep in mind that when you redistribute code, you have a responsibility not to break existing language features and that you should strive to avoid conflicts with third-party libraries.

But don't let all these caveats turn you away. Writing code that runs on both Ruby 1.8 and 1.9 is about the most friendly thing you can do in terms of open source Ruby, and will also be beneficial in other scenarios. Start by reviewing the guidelines in this appendix, then remember to keep testing your code on both versions of Ruby. As long as you keep things well organized and try as best as you can to minimize version-specific code, you should be able to get your project working on both Ruby 1.8 and 1.9 without conflicts. This gives you a great degree of flexibility, which is often worth the extra effort.

Leveraging Ruby's Standard Library

Most of this book has emphasized that understanding how to use tools effectively is just as important as having a nice collection of tools. However, that's not to say that knowing where to find the right tool for the job isn't an invaluable skill to have. In this appendix, we'll take a look at a small sampling of Ruby's vast standard library. What you will find is that it is essentially a treasure chest of goodies designed to make your Ruby programs more enjoyable to write.

Why Do We Need a Standard Library?

Because of RubyGems, we tend to leverage a lot of third-party software. For this reason, we are often more likely to resort to a Google search instead of a search of Ruby's API documentation when we want to solve a problem that isn't immediately handled in core Ruby. This isn't necessarily a bad thing, but it is important not to overlook the benefits that come with using a standard library when it is available. When all else is equal, the gains you'll get from using standard Ruby are easy to enumerate:

- Ruby standard libraries are typically distributed with Ruby itself, which means that no extra software needs to be installed to make them work.

- Standard libraries don't change rapidly. Their APIs tend to be stable and mature, and will likely outlast your application's development cycle. This removes the need for frequent compatibility updates that you might experience with third-party software.

- Except for a few obvious exceptions, Ruby standard libraries are guaranteed to run anywhere Ruby runs, avoiding platform-specific issues.

- Using standard libraries improves the understandability of your code, as they are available to everyone who uses Ruby. For open source projects, this might make contributions to your project easier, for the same reason.

These reasons are compelling enough to encourage us to check Ruby's standard library before doing a Google search for third-party libraries. However, it might be more convincing if you have some practical examples of what can be accomplished without resorting to dependency code.

I've handpicked 10 of the libraries I use day in and day out. This isn't necessarily meant to be a "best of" sampling, nor is it meant to point out the top 10 libraries you need to know about. We've implicitly and explicitly covered many standard libraries throughout the book, and some of those may be more essential than what you'll see here. However, I'm fairly certain that after reading this appendix, you'll find at least a few useful tricks in it, and you'll also get a clear picture of how diverse Ruby's standard library is.

Be sure to keep in mind that while we're looking at 10 examples here, there are more than 100 standard libraries packaged with Ruby, about half of which are considered mature. These vary in complexity from simple tools to solve a single task to full-fledged frameworks. Even though you certainly won't need to be familiar with every last package and what it does, it's important to be aware of the fact that what we're about to discuss is just the tip of the iceberg.

Now, on to the fun. I've included this appendix because I think it embodies a big part of the joy of Ruby programming to me. I hope that when reading through the examples, you feel the same way.

Pretty-Printer for Ruby Objects (pp)

As I mentioned before, Ruby standard libraries run the gamut from extreme simplicity to deep complexity. I figured we'd kick things off with something in the former category.

If you're reading this book, you've certainly made use of `Kernel#p` during debugging. This handy method, which calls `#inspect` on an object and then prints out its result, is invaluable for basic debugging needs. However, reading its output for even relatively modest objects can be daunting:

```
friends = [ { first_name: "Emily", last_name: "Laskin" },
            { first_name: "Nick",  last_name: "Mauro" },
            { first_name: "Mark",  last_name: "Maxwell" } ]

me = { first_name: "Gregory", last_name: "Brown", friends: friends }

p me # Outputs:

{:first_name=>"Gregory", :last_name=>"Brown", :friends=>[{:first_name=>"Emily",
:last_name=>"Laskin"}, {:first_name=>"Nick", :last_name=>"Mauro"}, {:first_name=
>"Mark", :last_name=>"Maxwell"}]]}
```

We don't typically write our code this way, because the structure of our objects actually means something to us. Luckily, the *pp* standard library understands this and provides much nicer human-readable output. The changes to use **pp** instead of **p** are fairly simple:

```ruby
require "pp"

friends = [ { first_name: "Emily", last_name: "Laskin" },
            { first_name: "Nick",  last_name: "Mauro" },
            { first_name: "Mark",  last_name: "Maxwell" } ]

me = { first_name: "Gregory", last_name: "Brown", friends: friends }

pp me # Outputs:

{:first_name=>"Gregory",
 :last_name=>"Brown",
 :friends=>
  [{:first_name=>"Emily", :last_name=>"Laskin"},
   {:first_name=>"Nick", :last_name=>"Mauro"},
   {:first_name=>"Mark", :last_name=>"Maxwell"}]}
```

Like when you use **p**, there is a hook to set up **pp** overrides for your custom objects. This is called `pretty_print`. Here's a simple implementation that shows how you might use it:

```ruby
require "pp"

class Person
  def initialize(first_name, last_name, friends)
    @first_name, @last_name, @friends = first_name, last_name, friends
  end

  def pretty_print(printer)
    printer.text "Person <#{object_id}>:\n" <<
                 "  Name: #@first_name #@last_name\n  Friends:\n"
    @friends.each do |f|
      printer.text "    #{f[:first_name]} #{f[:last_name]}\n"
    end
  end

end

friends = [ { first_name: "Emily", last_name: "Laskin" },
            { first_name: "Nick",  last_name: "Mauro" },
            { first_name: "Mark",  last_name: "Maxwell" } ]

person = Person.new("Gregory", "Brown", friends)
pp person #=> outputs:

Person <1013900>:
  Name: Gregory Brown
  Friends:
    Emily Laskin
    Nick Mauro
    Mark Maxwell
```

As you can see here, `pretty_print` takes an argument, which is an instance of the current `pp` object. Because `pp` inherits from `PrettyPrint`, a class provided by Ruby's *prettyprint* standard library, it provides a whole host of formatting helpers for indenting, grouping, and wrapping structured data output. We've stuck with the raw `text()` call here, but it's worth mentioning that there is a lot more available to you if you need it.

A benefit of indirectly displaying your output through a printer object is that it allows `pp` to give you an `inspect`-like method that returns a string. Try `person.pretty_print_inspect` to see how this works. The string represents exactly what would be printed to the console, just like `obj.inspect` would. If you wish to use `pretty_print_inspect` as your default inspect method (and therefore make p and `pp` work the same), you can do so easily with an alias:

```
class Person
  # other code omitted

  alias_method :inspect, :pretty_print_inspect
end
```

Generally speaking, `pp` does a pretty good job of rendering the debugging output for even relatively complex objects, so you may not need to customize its behavior often. However, if you do have a need for specialized output, you'll find that the `pretty_print` hook provides something that is actually quite a bit more powerful than Ruby's default `inspect` hook, and that can really come in handy for certain needs.

Working with HTTP and FTP (open-uri)

Like most other modern programming languages, Ruby ships with libraries for working with some of the most common network protocols, including FTP and HTTP. However, the `Net::FTP` and `Net::HTTP` libraries are designed primarily for heavy lifting at the low level. They are great for this purpose, but they leave something to be desired for when all that is needed is to grab a remote file or do some basic web scraping. This is where `open-uri` shines.

The way `open-uri` works is by patching `Kernel#open` to accept URIs. This means we can directly open remote files and work with them. For example, here's how we'd print out Ruby's license using `open-uri`:

```
require "open-uri"

puts open("http://www.ruby-lang.org/en/LICENSE.txt").read #=>

"Ruby is copyrighted free software by Yukihiro Matsumoto <matz@netlab.co.jp>.
You can redistribute it and/or modify it under either the terms of the GPL
(see COPYING.txt file), or the conditions below: ..."
```

If we encounter an HTTP error, an `OpenURI::HTTPError` will be raised, including the relevant error code:

```
>> open("http://majesticseacreature.com/a_totally_missing_document")
OpenURI::HTTPError: 404 Not Found
        from /usr/local/lib/ruby/1.8/open-uri.rb:287:in 'open_http'
        from /usr/local/lib/ruby/1.8/open-uri.rb:626:in 'buffer_open'
        from /usr/local/lib/ruby/1.8/open-uri.rb:164:in 'open_loop'
        from /usr/local/lib/ruby/1.8/open-uri.rb:162:in 'catch'
        from /usr/local/lib/ruby/1.8/open-uri.rb:162:in 'open_loop'
        from /usr/local/lib/ruby/1.8/open-uri.rb:132:in 'open_uri'
        from /usr/local/lib/ruby/1.8/open-uri.rb:528:in 'open'
        from /usr/local/lib/ruby/1.8/open-uri.rb:30:in 'open'
        from (irb):10
        from /usr/local/lib/ruby/1.8/uri/generic.rb:250

>> open("http://prism.library.cornell.edu/control/authBasic/authTest/")
OpenURI::HTTPError: 401 Authorization Required
        from /usr/local/lib/ruby/1.8/open-uri.rb:287:in 'open_http'
        from /usr/local/lib/ruby/1.8/open-uri.rb:626:in 'buffer_open'
        from /usr/local/lib/ruby/1.8/open-uri.rb:164:in 'open_loop'
        from /usr/local/lib/ruby/1.8/open-uri.rb:162:in 'catch'
        from /usr/local/lib/ruby/1.8/open-uri.rb:162:in 'open_loop'
        from /usr/local/lib/ruby/1.8/open-uri.rb:132:in 'open_uri'
        from /usr/local/lib/ruby/1.8/open-uri.rb:528:in 'open'
        from /usr/local/lib/ruby/1.8/open-uri.rb:30:in 'open'
        from (irb):7
        from /usr/local/lib/ruby/1.8/uri/generic.rb:250
```

The previous example was a small hint about another feature of *open-uri*, HTTP basic authentication. Notice what happens when we provide a username and password accessing the same URI:

```
>> open("http://prism.library.cornell.edu/control/authBasic/authTest/",
?>     :http_basic_authentication => ["test", "this"])
=> #<StringIO:0x2d1810>
```

Success! You can see here that *open-uri* represents the returned file as a `StringIO` object, which is why we can call `read` to get its contents. Of course, we can use most other I/O operations as well, but I won't get into that here.

As I mentioned before, *open-uri* also wraps `Net::FTP`, so you could even do something like download Ruby with it:

```
open("ftp://ftp.ruby-lang.org/pub/ruby/1.9/ruby-1.9.1-p0.tar.bz2") do |o|
  File.open(File.basename(o.base_uri.path), "w") { |f| f << o.read }
end
```

Here we see that even though the object returned by `open()` is a `StringIO` object, it includes some extra metadata, such as the `base_uri` of your request. These helpers are provided by the `OpenURI::Meta` module, and are worth looking over if you need to get more than just the contents of a file back.

Although there are some advanced features to `open-uri`, it is most useful for the simple cases shown here. Because it returns a `StringIO` object, this means that any fairly flexible interface can be extended to support remote file downloads. For a practical example, we can take a look at Prawn's image embedding, which assumes only that an object you pass to it must respond to #read:

```
Prawn::Document.generate("remote_images.pdf") do
  image open("http://prawn.majesticseacreature.com/media/prawn_logo.png")
end
```

This feature was accidentally enabled when we allowed the image() method to accept Tempfile objects. Because *open-uri* smoothly integrates with the rest of Ruby, you might find situations where it can come in handy in a similar way in your own applications.

Working with Dates and Times (date)

Core Ruby has a Time class, but we will encounter a lot of situations where we also need to work with dates, or combinations of dates and times. Ruby's *date* standard library gives us Date and DateTime, and extends Time with conversion methods for each of them. This library comes packed with a powerful parser that can handle all sorts of date formats, and a solid date formatting engine to output data based on a template. Here are just a couple of trivial examples to give you a sense of its flexibility:

```
>> Date.strptime("12/08/1985","%m/%d/%Y").strftime("%Y-%m-%d")
=> "1985-12-08"
>> Date.strptime("1985-12-08","%Y-%m-%d").strftime("%m/%d/%Y")
=> "12/08/1985"
>> Date.strptime("December 8, 1985","%b%e, %Y").strftime("%m/%d/%Y")
=> "12/08/1985"
```

Date objects can also be queried for all sorts of information, as well as manipulated to produce new days:

```
>> date = Date.today
=> #<Date: 2009-02-09 (4909743/2,0,2299161)>
>> date + 1
=> #<Date: 2009-02-10 (4909745/2,0,2299161)>
>> date << 1
=> #<Date: 2009-01-09 (4909681/2,0,2299161)>
>> date >> 1
=> #<Date: 2009-03-09 (4909799/2,0,2299161)>
>> date.year
=> 2009
>> date.month
=> 2
>> date.day
=> 9
>> date.wday
=> 1
>> date + 36
=> #<Date: 2009-03-17 (4909815/2,0,2299161)>
```

Here we've just scratched the surface, but in the interest of keeping a quick pace, we'll dive right into an example. So far, we've been looking at Date, but now we're going to

---

work with `DateTime`. The two are basically the same, except that the latter can hold time values as well:[*]

```
>> dtime = DateTime.now
=> #<DateTime: 2009-02-09T03:56:17-05:00 (...)>
>> [:month, :day, :year, :hour, :minute, :second].map { |attr| dtime.send(attr) }
=> [2, 9, 2009, 3, 56, 17]
>> dtime.between?(DateTime.now - 1, DateTime.now + 1)
=> true
>> dtime.between?(DateTime.now - 1, DateTime.now - 1)
=> false
```

What follows is a simplified look at a common problem: event scheduling. Basically, we want an object that provides functionality like this:

```
sched = Scheduler.new
sched.event "2009.02.04 10:00", "2009.02.04 11:30", "Eat Snow"
sched.event "2009.02.03 14:00", "2009.02.04 14:00", "Wear Special Suit"
sched.display_events_at '2009.02.04 10:20'
```

When given a specific date and time, `display_events_at` would look up all the events that were happening at that exact moment:

```
Events occurring around 10:20 on 02/04/2009
--------------------------------------------
14:00 (02/03) - 14:00 (02/04): Wear Special Suit
10:00 (02/04) - 11:30 (02/04): Eat Snow
```

This means that if we look a little later in the day, as you can see that in this particular example, although eating snow is a short-lived experience, the passion for wearing a special suit carries on:

```
sched.display_events_at '2009.02.04 11:45'

## OUTPUTS ##

Events occurring around 11:45 on 02/04/2009
--------------------------------------------
14:00 (02/03) - 14:00 (02/04): Wear Special Suit
```

As it turns out, implementing the `Scheduler` class is pretty straightforward, because `DateTime` objects can be used as endpoints in a Ruby range object. So when we look at these two events, what we're really doing is something similar to this:

```
>> a = DateTime.parse("2009.02.03 14:00") .. DateTime.parse("2009.02.04 14:00")
>> a.cover?(DateTime.parse("2009.02.04 11:45"))
=> true

>> b = DateTime.parse("2009.02.04 10:00") .. DateTime.parse("2009.02.04 11:30")
>> b.cover?(DateTime.parse("2009.02.04 11:45"))
=> false
```

[*] A `DateTime` is also similar to Ruby's `Time` object, but it is not constrained to representing only those dates that can be represented in Unix time. See *http://en.wikipedia.org/wiki/Unix_time*.

When you combine this with things we've already discussed, like flexible date parsing and formatting, you end up with a fairly vanilla implementation:

```ruby
require "date"

class Scheduler

  def initialize
    @events = []
  end

  def event(from, to, message)
    @events << [DateTime.parse(from) .. DateTime.parse(to),  message]
  end

  def display_events_at(datetime)
    datetime = DateTime.parse(datetime)
    puts "Events occurring around #{datetime.strftime("%H:%M on %m/%d/%Y")}"
    puts "-------------------------------------------"
    events_at(datetime).each do |range, message|
      puts "#{time_abbrev(range.first)} - #{time_abbrev(range.last)}: #{message}"
    end
  end

  private

  def time_abbrev(datetime)
    datetime.strftime("%H:%M (%m/%d)")
  end

  def events_at(datetime)
    @events.each_with_object([]) do |event, matched|
      matched << event if event.first.cover?(datetime)
    end
  end

end
```

We can start by looking at how **event()** works:

```ruby
def event(from, to, message)
  @events << [DateTime.parse(from) .. DateTime.parse(to),  message]
end
```

Here we see that each event is simply a tuple consisting of two elements: a datetime Range, and a message. We parse the strings on the fly using `DateTime.parse`. This method should typically be used with caution, as it is much more reliable to use `Date.strptime`, and much faster to construct a `DateTime` manually than it is to attempt to guess the date format. That having been said, there is no substitute when you cannot rely on a standardized date format, and it does a good job of providing a flexible interface when one is needed.

As this fairly pedestrian code completely covers storing events, what remains to be shown is how they are selectively retrieved and displayed. We'll start with the helper method that looks up what events are going on at a particular time:

```
def events_at(datetime)
  @events.each_with_object([]) do |event, matched|
    matched << event if event.first.cover?(datetime)
  end
end
```

Here, we build up our list of matching events by simply iterating over the event list and including those only those events in which the datetime `Range` covers the time in question. This, along with the self-explanatory `time_abbrev` code, is used to keep `display_events_at` nice and clean:

```
def display_events_at(datetime)
  datetime = DateTime.parse(datetime)
  puts "Events occurring around #{datetime.strftime("%H:%M on %m/%d/%Y")}"
  puts "-------------------------------------------"
  events_at(datetime).each do |range, message|
    puts "#{time_abbrev(range.first)} - #{time_abbrev(range.last)}: #{message}"
  end
end
```

Here, we're doing little more than parsing the date and time passed in as a string to get us a `DateTime` object, and then displaying the results of `events_at`. We take advantage of `strftime` for that, and recover the endpoints of the range to include in our output, to show exactly when an event starts and stops. There's really not much more to it.

Although this example is obviously a bit oversimplified, you'll find that similar problems crop up again and again. The key thing to remember is to take advantage of the ability of `DateTime` objects to be used within ranges, and whenever possible, to avoid parsing dates yourself. If you need finer granularity, use `strptime()`, but for many needs `parse()` will do the trick while providing a more flexible interface to your users.

We've covered some of the most common uses of Ruby's standard *date* library here, but there are of course plenty of other features for the edge case. As with the other topics in this appendix, hit up the API documentation if you need to know more.

Lexical Parsing with Regular Expressions (strscan)

Although Ruby's `String` object provides many powerful features that rely on regular expressions, it can be cumbersome to build any sort of parser with them. Most operations that you can do directly on strings work on the whole string at once, providing `MatchData` that can be used to index into the original content. This is great when a single pattern fits the bill, but when you want to consume some text in chunks, switching up strategies as needed along the way, things get a little more hairy. This is where the *strscan* library comes in.

When you require *strscan*, it provides a class called `StringScanner`. The underlying purpose of using this object is that it keeps track of where you are in the string as you consume parts of it via regex patterns. Just to clear up what this means, we can take a look at the example used in the RDoc:

```
s = StringScanner.new('This is an example string')
s.eos?                  # -> false

p s.scan(/\w+/)         # -> "This"
p s.scan(/\w+/)         # -> nil
p s.scan(/\s+/)         # -> " "
p s.scan(/\s+/)         # -> nil
p s.scan(/\w+/)         # -> "is"
s.eos?                  # -> false

p s.scan(/\s+/)         # -> " "
p s.scan(/\w+/)         # -> "an"
p s.scan(/\s+/)         # -> " "
p s.scan(/\w+/)         # -> "example"
p s.scan(/\s+/)         # -> " "
p s.scan(/\w+/)         # -> "string"
s.eos?                  # -> true

p s.scan(/\s+/)         # -> nil
p s.scan(/\w+/)         # -> nil
```

From this simple example, it's clear to see that the index is advanced only when a match is made. Once the end of the string is reached, there is nothing left to match. Although this may seem a little simplistic at first, it forms the essence of what `StringScanner` does for us. We can see that by looking at how it is used in the context of something a little more real.

We're about to look at how to parse JSON (JavaScript Object Notation), but the example we'll use is primarily for educational purposes, as it demonstrates an elegant use of `StringScanner`. If you have a real need for this functionality, be sure to look at the *json* standard library that ships with Ruby, as that is designed to provide the kind of speed and robustness you'll need in production.

In Ruby Quiz #155, James Gray builds up a JSON parser by hand-rolling a recursive descent parser using `StringScanner`. He actually covers the full solution in depth on the Ruby Quiz website (*http://rubyquiz.com/quiz155.html*), but this abridged version focuses specifically on his use of `StringScanner`. To keep things simple, we'll discuss roughly how he manages to get this small set of assertions to pass:

```
def test_array_parsing
  assert_equal(Array.new, @parser.parse(%Q{[]}))
  assert_equal( ["JSON", 3.1415, true],
    @parser.parse(%Q{["JSON", 3.1415, true]}) )
  assert_equal([1, [2, [3]]], @parser.parse(%Q{[1, [2, [3]]]}))
end
```

We can see by the general outline how this parser works:

```ruby
require "strscan"

class JSONParser
  AST = Struct.new(:value)

  def parse(input)
    @input = StringScanner.new(input)
    parse_value.value
  ensure
    @input.eos? or error("Unexpected data")
  end

  private

  def parse_value
    trim_space
    parse_object or
    parse_array or
    parse_string or
    parse_number or
    parse_keyword or
    error("Illegal JSON value")
  ensure
    trim_space
  end


  # ...

end
```

Essentially, a `StringScanner` object is built up using the original JSON string. Then, the parser recursively walks down through the structure and parses the data types it encounters. Once the parsing completes, we expect that we'll be at the end of the string, otherwise some data was left unparsed, indicating corruption.

Looking at the way `parse_value` is implemented, we see the benefit of using `StringScanner`. Before an actual value is parsed, whitespace is trimmed on both ends using the `trim_space` helper. This is exactly as simple as you might expect it to be:

```ruby
def trim_space
  @input.scan(/\s+/)
end
```

Of course, to make things a little more interesting, and to continue our job, we need to peel back the covers on `parse_array`:

```ruby
def parse_array
  if @input.scan(/\[\s*/) #1
    array       = Array.new
    more_values = false
    while contents = parse_value rescue nil #2
      array << contents.value
      more_values = @input.scan(/\s*,\s*/) or break
    end
```

```
        error("Missing value") if more_values
        @input.scan(/\s*\]\s*/) or error("Unclosed array") #3
        AST.new(array)
      else
        false
      end
    end
```

The beauty of JSON (and this particular parsing solution) is that it's very easy to see what's going on. On a successful parse, this code takes three simple steps. First, it detects the opening [, indicating the start of a JSON array. If it finds that, it creates a Ruby array to populate. Then, the second step is to parse out each value, separated by commas and optional whitespace. To do this, the parser simply calls `parse_value` again, taking advantage of recursion as we mentioned before. Finally, the third step is to seek a closing], which, when found, ends this stage of parsing and returns a Ruby array wrapped in the AST struct this parser uses.

Going back to our three assertions, we can trace them one by one. The first one was meant to test parsing an empty array:

```
assert_equal(Array.new, @parser.parse(%Q{[]}))
```

This one is the most simple to trace, predictably. When `parse_value` is called to capture the contents in the array, it will error out, because no JSON objects start with]. James is using a clever trick that banks on a failed parse, because that allows him to short-circuit processing the contents. This error is swallowed, leaving the contents empty. The string is then scanned for the closing], which is found, and an AST-wrapped empty Ruby array is returned.

The second assertion is considerably more tricky:

```
assert_equal( ["JSON", 3.1415, true],
  @parser.parse(%Q{["JSON", 3.1415, true]}) )
```

Here, we need to rely on `parse_value`'s ability to parse strings, numbers, and booleans. All three of these are done using techniques similar to those shown so far, but a string is a little hairy due to some tricky edge cases. However, to give you a few extra samples, we can take a look at the other two:

```
def parse_number
  @input.scan(/-?(?:0|[1-9]\d*)(?:\.\d+)?(?:[eE][+-]?\d+)?\b/) and
    AST.new(eval(@input.matched))
end

def parse_keyword
  @input.scan(/\b(?:true|false|null)\b/) and
    AST.new(eval(@input.matched.sub("null", "nil")))
end
```

In both cases, James takes advantage of the similarities between Ruby and JSON when it comes to numbers and keywords, and essentially just `eval`s the results after a bit of massaging. The numeric pattern is a little hairy, and you don't necessarily need to understand it. Instead, the interesting thing to note about these two examples is their use of `StringScanner#matched`. As the name suggests, this method returns the actual string that was just matched by the pattern. This is a common way to extract values while conditionally scanning for matches.

This pretty much wraps up the interesting bits about getting the second assertion to pass. Here, the parser just keeps attempting to pull off new values if it can, while the array code wipes out any intermediate commas. Once the values are exhausted, the] is then searched for, as before.

The third and final case for array parsing may initially seem complicated:

```
assert_equal([1, [2, [3]]], @parser.parse(%Q{[1, [2, [3]]]}))
```

However, if you recall that the way `parse_array` works is to repeatedly call `parse_value` until all its elements are consumed, it's clear what is going on. Because an array can be parsed by `parse_value` just the same as any other job, the nested arrays have no trouble repeating the same process to find their elements, which can also be arrays. At some point, this process bottoms out, and the whole structure is built up. That means that we actually get to pass this third assertion *for free*, as the implementation already uses recursive calls through `parse_value`.

Although this doesn't cover 100% of how James's parser works, it gives you a good sense of when `StringScanner` might be a good tool to have around. You can see how powerful it is to keep a single reference to a `StringScanner` and use it in a number of different methods to consume a string part by part. This allows better decomposition of your program, and simplifies the code by removing some of the low-level plumbing from the equation. So next time you want to do regular expression processing on a string chunk by chunk rather than all at once, you might want to give `StringScanner` a try.

Cryptographic Hash Functions (digest)

Though it might not be something we do every day, having easy access to the common cryptographic hash functions can be handy for all sorts of things. The *digest* standard library provides several options, including MD5, SHA1, and SHA2. We'll cover three simple use cases here: calculating the checksum of a file, uniquely hashing files based on their content, and encrypted password storage.

I won't get into the details about the differences between various hashing algorithms or their limitations. Though they all have a potential risk for what is known as a *collision*, where two distinct content keys are hashed to the same value, this is rare enough to not need to worry about in most practical scenarios. Of course, if you're new to encryption in general, you will want to read up on these techniques elsewhere before attempting to use them for anything nontrivial. Assuming that you accept this responsibility, we can move on to see how these hashing functions can be used in your Ruby applications.

We'll start with checksums, because these are pretty easy to find in the wild. If you've downloaded open source software before, you've probably seen MD5 or SHA256 hashes before. I'll be honest: most of the time I just ignore these, but they do come in handy when you want to verify that an automated download completed correctly. They're also useful if you have a tendency toward paranoia and want to be sure that the file you are receiving is really what you think it is. Using the Ruby 1.9.1 release notes themselves as an example, we can see what a digitally signed file download looks like:

```
== Location
* ftp://ftp.ruby-lang.org/pub/ruby/1.9/ruby-1.9.1-p0.tar.bz2
  SIZE:   7190271 bytes
  MD5:    0278610ec3f895ece688de703d99143e
  SHA256: de7d33aeabdba123404c21230142299ac1de88c944c9f3215b816e824dd33321
```

Once we've downloaded the file, pulling the relevant hashes is trivial. Here's how we'd grab the MD5 hash:

```
>> require "digest/md5"
=> true
>> Digest::MD5.hexdigest(File.binread("ruby-1.9.1-p0.tar.bz2"))
=> "0278610ec3f895ece688de703d99143e"
```

If we preferred the slightly more secure SHA256 hash, we don't need to work any harder:

```
>> require "digest/sha2"
=> true
>> Digest::SHA256.hexdigest(File.binread("ruby-1.9.1-p0.tar.bz2"))
=> "de7d33aeabdba123404c21230142299ac1de88c944c9f3215b816e824dd33321"
```

As both of these match the release notes, we can be reasonably sure that nothing nefarious is going on, and also that our file integrity has been preserved. That's the most common use of this form of hashing.

Of course, in addition to identifying a particular file uniquely, cryptographic hashes allow us to identify the uniqueness of a file's content. If you've used the revision control system git, you may have noticed that the revisions are actually identified by SHA1 hashes that describe the changesets. We can do similar things in our Ruby applications.

For example, in Prawn, we support embedding images in PDF documents. Because these images can be from any number of sources ranging from a temp file to a directly downloaded image from the Web, we cannot rely on unique filenames mapping to unique images. Processing images can be pretty costly, especially when we do things like split out alpha channels for PNGs, so we want to avoid reprocessing images when we can avoid it. The solution to this problem is simple: we use SHA1 to generate a hexdigest for the image content and then use that as a key into a hash. A rough approximation of what we're doing looks like this:

```
require "digest/sha1"

def image_registry(raw_image_data)
  img_sha1 = Digest::SHA1.hexdigest(raw_image_data)
  @image_registry[img_sha1] ||= build_image_obj(raw_image_data)
end
```

This technique clearly isn't limited to PDF generation. To name just a couple of other use cases, I use a similar hashing technique to make sure the content of my blog has changed before reuploading the static files it generates, so it uploads only the files it needs. I've also seen this used in the context of web applications to prevent identical content from being copied again and again to new files. Fundamentally, these ideas are nearly identical to the previous code sample, so I won't illustrate them explicitly.

However, while we're on the topic of web applications, we can work our way into our last example: secure password storage.

It should be pretty obvious that even if we restrict access to our databases, we should not store passwords in clear text. We have a responsibility to offer users a reasonable amount of privacy, and through cryptographic hashing, even administrators can be kept in the dark about what individual users' passwords actually are. Using the techniques already shown, we get most of the way to a solution.

The following example is from an ActiveRecord model as part of a Rails application, but it is fairly easily adaptable to any system in which the user information is remotely stored outside of the application itself. Regardless of whether you are familiar with ActiveRecord, the code should be fairly straightforward to follow with a little explanation. Everything except the relevant authentication code has been omitted, to keep things well focused:

```
class User < ActiveRecord::Base

  def password=(pass)
    @password = pass
    salt = [Array.new(6){rand(256).chr}.join].pack("m").chomp
    self.password_salt, self.password_hash =
      salt, Digest::SHA256.hexdigest(pass + salt)
  end

  def self.authenticate(username,password)
    user = find_by_username(username)
    hash = Digest::SHA256.hexdigest(password + user.password_salt)
    if user.blank? || hash != user.password_hash
      raise AuthenticationError, "Username or password invalid"
    end

    user
  end

end
```

Here we see two functions: one for setting an individual user's password, and another for authenticating and looking up a user by username and password. We'll start with setting the password, as this is the most crucial part:

```ruby
def password=(pass)
  @password = pass
  salt = [Array.new(6){rand(256).chr}.join].pack("m").chomp
  self.password_salt, self.password_hash =
    salt, Digest::SHA256.hexdigest(pass + salt)
end
```

Here we see that the password is hashed using `Digest::SHA256`, in a similar fashion to our earlier examples. However, this password isn't directly hashed, but instead, is combined with a `salt` to make it more difficult to guess. This technique has been shown in many Ruby cookbooks and tutorials, so you may have encountered it before. Essentially, what you are seeing here is that for each user in our database, we generate a random six-byte sequence and then pack it into a base64-encoded string, which gets appended to the password before it is hashed. This makes several common attacks much harder to execute, at a minimal complexity cost to us.

An important thing to notice is that what we store is the fingerprint of the password after it has been salted rather than the password itself, which means that we never store the original content and it cannot be recovered. So although we can tell whether a given password matches this fingerprint, the original password cannot be retrieved from the data we are storing.

If this more or less makes sense to you, the `authenticate` method will be easy to follow now:

```ruby
def self.authenticate(username,password)
  user = find_by_username(username)
  hash = Digest::SHA256.hexdigest(password + user.password_salt)
  if user.blank? || hash != user.password_hash
    raise AuthenticationError, "Username or password invalid"
  end

  user
end
```

Here, we first retrieve the user from the database. Assuming that the username is valid, we then look up the `salt` and add it to our bare password string. Because we never stored the actual password, but only its salted hash, we call `hexdigest` again and compare the hash to the one stored in the database. If they match, we return our user object and all is well; if they don't, an error is raised. This completes the cycle of secure password storage and authentication and demonstrates the role that cryptographic hashes play in it.

With that, we've probably talked enough about `digest` for now. There are some more advanced features available, but as long as you know that `Digest::MD5`, `Digest::SHA1` and `Digest::SHA256` exist and how to call `hexdigest()` on each of them, you have all you'll need to know for most occasions. Hopefully, the examples here have illustrated some of the common use cases, and helped you think of your own in the process.

Mathematical Ruby Scripts (mathn)

The *mathn* standard library, when combined with the core `Math` module, serves to make mathematical operations more pleasant in Ruby. The main purpose of *mathn* is to pull in other standard libraries and integrate them with the rest of Ruby's numeric system. You'll notice this right away when doing basic arithmetic:

```
>> 1 / 2
=> 0
>> Math.sqrt(-1)
Errno::EDOM: Numerical argument out of domain - sqrt ..

>> require "mathn"
=> true
>> 1 / 2
=> 1/2
>> 1 / 2  + 5 / 7
=> 17/14
>> Math.sqrt(-1)
=> (0+1i)
```

As you can see, integer division gives way when *mathn* is loaded, in favor of returning `Rational` objects. These behave like the fractions you learned in grade school, and keep values in exact terms rather than expressing them as floats where possible. Numbers also gracefully extend into the `Complex` field, without error. Although this sort of behavior might seem unnecessary for day-to-day programming needs, it can be very helpful for mathematical applications.

In addition to changing the way basic arithmetic works, *mathn* pulls in a few of the higher-level mathematical constructs. For those interested in enumerating prime numbers (for whatever fun reason you might have in mind), a class is provided. To give you a peek at how it works, we can do things like ask for the first 10 primes or how many primes exist up to certain numbers:

```
>> Prime.first(10)
=> [2, 3, 5, 7, 11, 13, 17, 19, 23, 29]

>> Prime.find_index { |e| e > 1000 }
=> 168
```

In addition to enabling `Prime`, *mathn* also allows you to use `Matrix` and `Vector` without an explicit `require`:

```
>> Vector[1,2,3] * 3
=> Vector[3, 6, 9]
>> Matrix[[5,1,2],[3,1,4]].transpose
=> Matrix[[5, 3], [1, 1], [2, 4]]
```

These classes can do all sorts of useful linear algebra functions, but I don't want to overwhelm the casual Rubyist with mathematical details. Instead, we'll look at a practical use of them and leave the theory as a homework assignment. Consider the simple drawing in Figure B-1.

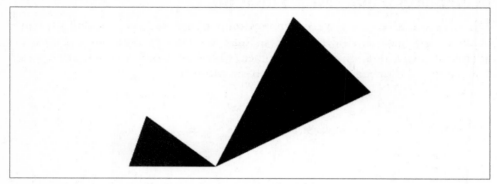

Figure B-1. A pair of triangles with a mathematical relationship

We see two rather exciting triangles, nuzzling up against each other at a single point. As it turns out, the smaller triangle is nothing more than a clone of the larger one, reflected, rotated, and scaled to fit. Here's the code that makes all that happen:†

```ruby
include Math

Canvas.draw("triangles.pdf") do
  points = Matrix[[0,0], [100,200], [200,100]]

  paint_triangle(*points)

  # reflect across y-axis
  points *= Matrix[[-1, 0],[0,1]]

  # rotate so bottom is flush with x axis.
  theta = -atan(1/2)
  points *= Matrix[[cos(theta), -sin(theta)],
                   [sin(theta),  cos(theta)]]

  # scale down by 50%
  points  *= 1/2
  paint_triangle(*points)
end
```

You don't need to worry about the graphics-drawing code. Instead, focus on the use of `Matrix` manipulations here, and watch what happens to the points in each step. We start off with our initial triangle's coordinates, as such:

```ruby
>> points = Matrix[[0,0], [100,200], [200,100]]
=> Matrix[[0, 0], [100, 200], [200, 100]]
```

† To run this example, you'll need my Prawn-based helpers. These are included in this book's git repository.

Then, we multiply by a 2 × 2 matrix that performs a reflection across the *y*-axis:

```
>> points *= Matrix[[-1, 0],[0,1]]
=> Matrix[[0, 0], [-100, 200], [-200, 100]]
```

Notice here that the *x* values are inverted, while the *y* value is left untouched. This is what translates our points from the right side to the left. Our next task uses a bit of trigonometry to rotate our triangle to lie flat along the *x*-axis. Notice here that we use the arctan of 1/2, because the bottom-edge triangle on the right rises halfway toward the upper boundary before terminating. If you aren't familiar with how this calculation works, don't worry—just observe its results:

```
>> theta = -atan(1/2)
=> -0.463647609000806
>> points *= Matrix[[cos(theta), -sin(theta)],
?>               [sin(theta), cos(theta)] ]
=> Matrix[[0.0, 0.0], [-178.885438199983, 134.164078649987], [-223.606797749979, 0.0]]
```

The numbers got a bit ugly after this calculation, but there is a key observation to make here. The triangle's dimensions were preserved, but two of the points now lie on the *x*-axis. This means our rotation was successful.

Finally, we do scalar multiplication to drop the whole triangle down to half its original size:

```
>> points *= 1/2
=> Matrix[[0.0, 0.0], [-89.4427190999915, 67.0820393249935], [-111.803398874989, 0.0]]
```

This completes the transformation and shows how the little triangle was developed simply by manipulating the larger one. Although this is certainly a bit of an abstract example, it hopefully serves as sufficient motivation for learning a bit more about matrixes. Although they can certainly be used for more hardcore calculations, simple linear transformations such as the ones shown in this example come cheap and easy and demonstrate an effective way to do some interesting graphics work.

Although truly hardcore math might be better suited for a more special-purpose language, Ruby is surprisingly full-featured enough to write interesting math programs with. As this particular topic can run far deeper than I have time to discuss, I will leave further investigation to the interested reader. The key thing to remember is that *mathn* puts Ruby in a sort of "math mode" by including some of the most helpful standard libraries and modifying the way that Ruby does its basic arithmetic. This feature is so useful that *irb* includes a special switch -m, which essentially requires *mathn* and then includes the Math module in at the top level.

A small caveat to keep in mind when working with *mathn* is that it is fairly aggressive about the changes it makes. If you are building a Ruby library, you may want to be a bit more conservative and use the individual packages it enables one by one rather than having to deal with the consequences of potentially breaking code that relies on behaviors such as integer division.

All that having been said, if you're working on your math homework, or building a specialized mathematical application in Ruby, feel free to go wild with all that *mathn* has to offer.

Working with Tabular Data (csv)

If you need to represent a data table in plain-text format, CSV (comma-separated value) files are about as simple as you can get. These files can easily be processed by almost any programming language, and Ruby is no exception. The *csv* standard library is fast for pure Ruby, internationalized, and downright pleasant to work with.

In the most simple cases, it'd be hard to make things easier. For example, say you had a CSV file (*payments.csv*) that looked like this:

```
name,payment
Gregory Brown,100
Joe Comfort,150
Jon Juraschka,200
Gregory Brown,75
Jon Juraschka,250
Jia Wu,25
Gregory Brown,50
Jia Wu,75
```

If you want to just slurp this into an array of arrays, it can't be easier:

```
>> require "csv"
=> true
>> CSV.read("payments.csv")
=> [["name", "payment"], ["Gregory Brown", "100"], ["Joe Comfort", "150"],
    ["Jon Juraschka", "200"], ["Gregory Brown", "75"], ["Jon Juraschka", "250"],
    ["Jia Wu", "25"], ["Gregory Brown", "50"], ["Jia Wu", "75"]]
```

Of course, slurping files isn't a good idea if you want to handle only a subset of data, but *csv* makes row-by-row handling easy. Here's an example of how you'd capture only my records:

```
>> data = []
=> []
>> CSV.foreach("payments.csv") { |row| data << row if row[0] == "Gregory Brown" }
=> nil
>> data
=> [["Gregory Brown", "100"], ["Gregory Brown", "75"], ["Gregory Brown", "50"]]
```

A common convention is to have the first row of a CSV file represent header data. *csv* can give you nicer accessors in this case:

```
>> data
=> []
>> CSV.foreach("payments.csv", :headers => true) do |row|
?>   data << row if row['name'] == "Gregory Brown"
>> end
=> nil
```

```
>> data
=> [#<CSV::Row "name":"Gregory Brown" "payment":"100">,
    #<CSV::Row "name":"Gregory Brown" "payment":"75">,
    #<CSV::Row "name":"Gregory Brown" "payment":"50">]
```

`CSV::Row` is a sort of hash/array hybrid. The primary feature that distinguishes it from a hash is that it allows for duplicate field names. Here's an example of how that works. Given a simple file with nonunique column names like this (*phone_numbers.csv*):

```
applicant,phone_number,spouse,phone_number
James Gray,555 555 5555,Dana Gray,123 456 7890
Gregory Brown,098 765 4321,Jia Wu,222 222 2222
```

we can extract both `"phone_number"` fields, as shown here:

```
>> data = CSV.read("phone_numbers.csv", :headers => true)
=> #<CSV::Table mode:col_or_row row_count:3>
>> data.map { |r| r["phone_number"], r["phone_number",2] }
=> [["555 555 5555", "123 456 7890"], [" 098 765 4321", "222 222 2222"]]
```

We see that `CSV::Row#[]` takes an optional second argument that is an offset from which to begin looking for a field name. For this particular data, `r["phone_number",0]` and `r["phone_number",1]` would resolve as the first phone number field; an index of 2 or 3 would look up the second phone number. If we know the names of the columns near each phone number, we can do this in a bit of a smarter way:

```
>> data.map { |r| [ r["phone_number", r.index("applicant")],
?>                  r["phone_number", r.index("spouse")] ] }
=> [[" 555 555 5555", "123 456 7890"], ["098 765 4321", "222 222 2222"]]
```

Although this still depends on ordinal positioning to some extent, it allows us to do a relative index lookup. If we know that "phone number" is always going to be next to "applicant" and "spouse," it doesn't matter which column they start at. Whenever you can take advantage of this sort of flexibility, it's a good idea to do so.

So far, we've talked about reading files, but the *csv* library handles writing as well. Rather than continue with our *irb*-based exploration, I'll just combine the features that we've already gone over with a couple new ones, so that we can look at a tiny but fully functional script.

Our task is to convert the previously mentioned *payments.csv* file into a summary report (*payment_summary.csv*), which will look like this:

```
name,total payments
Gregory Brown,225
Joe Comfort,150
Jon Juraschka,450
Jia Wu,100
```

Here, we've done a grouping on name and summed up the payments. If you thought this might be a complicated process, you thought wrong. Here's all that needs to be done:

```ruby
require "csv"

@totals = Hash.new(0)

csv_options = {:headers => true, :converters => :numeric }

CSV.foreach("payments.csv", csv_options) do |row|
  @totals[row['name']] += row['payment']
end

CSV.open("payment_summary.csv", "w") do |csv|
  csv << ["name","total payments"]
  @totals.each { |row| csv << row }
end
```

The core mechanism for doing the grouping-and-summing operation is just a hash with default values of zero for unassigned keys. If you haven't seen this technique before, be sure to make a note of it, because you'll see it all over Ruby scripts. The rest of the work is easy once we exploit this little trick.

As far as processing the initial CSV file goes, the only new trick we've added is to specify the option :converters => :numeric. This tells *csv* to hit each cell with a check to see whether it contains a valid Ruby number. It then does the right thing and converts it to a Fixnum or Float if there's a match. This lets us normalize our data as soon as it's loaded, rather than litter our code with to_i and to_f calls.

For this reason, the foreach loop is nothing more than simple addition, keying the name to a running total of payments.

Finally, we get to the writing side of things. We use CSV.open in a similar way to how we might use File.open, and we populate a CSV object by shoving arrays that represent rows into it. This code is a little prettier than it might be in the general case, as we're working with only two columns, but you should be able to see that the process is relatively straightforward nonetheless.

Here we see a useful little script based on the *csv* library weighing in at around 10 lines of code. As impressive as that might be, we haven't even scratched the surface on this one, so be sure to dig deeper if you have a need for processing tabular datafiles. One thing that I didn't show at all is that *csv* handles reading and writing from strings just as well as it does files, which may be useful in web applications and other places where there is a need to stream files rather than work directly with the filesystem. Another is dealing with different column and row record separators. Luckily, the *csv* library is comparably well documented, so all of these things are just a quick API documentation search away.

A great thing about the newly revamped *csv* standard library is that you don't necessarily need to upgrade to Ruby 1.9 to use it. It started as a third-party alternative to Ruby 1.8's CSV standard library, under the name FasterCSV, and this project is still supported under Ruby 1.8.6. So if you like what you see here, and you want to use it in some of your legacy Ruby code, you can always install the *fastercsv* gem and be up and running.

Transactional Filesystem-Based Data Storage (pstore)

PStore provides a simple, transactional database for storing Ruby objects within a file. This gives you a persistence layer without relying on any external resources, which can be very handy. Using PStore is so simple that I can forgo most of the details and jump right into some code that I use for a Sinatra microapp at work. What follows is a very simple backend for storing replies to an anonymous survey:

```ruby
class SuggestionBox
  def initialize(filename="suggestions.pstore")
    @filename = filename
  end

  def store
    @store ||= PStore.new(@filename)
  end

  def add_reply(reply)
    store.transaction do
      store[:replies] ||= []
      store[:replies] << reply
    end
  end

  def replies(readonly=true)
    store.transaction do
      store[:replies]
    end
  end

  def clear_replies
    store.transaction do
      store[:replies] = []
    end
  end
end
```

In our application, the usage of this object for storing responses is quite simple. Given that box is just a SuggestionBox in the following code, we just have a single call to add_reply that looks something like this:

```ruby
box.add_reply(:question1 => params["question1"],
              :question2 => params["question2"])
```

Later, when we need to generate a PDF report of all the replies in the suggestion box, we do something like this to extract the responses to the two questions:

```ruby
question1_replies = []
question2_replies = []
box.replies.each do |reply|
```

```
    question1_replies << reply[:question1]
    question2.replies << reply[:question2]
  end
```

So that covers the usage, but let's go back in a little more detail to the implementation. You can see that our **store** is initialized by just constructing a new **PStore** object and passing it a filename:

```
def store
  @store ||= PStore.new(@filename)
end
```

Then, when it comes to using our **PStore**, it basically looks like we're dealing with a hash-like object, but all of our interactions with it are through these **transaction** blocks:

```
def add_reply(reply)
  store.transaction do
    store[:replies] ||= []
    store[:replies] << reply
  end
end

def replies
  store.transaction(readonly=true) do
    store[:replies]
  end
end

def clear_replies
  store.transaction do
    store[:replies] = []
  end
end
```

So the real question here is what do we gain? The answer is, predictably, a whole lot.[‡]

By using **PStore**, we can be sure that only one write-mode transaction is open at a time, preventing issues with partial reads/writes in multiprocessed applications. This means that if we attempt to produce a report against **SuggestionBox** while a new suggestion is being written, our report will wait until the write operation completes before it processes. However, when all transactions are read-only, they will not block each other, allowing them to run concurrently.

Every transaction reloads the file at its start, keeping things up-to-date and synchronized. Every write that is done checks the MD5 sum of the contents to avoid unnecessary writes for unchanging data. If something goes wrong during a write, all the write operations in a transaction are rolled back and an exception is raised. In short, **PStore** provides a fairly robust persistence framework that is suitable for use across multiple applications or threads.

[‡] The following paragraph summarizes a *ruby-talk* post from Ara T. Howard, found at *http://blade.nagaokaut .ac.jp/cgi-bin/scat.rb/ruby/ruby-talk/177666*.

Of course, though it is great for what it does, PStore has notable limitations. Because it loads the entire dataset on every read, and writes the whole dataset on every write, it is very I/O-intensive. Therefore, it's not meant to handle very high load or large datasets. Additionally, as it is essentially nothing more than a file-based Hash object, it cannot serve as a substitute for some sort of SQL server when dealing with relational data that needs to be efficiently queried. Finally, because it uses the core utility Marshal to serialize objects to disk,§ PStore cannot be used to store certain objects. These include anonymous classes and Proc objects, among other things.

Despite these limitations, PStore has a very wide sweet spot in which it is the right way to go. Whenever you need to persist a modest amount of nonrelational data and possibly share it across processes or threads, it is usually the proper tool for the job. Although it is possible to code up your own persistence solutions on top of Ruby's raw serialization support, PStore solves most of the common needs in a rather elegant way.

Human-Readable Data Serialization (json)

JavaScript Object Notation (JSON) (*http://json.org/*) is an object serialization format that has been gaining a ton of steam lately. With the rise of a service-oriented Web, the need for a simple, language-independent data serialization format has become more and more apparent.

Historically, XML has been used for interoperable data serialization. However, using XML for this is a bit like going bird hunting with a bazooka: it's just way more firepower than the job requires. JSON aims to do one thing and do it well, and these constraints give rise to a human-readable, human-editable, easy-to-parse, and easy-to-produce data interchange format.

The primitive constructs provided by JSON are limited to hashes (called *objects* in JSON), arrays, strings, numbers, and the conditional triumvirate of true, false, and nil (called null in JSON). It's easy to see that these concepts trivially map to core Ruby objects. Let's take a moment to see how each of these data types are represented in JSON:

```
require "json"

hash = { "Foo" => [Math::PI, 1, "kittens"],
         "Bar" => [false, nil, true], "Baz" => { "X" => "Y" } } #...

puts hash.to_json #=> Outputs
{"Foo":[3.14159265358979,1,"kittens"],"Bar":[false,null,true],"Baz":{"X":"Y"}}
```

There isn't really much to it. In fact, JSON is somewhat syntactically similar to Ruby. Though the similarity is only superficial, it is nice to be able to read and write structures in a format that doesn't feel completely alien.

---

§ The *yaml/store* library will allow you to use YAML in place of Marshal, but with many of the same limitations.

If we go the other direction, from JSON into Ruby, you'll see that the transformation is just as easy:

```ruby
require "json"

json_string = '{"Foo":[3.14159265358979,1,"kittens"], ' +
              '"Bar":[false,null,true],"Baz":{"X":"Y"}}'

hash = JSON.parse(json_string)

p hash["Bar"] #=> Outputs
[false,nil,true]

p hash["Baz"] #=> Outputs
{ "X"=>"Y" }
```

Without knowing much more about Ruby's *json* standard library, you can move on to building useful things. As long as you know how to navigate the nested hash and array structures, you can work with pretty much any service that exposes a JSON interface as if it were responding to you with Ruby structures. As an example, we can look at a fairly simple interface that does a web search and processes the JSON dataset it returns:

```ruby
require "json"
require "open-uri"
require "cgi"

module GSearch
  extend self

  API_BASE_URI =
    "http://ajax.googleapis.com/ajax/services/search/web?v=1.0&q="

  def show_results(query)
    results = response_data(query)
    results["responseData"]["results"].each do |match|
      puts CGI.unescapeHTML(match["titleNoFormatting"]) + ":\n  " + match["url"]
    end
  end

  def response_data(query)
    data = open(API_BASE_URI + URI.escape(query),
                "Referer" => "http://rubybestpractices.com").read
    JSON.parse(data)
  end

end
```

Here we're using *json* and the *open-uri* library, which was discussed earlier in this appendix as a way to wrap a simple Google web search. When run, this code will print out a few page titles and their URLs for any query you enter. Here's a sample of GSearch in action:

```
GSearch.show_results("Ruby Best Practices") # OUTPUTS

Ruby Best Practices: Rough Cuts Version | O'Reilly Media:
   http://oreilly.com/catalog/9780596156749/
Ruby Best Practices: The Book and Interview with Gregory Brown:
   http://www.rubyinside.com/ruby-best-practices-gregory-brown-interview-1332.html
On Ruby: A 'Ruby Best Practices' Blogging Contest:
   http://on-ruby.blogspot.com/2008/12/ruby-best-practices-blogging-contest.html
Gluttonous : Rails Best Practices, Tips and Tricks:
   http://glu.ttono.us/articles/2006/02/06/rails-best-practices-tips-and-tricks
```

Maybe by the time this book comes out, we'll have nabbed all four of the top spots, but that's beside the point. You'll want to notice that the GSearch module interacts with the *json* library in a sum total of one line, in order to convert the dataset into Ruby. After that, the rest is business as usual.

The interesting thing about this particular example is that I didn't read any of the documentation for the search API. Instead, I tried a sample query, converted the JSON to Ruby, and then used Hash#keys to tell me what attributes were available. From there I continued to use ordinary Ruby reflection and inspection techniques straight from *irb* to figure out which fields were needed to complete this example. By thinking of JSON datasets as nothing more than the common primitive Ruby objects, you can accomplish a lot using the skills you're already familiar with.

After seeing how easy it is to consume JSON, you might be wondering how you'd go about producing it using your own custom objects. As it turns out, there really isn't that much to it. Say, for example, you had a Point class that was responsible for doing some calculations, but that at its essence it was basically just an ordered pair representing an [x,y] coordinate. Producing the JSON to match this is easy:

```ruby
require "json"

class Point

  def initialize(x,y)
    @x, @y = x, y
  end

  def distance_to(point)
    Math.hypot(point.x - x, point.y - y)
  end

  attr_reader :x, :y

  def to_json(*args)
    [x,y].to_json(*args)
  end

end

point_a = Point.new(1,2)
puts point_a.to_json #=> "[1,2]"
```

```ruby
point_data = JSON.parse('[4,6]')
point_b = Point.new(*point_data)

puts point_b.distance_to(point_a) #=> 5.0
```

Here, we have simply represented our core data in primitives and then wrapped our object model around it. In many cases, this is the most simple, implementation-independent way to represent one of our objects.

However, in some cases you may wish to let the object internally interpret the structure of a JSON document and do the wrapping for you. The Ruby *json* library provides a simple hook that depends on a bit of metadata to convert our parsed JSON into a customized higher-level Ruby object. If we rework our example, we can see how it works:

```ruby
require "json"

class Point
  def initialize(x,y)
    @x, @y = x, y
  end

  def distance_to(point)
    Math.hypot(point.x - x, point.y - y)
  end

  attr_reader :x, :y

  def to_json(*args)
    { 'json_class' => self.class.name,
      'data' => [@x, @y] }.to_json(*args)
  end

  def self.json_create(obj)
    new(*obj['data'])
  end
end

point_a = Point.new(1,2)
puts point_a.to_json #=> {"json_class":"Point","data":[1,2]}


point_b = JSON.parse('{"json_class":"Point","data":[4,6]}')
puts point_b.distance_to(point_a) #=> 5.0
```

Although a little more work needs to be done here, we can see that the underlying mechanism for a direct Ruby→JSON→Ruby round trip is simple. The JSON library depends on the attribute `json_class`, which points to a string that represents a Ruby class name. If this class has a method called `json_create`, the parsed JSON data is passed to this method and its return value is returned by `JSON.parse`. Although this approach involves rolling up our sleeves a bit, it is nice to see that there is not much magic to it.

Although this adds some extra noise to our JSON output, it does not add any new constructs, so there is not an issue with other programming languages being able to parse it and use the underlying data. It simply comes with the added benefit of Ruby applications being able to simply map raw primitive data to the classes that wrap them.

Depending on your needs, you may prefer one technique over the other. The benefit of providing a simple to_json hook that produces raw primitive values is that it keeps your serialized data completely implementation-agnostic. This will come in handy if you need to support a wide range of clients. The benefit of using the "json_class" attribute is that you do not have to think about manually building up high-level objects from your object data. This is most beneficial when you are serving up data to primarily Ruby clients, or when your data is complex enough that manually constructing objects would be painful.

No matter what your individual needs are, it's safe to say that JSON is something to keep an eye on moving forward. Ruby's implementation is fast and easy to work with. If you need to work with or write your own web services, this is definitely a tool you will want to familiarize yourself with.

Embedded Ruby for Code Generation (erb)

Code generation can be useful for dynamically generating static files based on a template. When we need this sort of functionality, we can turn to the *erb* standard library. ERB stands for *Embedded Ruby*, which is ultimately exactly what the library facilitates.

In the most basic case, a simple ERB template[||] might look like this:

```
require 'erb'

x = 42
template = ERB.new("The value of x is: <%= x %>")
puts template.result(binding)
```

The resulting text looks like this:

```
The value of x is: 42
```

If you've not worked with ERB before, you may be wondering how this differs from ordinary string interpolation, such as this:

```
x = 42
puts "The value of x is: #{x}"
```

The key difference to recognize here is the way the two strings are evaluated. When we use string interpolation, our values are substituted immediately. When we evaluate an ERB template, we do not actually evaluate the expression inside the <%= ... %> until we call ERB#result. That means that although this code does not work at all:

[||] Credit: this is the first example in the ERB API documentation.

```
string = "The value of x is: #{x}"
x = 42
puts string
```

the following code will work without any problems:

```
require 'erb'

template = ERB.new("The value of x is: <%= x %>")
x = 42

puts template.result(binding)
```

This is the main reason why ERB can be useful to us. We can write templates ahead of time, referencing variables and methods that may not exist yet, and then bind them just before rendering time using `binding`.

We can also include some logic in our files, to determine what should be printed:

```
require "erb"

class A

  def initialize(x)
    @x = x
  end

  attr_reader :x

  public :binding

  def eval_template(string)
    ERB.new(string,0,'<>').result(binding)
  end

end

template = <<-EOS
<% if x == 42 %>
You have stumbled across the Answer to the Life, the Universe, and Everything
<% else %>
The value of x is <%= x %>
<% end %>
EOS

foo = A.new(10)
bar = A.new(21)
baz = A.new(42)

[foo, bar, baz].each { |e| puts e.eval_template(template) }
```

Here, we run the same template against three different objects, evaluating it within the context of each of their bindings. The more complex `ERB.new` call here sets the `safe_level` the template is executed in to 0 (the default), but this is just because we want to provide the third argument, `trim_mode`. When `trim_mode` is set to "<>", the newlines are omitted for lines starting with <% and ending with %>. As this is useful for embedding logic, we need to turn it on to keep the generated string from having ugly stray newlines. The final output of the script looks like this:

```
The value of x is 10
The value of x is 21
You have stumbled across the Answer to the Life, the Universe, and Everything
```

As you can see, ERB does not emit text when it is within a conditional block that is not satisfied. This means a lot in the way of building up dynamic output, as you can use all your normal control structures to determine what text should and should not be rendered.

The documentation for the *erb* library is quite good, so I won't attempt to dig much deeper here. Of course, no mention of ERB would be complete without an example of HTML templating. Although the API documentation goes into much more complicated examples, I can't resist showing the template that I use for rendering entries in my blog engine.# This doesn't include the site layout, but just the code that gets run for each entry:

```
<h2><%= title %></h2>

<%= entry %>

<div align="right">
<p><small>Written by <%= Blaag::AUTHOR %> on
<%= published_date.strftime("%Y.%m%.%d") %> at
<%= published_date.strftime("%H:%M" )%>  | <%= related %>
</small>
  </p>
</div>
```

This code is evaluated in the context of a `Blaag::Entry` object, which, as you can clearly see, does most of the heavy lifting through helper methods. Although this example might be boring and a bit trivial, it shows something worth keeping in mind. Just because you can do all sorts of logic in your ERB templates doesn't mean that you should. The fact that these templates can be evaluated in a custom binding means that you are able to keep your code where it should be while avoiding messy string interpolation. If your ERB templates start to look more like Ruby scripts than templates, you'll want to clean things up before you start pulling your hair out.

Using `ERB` for templating can really come in handy. Whether you need to generate a form letter or just plug some values into a complicated data format, the ability to late-bind data to a template and generate dynamic content on the fly from static templates is powerful indeed. Just be sure to keep in mind that ERB is meant to supplement your ordinary code rather than replace it, and you'll be able to take advantage of this useful library without creating a big mess.

See *http://github.com/sandal/blaag*.

Conclusions

Hopefully these examples have shown the diversity you can come to expect from Ruby's standard library. What you have probably noticed by now is that there really is a lot there—so much so that it might be a little overwhelming at first. Another observation you may have made is that there seems to be little consistency in interface between the libraries. This is because many were written by different people at different stages in Ruby's evolution.

However, assuming that you can tolerate the occasional wart, a solid working knowledge of what is available in Ruby's standard libraries is a key part of becoming a masterful Rubyist. It goes beyond simply knowing about and using these tools, though. Many of the libraries discussed here are written in pure Ruby, which means that you can actually learn a lot by grabbing a copy of Ruby's source and reading through their implementations. I know I've learned a lot in this manner, so I wholeheartedly recommend it as a way to test and polish your Ruby chops.

Ruby Worst Practices

If you've read through most of this book, you'll notice that it doesn't have much of a "Do this, not that" theme. Ruby as a language doesn't fit well into that framework, as there are always exceptions to any rule you can come up with.

However, there are certainly a few things you really shouldn't do, unless you know exactly why you are doing them. This appendix is meant to cover a handful of those scenarios and show you some better alternatives. I've done my best to stick to issues that I've been bit by myself, in the hopes that I can offer some practical advice for problems you might actually have run into.

A bad practice in programming shouldn't simply be characterized as some ill-defined aesthetic imposed upon folks by the "experts." Instead, we can often track antipatterns in code down to either flaws in the high-level design of an object-oriented system, or failed attempts at cleverness in the underlying feature implementations. These bits of unsavory code produced by bad habits or the misunderstanding of certain Ruby peculiarities can be a drag on your whole project, creating substantial technical debt as they accumulate.

We'll start with the high-level design issues and then move on to the common sticking points when implementing tricky Ruby features. Making an improvement to even a couple of these problem areas will make a major difference, so even if you already know about most of these pitfalls, you might find one or two tips that will go a long way.

Not-So-Intelligent Design

Well-designed object-oriented systems can be a dream to work with. When every component seems to fit together nicely, with clear, simple integration code between the major subsystems, you get the feeling that the architecture is working for you, and not against you.

If you're not careful, all of this can come crashing down. Let's look at a few things to watch out for, and how to get around them.

Class Variables Considered Harmful

Ruby's class variables are one of the easiest ways to break encapsulation and create headaches for yourself when designing class hierarchies. To demonstrate the problem, I'll show an example in which class variables were tempting but ultimately the wrong solution.

In my abstract formatting library *fatty*, I provide a formatter base class that users must inherit from to make use of the system. This provides helpers that build up anonymous classes for certain formats. To get a sense of what this looks like, check out this example:

```ruby
class Hello < FattyRBP::Formatter
  format :text do
    def render
      "Hello World"
    end
  end

  format :html do
    def render
      "<b>Hello World</b>"
    end
  end
end

puts Hello.render(:text) #=> "Hello World"
puts Hello.render(:html) #=> "<b>Hello World</b>"
```

Though I've omitted most of the actual functionality that *fatty* provides, a simple implementation of this system using class variables might look like this:

```ruby
module FattyRBP
  class Formatter
    @@formats = {}

    def self.format(name, options={}, &block)
      @@formats[name] = Class.new(FattyRBP::Format, &block)
    end

    def self.render(format, options={})
      @@formats[format].new(options).render
    end
  end

  class Format
    def initialize(options)
      # not important
    end

    def render
      raise NotImplementedError
    end
  end
end
```

This code will make the example shown earlier work as advertised. Now let's see what happens when we add another subclass into the mix:

```ruby
class Goodbye < FattyRBP::Formatter
  format :text do
    def render
      "Goodbye Cruel World!"
    end
  end
end

puts Goodbye.render(:text) #=> "Goodbye Cruel World!"
```

At first glance, things seem to be working. But if we dig deeper, we see two problems:

```ruby
# Should not have changed
puts Hello.render(:text) #=> "Goodbye Cruel World!"

# Shouldn't exist
puts Goodbye.render(:html) #=> "<b>Hello World</b>"
```

And here, we see the problem with class variables. If we think of them as class-level state, we'd be wrong. They are actually class-hierarchy variables that can have their state modified by any subclass, whether direct or many levels down the ancestry chain. This means they're fairly close to global state in nature, which is usually a bad thing. So unless you were actually counting on this behavior, an easy fix is to just dump class variables and use class instance variables instead:

```ruby
module FattyRBP
  class Formatter

    def self.formats
      @formats ||= {}
    end

    def self.format(name, options={}, &block)
      formats[name] = Class.new(FattyRBP::Format, &block)
    end

    def self.render(format, options={})
      formats[format].new(options).render
    end
  end

  class Format
    def initialize(options)
      # not important
    end
  end
end
```

Although this prevents direct access to the variable from instances, it is easy to define accessors at the class level. The benefit is that each subclass carries its own instance variable, just like ordinary objects do. With this new code, everything works as expected:

```
puts Hello.render(:text)    #=> "Hello World"
puts Hello.render(:html)    #=> "<b>Hello World</b>"
puts Goodbye.render(:text)  #=> "Goodbye Cruel World"

puts Hello.render(:text)    #=> "Hello World"
puts Goodbye.render(:html)  #=> raises an error
```

So the moral of the story here is that class-level state should be stored in class instance variables if you want to allow subclassing. Reserve class variables for data that needs to be shared across an entire class hierarchy.

Hardcoding Yourself Into a Corner

One good practice is to provide alternative constructors for your classes when there are common configurations that might be generally useful. One such example is in Prawn, when a user wants to build up a document via a simplified interface and then immediately render it to file:

```
Prawn::Document.generate("hello.pdf") do
  text "Hello Prawn!"
end
```

Implementing this method was very simple, as it simply wraps the constructor and calls an extra method to render the file afterward:

```
module Prawn
  class Document

    def self.generate(filename,options={},&block)
      pdf = Prawn::Document.new(options,&block)
      pdf.render_file(filename)
    end

  end
end
```

However, some months down the line, a bug report made me realize that I made a somewhat stupid mistake here. I accidentally prevented users from being able to write code like this:

```
class MyDocument < Prawn::Document
  def say_hello
    text "Hello MyDocument"
  end
end

MyDocument.generate("hello.pdf") do
  say_hello
end
```

The problem, of course, is that `Prawn::Document.generate` hardcodes the constructor call, which prevents subclasses from ever being instantiated via `generate`. The fix is so easy that it is somewhat embarrassing to share:

```ruby
module Prawn
  class Document

    def self.generate(filename,options={},&block)
      pdf = new(options,&block)
      pdf.render_file(filename)
    end

  end
end
```

By removing the explicit receiver, we now construct an object based on whatever `self` is, rather than only building up `Prawn::Document` objects. This affords us additional flexibility at virtually no cost. In fact, because hardcoding the name of the current class in your method definitions is almost always an accident, this applies across the board as a good habit to get into.

Although much less severe, the same thing goes for class method definitions as well. Throughout this book, you will see class methods defined using `def self.my_method` rather than `def MyClass.my_method`. The reason for this is much more about maintainability than it is about style. To illustrate this, let's do a simple comparison. We start off with two boring class definitions for the classes `A` and `B`:

```ruby
class A
  def self.foo
    # ..
  end

  def self.bar
    # ..
  end
end

class B
  def B.foo
    # ...
  end

  def B.bar
    # ...
  end
end
```

These two are functionally equivalent, each defining the class methods `foo` and `bar` on their respective classes. But now, let's refactor our code a bit, renaming `A` to `C` and `B` to `D`. Observe the work involved in doing each:

```
class C
  def self.foo
    # ..
  end

  def self.bar
    # ..
  end
end

class D
  def D.foo
    # ...
  end

  def D.bar
    # ...
  end
end
```

To rename A to C, we simply change the name of our class, and we don't need to touch the method definitions. But when we change B to D, each and every method needs to be reworked. Though this might be OK for an object with one or two methods at the class level, you can imagine how tedious this could be when that number gets larger.

So we've now found two points against hardcoding class names, and could probably keep growing the list if we wanted. But for now, let's move on to some even higher-level design issues.

When Inheritance Becomes Restrictive

Inheritance is very nice when your classes have a clear hierarchical structure between them. However, it can get in the way when used inappropriately. Problems begin to crop up when we try to model cross-cutting concerns using ordinary inheritance. For examples of this, it's easy to look directly into core Ruby.

Imagine if `Comparable` were a class instead of a module. Then, you would be writing code like this:

```
class Person < Comparable

  def initialize(first_name, last_name)
    @first_name = first_name
    @last_name  = last_name
  end

  attr_reader :first_name, :last_name

  def <=>(other_person)
    [last_name, first_name] <=> [other_person.last_name, other_person.first_name]
  end

end
```

However, after seeing this, it becomes clear that it'd be nice to use a `Struct` here. If we ignore the features provided by `Comparable` here for a moment, the benefits of a struct to represent this simple data structure become obvious.

```ruby
class Person < Struct.new(:first_name, :last_name)
  def full_name
    "#{first_name} #{last_name}"
  end
end
```

Because Ruby supports single inheritance only, this example clearly demonstrates the problems we run into when relying too heavily on hierarchical structure. A `Struct` is certainly not always `Comparable`. And it is just plain silly to think of all `Comparable` objects being `Struct` objects. The key distinction here is that a `Struct` defines what an object is made up of, whereas `Comparable` defines a set of features associated with certain objects. For this reason, the real Ruby code to accomplish this modeling makes a whole lot of sense:

```ruby
class Person < Struct.new(:first_name, :last_name)

  include Comparable

  def <=>(other_person)
    [last_name, first_name] <=> [other_person.last_name, other_person.first_name]
  end

  def full_name
    "#{first_name} #{last_name}"
  end

end
```

Keep in mind that although we are constrained to exactly one superclass, we can include as many modules as we'd like. For this reason, modules are often used to implement features that are completely orthogonal to the underlying class definition that they are mixed into. Taking an example from the Ruby API documentation, we see `Forwardable` being used to very quickly implement a simple `Queue` structure by doing little more than delegating to an underlying `Array`:

```ruby
require "forwardable"

class Queue
  extend Forwardable

  def initialize
    @q = [ ]
  end

  def_delegator :@q, :push, :enq
  def_delegator :@q, :shift, :deq

  def_delegators :@q, :clear, :first, :push, :shift, :size
end
```

Although `Forwardable` would make no sense anywhere in a class hierarchy, it accomplishes its task beautifully here. If we were constrained to a purely inheritance-based model, such cleverness would not be so easy to pull off.

The key thing to remember here is not that you should avoid inheritance at all costs, by any means. Instead, you should simply remember not to go out of your way to construct an artificial hierarchical structure to represent cross-cutting or orthogonal concerns. It's important to remember that Ruby's core is not special or magical in its abundant use of mixins, but instead, is representative of a very pragmatic and powerful object model. You can and should apply this technique within your own designs, whenever it makes sense to do so.

The Downside of Cleverness

Ruby lets you do all sorts of clever, fancy tricks. This cleverness is a big part of what makes Ruby so elegant, but it also can be downright dangerous in the wrong hands. To illustrate this, we'll look at the kind of trouble you can get in if you aren't careful.

The Evils of eval( )

Throughout this book, we've dynamically evaluated code blocks all over the place. However, what you have not seen much of is the use of `eval()`, `class_eval()`, or even `instance_eval()` with a string. Some might wonder why this is, because `eval()` can be so useful! For example, imagine that you are exposing a way for users to filter through some data. You would like to be able to support an interface like this:

```ruby
user1 = User.new("Gregory Brown", balance: 2500)
user2 = User.new("Arthur Brown", balance: 3300)
user3 = User.new("Steven Brown", balance: 3200)

f = Filter.new([user1, user2, user3])
f.search("balance > 3000") #=> [user2, user3]
```

Armed with `instance_eval`, this task is so easy that you barely bat an eye as you type out the following code:

```ruby
class User
  def initialize(name, options)
    @name    = name
    @balance = options[:balance]
  end

  attr_reader :name, :balance
end

class Filter
  def initialize(enum)
    @collection = enum
  end
```

```
def search(query)
  @collection.select { |e| e.instance_eval(query) }
end
end
```

Running the earlier example, you see that this code works great, exactly as expected. But unfortunately, trouble strikes when you see queries like this:

```
>> f.search("@balance = 0")
=> [#<User:0x40caa4 @name="Gregory Brown", @balance=0>,
    #<User:0x409138 @name="Arthur Brown", @balance=0>,
    #<User:0x402874 @name="Steven Brown", @balance=0>]
```

Or, perhaps even scarier:

```
>> f.search("system('touch hacked')")
=> [#<User:0x40caa4 @name="Gregory Brown", ...]
>> File.exist?('hacked')
=> true
```

Because the ability for user-generated strings to execute arbitrary system commands or damage the internals of an object aren't exactly appealing, you code up a regex filter to protect against this:

```
def search(query)
  raise "Invalid query" unless query =~ /^(\w+) ([><!]=?|==) (\d+)$/
  @collection.select { |e| e.instance_eval(query) }
end
```

This protects against the two issues we saw before, which is great:

```
>> f.search("system('touch hacked')")
RuntimeError: Invalid query
        from (irb):33:in `search'
        from (irb):38
        from /Users/sandal/lib/ruby19_1/bin/irb:12:in `<main>'

>> f.search("@balance = 0")
RuntimeError: Invalid query
        from (irb):33:in `search'
        from (irb):39
        from /Users/sandal/lib/ruby19_1/bin/irb:12:in `<main>'
```

But if you weren't paying very close attention, you would have missed that we got our anchors wrong. That means there's still a hole to be exploited here:

```
>> f.search("balance == 0\nsystem('touch hacked_again')")
=> [#<User:0x40caa4 @name="Gregory Brown", @balance=0  ...]
>> File.exist?('hacked_again')
=> true
```

Because our regex checked the first line and not the whole string, we were able to sneak by the validation. Arguably, if you're very careful, you could come up with the right pattern and be reasonably safe. But as you are already validating the syntax, why play with fire? We can rewrite this code to accomplish the same goals with none of the associated risks:

```ruby
def search(query)
  data = query.match(/^(?<attr>\w+) (?<op>[><!]=?|==) (?<val>\d+)$/)
  @collection.select do |e|
    attr = e.public_send(data[:attr])
    attr.public_send(data[:op], Integer(data[:val]))
  end
end
```

Here, we don't expose any of the object's internals, preserving encapsulation. Because we parse out the individual components of the statement and use `public_send` to pass the messages on to our objects, we have completely eliminated the possibility of arbitrary code execution. All in all, this code is much more secure and easier to debug. As it turns out, this code will actually perform considerably better as well.

Every time you use `eval(string)`, Ruby needs to fire up its parser and tree walker to execute the code you've embedded in your string. This means that in cases in which you just need to process a few values and then do something with them, using a targeted regular expression is often a much better option, as it greatly reduces the amount of work the interpreter needs to do.

For virtually every situation in which you might turn to a raw string `eval()`, you can work around it using the tools Ruby provides. These include all sorts of methods for getting at whatever you need, including `instance_variable_get`, `instance_variable_set`, `const_get`, `const_set`, `public_send`, `send`, `define_method`, `method()`, and even `Class.new`/`Module.new`. These tools allow you to dynamically manipulate Ruby code without evaluating strings directly. For more details, you'll definitely want to read Chapter 3, *Mastering the Dynamic Toolkit*.

Blind Rescue Missions

Ruby provides a lot of different ways to handle exceptions. They run the gamut all the way from capturing the full stack trace to completely ignoring raised errors. This flexibility means that exceptions aren't necessarily treated with the same gravity in Ruby as in other languages, as they are very simple to rescue once they are raised. In certain cases, folks have even used `rescue` as a stand-in replacement for conditional statements. The classic example follows:

```ruby
name = @user.first_name.capitalize rescue "Anonymous"
```

Usually, this is done with the intention of capturing the `NoMethodError` raised by something like `first_name` being `nil` here. It accomplishes this task well, and looks slightly nicer than the alternative:

```ruby
name = @user.first_name ? @user.first_name.capitalize : "Anonymous"
```

However, the downside of using this trick is that you will most likely end up seeing this code again, at the long end of a painful debugging session. For demonstration purposes, let's assume our `User` is implemented like this:

```
require "pstore"

class User

  def self.data
    @data ||= PStore.new("users.store")
  end

  def self.add(id, user_data)
    data.transaction do
      data[id] = user_data
    end
  end

  def self.find(id)
    data.transaction do
      data[id] or raise "User not found"
    end
  end

  def initialize(id)
    @user_id = id
  end

  def attributes
    self.class.find(@user_id)
  end

  def first_name
    attributes[:first_name]
  end

end
```

What we have here is basically a PStore-backed user database. It's not terribly important to understand every last detail, but the code should be fairly easy to understand if you play around with it a bit.

Firing up *irb*, we can see that the rescue trick works fine for cases in which User#first_name returns nil:

```
>> require "user"
=> true

>> User.add('sandal', email: 'gregory@majesticseacreature.com')

=> {:email=>"gregory@majesticseacreature.com"}
>> @user = User.new('sandal')
=> #<User:0x48c448 @user_id="sandal">
>> name = @user.first_name.capitalize rescue "Anonymous"
=> "Anonymous"
=> #<User:0x49ab74 @user_id="sandal">
>> @user.first_name
=> nil
```

```
>> @user.attributes
=> {:email=>"gregory@majesticseacreature.com"}
```

Ordinary execution also works fine:

```
>> User.add('jia', first_name: "Jia", email: "jia@majesticseacreature.com")

=> {:first_name=>"Jia", :email=>"jia@majesticseacreature.com"}
>> @user = User.new('jia')
=> #<User:0x492154 @user_id="jia">
>> name = @user.first_name.capitalize rescue "Anonymous"
=> "Jia"
>> @user.attributes
=> {:first_name=>"Jia", :email=>"jia@majesticseacreature.com"}
>> @user.first_name
=> "Jia"
>> @user = User.new('sandal')
```

It seems like everything is in order; however, you don't need to look far. Notice that this line will succeed even if **@user** is undefined:

```
>> @user = nil
=> nil
>> name = @user.first_name.capitalize rescue "Anonymous"
=> "Anonymous"
```

This means you can't count on catching an error when a typo or a renamed variable creeps into your code. This weakness of course propagates down the chain as well:

```
>> name = @user.a_fake_method.capitalize rescue "Anonymous"
=> "Anonymous"
>> name = @user.a_fake_method.cannot_fail rescue "Anonymous"
=> "Anonymous"
```

Of course, issues with a one-liner like this should be easy enough to catch even without an exception. This is most likely the reason why this pattern has become so common. However, this is usually an oversight, because the problem exists deeper down the bunny hole as well. Let's introduce a typo into our user implementation:

```
class User

  def first_name
    attribute[:first_name]
  end

end
```

Now, we go back and look at one of our previously working examples:

```
>> @user = User.new('jia')
=> #<User:0x4b8548 @user_id="jia">
>> name = @user.first_name.capitalize rescue "Anonymous"
=> "Anonymous"
>> @user.first_name
NameError: undefined local variable or method `attribute' for #<User:0x4b8548 ...>
        from (irb):23:in `first_name'
```

```
    from (irb):32
    from /Users/sandal/lib/ruby19_1/bin/irb:12:in `<main>'
```

Hopefully, you're beginning to see the picture. Although good testing and extensive quality assurance can catch these bugs, using this conditional modifier `rescue` hack is like putting blinders on your code. Unfortunately, this can also go for code of the form:

```
def do_something_dangerous
  might_raise_an_error
rescue
  "default value"
end
```

Pretty much any `rescue` that does not capture a specific error may be a source of silent failure in your applications. The only real case in which an unqualified `rescue` might make sense is when it is combined with a unqualified `raise`, which causes the same error to resurface after executing some code:

```
begin
  # do some stuff
rescue => e
  MyLogger.error "Error doing stuff: #{e.message}"
  raise
end
```

In other situations, be sure to either know the risks involved, or avoid this technique entirely. You'll thank yourself later.

Doing method_missing Wrong

One thing you really don't want to do is mess up a `method_missing` hook. Because the purpose of `method_missing` is to handle unknown messages, it is a key feature for helping to find bugs in your code.

In Chapter 3, *Mastering the Dynamic Toolkit*, we covered some examples of how to use `method_missing` properly. Here's an example of how to do it wrong:

```
class Prawn::Document

  # Provides the following shortcuts:
  #
  #    stroke_some_method(*args) #=> some_method(*args); stroke
  #    fill_some_method(*args) #=> some_method(*args); fill
  #    fill_and_stroke_some_method(*args) #=> some_method(*args); fill_and_stroke
  #
  def method_missing(id,*args,&block)
    case(id.to_s)
    when /^fill_and_stroke_(.*)/
      send($1,*args,&block); fill_and_stroke
    when /^stroke_(.*)/
      send($1,*args,&block); stroke
    when /^fill_(.*)/
      send($1,*args,&block); fill
    end
```

```
    end

  end
```

Although this may look very similar to an earlier example in this book, it has a critical flaw. Can you see it? If not, this *irb* session should help:

```
>> pdf.fill_and_stroke_cirlce([100,100], :radius => 25)
=> "0.000 0.000 0.000 rg\n0.000 0.000 0.000 RG\nq\nb\n"
>> pdf.stroke_the_pretty_kitty([100,100], :radius => 25)
=> "0.000 0.000 0.000 rg\n0.000 0.000 0.000 RG\nq\nb\nS\n"
>> pdf.donuts
=> nil
```

By coding a `method_missing` hook without delegating to the original `Object` definition, we have effectively muted our object's ability to complain about messages we really didn't want it to handle. To add insult to injury, failure cases such as `fill_and_stroke_cirlce` and `stroke_the_pretty_kitty` are doubly confusing, as they return a non-nil value, even though they do not produce meaningful results.

Luckily, the remedy to this is simple. We just add a call to **super** in the catchall case:

```
def method_missing(id,*args,&block)
  case(id.to_s)
  when /^fill_and_stroke_(.*)/
    send($1,*args,&block); fill_and_stroke
  when /^stroke_(.*)/
    send($1,*args,&block); stroke
  when /^fill_(.*)/
    send($1,*args,&block); fill
  else
    super
  end
end
```

Now, if we rerun our earlier examples, you will see much more predictable behavior, in line with what we'd expect if we had no hook set up in the first place:

```
>> pdf.fill_and_stroke_cirlce([100,100], :radius => 25)
NoMethodError: undefined method `cirlce' for #<Prawn::Document:0x4e59f8>
        from prawn/lib/prawn/graphics/color.rb:68:in `method_missing'
        from prawn/lib/prawn/graphics/color.rb:62:in `method_missing'
        from (irb):4
        from /Users/sandal/lib/ruby19_1/bin/irb:12:in `<main>'

>> pdf.stroke_the_pretty_kitty([100,100], :radius => 25)
NoMethodError: undefined method `the_pretty_kitty' for #<Prawn::Document:0x4e59f8>
        from prawn/lib/prawn/graphics/color.rb:68:in `method_missing'
        from prawn/lib/prawn/graphics/color.rb:64:in `method_missing'
        from (irb):5
        from /Users/sandal/lib/ruby19_1/bin/irb:12:in `<main>'

>> pdf.donuts
NoMethodError: undefined method `donuts' for #<Prawn::Document:0x4e59f8>
        from prawn/lib/prawn/graphics/color.rb:68:in `method_missing'
```

```
from (irb):6
from /Users/sandal/lib/ruby19_1/bin/irb:12:in `<main>'
```

An important thing to remember is that in addition to ensuring that you call **super** from within your `method_missing()` calls, you are also responsible for maintaining the method's signature. It's possible to write a hook that captures only a missing method's name while ignoring its arguments and associated block:

```
def method_missing(id)
  # ...
end
```

However, if you set things up this way, even when you call **super**, you'll be breaking things farther up the chain, as `Object#method_missing` expects the whole signature of the function call to remain intact. So it's not only delegating to the original that is important, but delegating without information loss.

If you're sure to act responsibly with your `method_missing` calls, it won't be that dangerous in most cases. However, if you get sloppy here, it is virtually guaranteed to come back to haunt you. If you get into this habit right away, it'll be sure to save you some headaches down the line.

Conclusions

This appendix doesn't come close to covering all the trouble that you can get yourself into with Ruby. It does, however, cover some of the most common sources of trouble and confusion and shows some much less painful alternatives.

When it comes to design, much can be gained by simply reducing complexity. If the path you're on seems too difficult, odds are that it can be made a lot easier if you just think about it in a different way. As for "clever" implementation tricks and shortcuts, they can be more trouble than they're worth if they come at the expense of clarity or maintainability of your code.

Put simply, the worst practices in Ruby are ones that make you work much harder than you have to. If you start to introduce code that seems really cool at first, but later is shown to introduce complicated faults at the corner cases, it is generally wise to just rip it out and start fresh with something a little less exciting that's more reliable.

If you maintain the balancing act between creative approaches to your problems and ones that work without introducing excess complexity, you'll have a very happy time writing Ruby code. Because Ruby gives you the power to do both good and evil, it's ultimately up to you how you want to maintain your projects. However, code that is maintainable and predictable is much more of a joy to work with than fragile and sloppy hacks that have been simply duct-taped together.

Now that we have reached the very end of this book, I trust that you have the skills necessary to go out and find Ruby Best (and Worst) Practices on your own. The real challenge is knowing the difference between the two, and that ability comes only with practical experience gained by working on and investigating real problems. This book has included enough real-world examples to give you a head start in that area, but the heavy lifting needs to be done by you.

I hope you have enjoyed this wild ride through Ruby with me, and I really hope that something or the other in this book has challenged or inspired you. Please go out now and write some good open source Ruby code, and maybe you'll make a guest appearance in the second edition!

Index

Symbols

&block syntax, 46
    using with instance_eval( ), 47
* (array splat operator), 33
*args idiom, 40
<=> (spaceship) operator, 53

A

ActiveRecord, object-relational mapping
    (ORM), 52
activesupport gem
    test( ) method, 4
Adobe Font Metrics file, parser for, 99–103
aliasing
    aliases, collisions in, 80
    alias_method( ), 79
    modification via, 79–81
anchors in regular expressions, 105
anonymous classes
    defined, 85
    generation by calls to Class.new( ), 84
    looking up by extension name, 88
APIs, designing, 31–55
    avoiding surprises, 48–55
        method? and method!, 50–53
        summary of practices, 54
        using attr_reader, attr_writer, and
            attr_accessor, 48–50
        using custom operators, 53
    designing for convenience, Ruport Table( )
        method, 31–34
    flexible argument processing, 35–40
    guidelines for design of methods, 40
    using code blocks, 40–48

append operator, 53
argument processing, flexible, 35–40
    ordinal arguments with optional
        parameters, 36
    pseudo-keyword arguments, 37
    standard ordinal arguments, 36
    treating arguments as an array, 38–40
arguments
    block, 245
    multisplat, 244
array splat operator (*), 33
Array#each method, 42
arrays
    adding elements to end of, 129
    parsing, 261
    treating arguments as, 38–40
    using for caching in memoization, 139
ASCII strings, transcoding and, 185
assertions, custom, building for testing, 29
assert_block( ) function, using to build custom
    assertions, 29
assert_equal( ) method, 262
assert_nothing_raised( ) method, 12
assert_raises( ) method, 12
attribute writers in instance_eval-based
    interfaces, 69
attr_reader, attr_writer, and attr_accessor, 48–
    50
authentication
    HTTP, 255
    LDAP authentication module, 135
automated behavior verification, 6

We'd like to hear your suggestions for improving our indexes. Send email to *index@oreilly.com*.

Hash.new method, 140
hashes
    option hashes, forwarding, 34
    pseudo-keyword arguments, 37
helper functions for testing, 27
hexdigest( ) method, 267
    calling on Digest::MD5, 264
    calling on Digest::SHA1, 264
    calling on Digest::SHA256, 264
hooks, registering, 88–95
    detecting newly added functionality, 89–91
    tracking inheritance, 91–93
    tracking mixins, 93–95
HTML templating with ERB, 281
HTTP, working with, using open-uri, 254

I

images, embedding in PDF documents, 264
include( ) method, 93
infinite lists, 145–149
    building up recursively using lazy_stream,
        149
    creating custom LazyStream::Node objects,
        147
    object representing even sequence of
        numbers, 145
    summary of important concepts, 149
    using filters and transforms with
        lazy_stream, 148
    using LazyStream::Node objects to create
        step iterator, 147
    using lazy_stream.rb to iterate over range of
        numbers, 146
INFO logging level, 173
inheritance
    restrictive, 288–290
    tracking, 91–93
inline styling, 5
input and output
    network I/O via sockets, 43–45
    temporary files, 114
    testing complex output, 22–26
    using StringIO as mock for IO objects, 19
inspect output, improving, 162
InspectTemplate module, 163
install instructions, 212
instance_eval( ) method, 58
    interfaces based on, attribute writers and,
        69

making optional, 63–65
    using with &block syntax, 47
instance_methods( ), 58
instance_variable_get( ) function, 162
integer division, 267
iterative design, 9
iterators
    blocks as, 40
    building custom, 42

J

JSON (JavaScript Object Notation), 275
    converting JSON to Ruby, 276
    converting parsed JSON into custom higher-
        level Ruby object, 278
    parsing, 260
    primitive constructs provided by, 275
    producing, using your custom objects, 277
JSON array, starting and end points, 262
json standard library, 275–279
json_class attribute, 278
json_create method, 278

K

kcode system, 192
Kernel module, 90
Kernel#gem method, 232
Kernel#open, patching to accept URIs, 254
Kernel#p method, 160
    improving output, 162
Kernel#require method, 79
Kernel#y method, 164
keyword arguments, Ruby and, 37
Ku flag, 192

L

L10n (localization), 177, 195–204
    dealing with names of people, 203
    doing as late as possible to avoid effects on
        business logic, 200
    guidelines for, 203
    localized version of Rock, Paper, Scissors
        game, 199
    passing all strings shown to viewer through
        translation filter, 200
    view level localization of Rock, Paper,
        Scissors game, 201

module_function, 134
mooch script, 109
multibyte character encodings, 193
multilingualization (see m17n)
multisplat arguments, 244
mutable state, minimizing, and reducing side
        effects, 129–133
    code free of side effects, 129
    guidelines for, 132
    recursive solution, 130
    rewriting naive_map to be stateless, 129
    rewriting recursive solution iteratively, 131
    using Enumerable#inject instead of
        recursion, 131

N

names of people, localizing, 203
namespaces
    collection of functions under single
        namespace, 133
    using to segment Rake tasks, 236
Net::FTP module, 255
new( ) method, object modification and, 82
:nodoc: directive, 223
nokogiri gem, 25
NoMethodError, 68
nongreedy quantifiers, 108
normalize_encoding methods, 187

O

Object class, inclusion of modules at runtime,
    90
Object#inspect method, 160
Object#to_proc, 150
object-relational mapping (ORM),
    ActiveRecord, 52
Object.method_added( ) function, 90
objects, 57
    implementing per-object behavior, 70–74
        key concepts, 74
    modifying, 81
    per-object customization not affecting class
        definition, 71
Oniguruma, 246
open-uri standard library, 254–256
    using with json, 276
OpenURI::HTTPError, 254
OpenURI::Meta module, 255

operators, custom, 53
options hashes
    forwarding, 34
    mandatory arguments and, 38
ordinal arguments
    with optional parameters, 36
    standard, 36

P

parameterized subclassing, 84
parsers, 108
    parser for Adobe Font Metrics file, 99–103
    RSS and XML, 24
parse_array method, 261
parse_value method, 261
    parsing strings, numbers, and booleans,
        262
password storage, secure, 265
passwords, setting, 266
Pathname module, 109
Patterson, Aaron, 25
PDF documents, embedding images in, 264
PDF::Writer, managing memory consumption
    issue, 82
performance
    recursion and, 131
    text processing and file management, 120
    using Memoizable module versus manual
        caching, 143
pp (prettyprint) standard library, 162, 252–
    254
prawn gem, dependencies, 231–233
Prawn PDF generation library, 4
    inline styling support, 5
prawn/compatibility.rb, 242
Prawn::Document#inspect output, 160
Prawn::Document#render_file method, 185
Prawn::Document, documentation, 220
Prawn::Font#normalize_encoding method,
    187
Prawn::Font::TTF#normalize_encoding
    method, 187
pre/postprocessing, using blocks to abstract,
    43–45
pretty-printer for Ruby objects (pp), 252–254
PrettyPrint class, 254
pretty_print method, 253
pretty_print_inspect method, 254
Prime class, 267

Proc objects, 150
    lazy evaluation, 122
    new syntax in Ruby 1.9, 245
Proc#arity method, 65
procedures, higher-order, 150–151
project maintenance, 205–238
    API documentation via RDoc, 220–227
        basic documentation guidelines, 220–222
        output control with RDoc directives, 222–227
    conventions to know about, 211–219
        examples, 217–219
        executables, 216
        library layout, 213–216
        README file contents, 211–213
        summary of key points, 219
        tests, 216
    exploring well-organized project, 206–210
    Rake, 234–237
    RubyGems package manager, 228–234
        dependencies, 231–233
        summary of key points, 233
        writing gem specification, 228–231
project management utilities in Ruby, 205
Promise objects, 124
promise( ) method, 123
pseudo-keyword arguments, 37
pseudo-keyword hash syntax, 244
PStore objects, constructing and using, 274
pstore standard library, 273–275
    API documentation, 221

Q

quantifiers in regular expressions, 106

R

Rake, 205, 234–237
    custom tasks, 235
    rake build command, 235
    rake rdoc task, 234
    Rakefiles, 236
    rubyforge command-line utility, 235
    summary of key points, 237
    uploading website documentation via scp, 236
rake install task, Haml project, 209
rake task listing, Haml project, 206

rake test command, 208
    using to automate running of test suite, 13
Rake::GemPackageTask, 209
Rational objects, 267
RDoc, 205
    API documentation via, 220–227
        basic documentation guidelines, 220–222
        controlling output with directives, 222–227
    generated from source, 207
    generation of, details in gemspec, 230
    website, 222
README file
    contents of, 211–213
    Haml project, 206
read_to_char, 194
recursion
    drawbacks in Ruby, 130
    performance problems with, 131
    reducing with memoization, 139
    rewriting recursive solutions iteratively, 131
    using Enumerable#inject instead of, 131
refactoring, 2
    using automated behavior verification, 6
reflection, 58–61
    determining names of instance methods, 61
reflection, using to inspect code, 160–162
Regexp.escape( ) method, 180
regular expressions, 104–108
    anchors in, 105
    caution with quantifiers, 106
    defining to match text in encoding different from source, 179
    escaping special characters, 180
    guidelines for, 108
    lexical parsing with (strscan), 259–263
    Oniguruma engine, 246
    special characters in pattern syntax, 104
    specifying character encoding for, 183
    writing clean, tight patterns, 105
reports, writing from CSV files, 271
require statements for testing, 27
requires, 213–216
    deeply nested classes in projects, 214
rescuing a failure and reraising an error, 167

resources (external), removing dependencies on, 15

revision control system, git, 264

RSpec code, 62

RSS feed, testing, 22–26

Ruby Quiz website, 260

Ruby worst practices, 283–298
    downside of cleverness, 290
        evils of eval( ), 290–292
        method_missing, 295–297
        rescuing exceptions, 292–295
    unintelligent design, 283
        class variables, 284–286
        hardcoding class names, 286–288
        inheritance becoming restrictive, 288–290

RubyGems, 79, 205
    package manager, 228–234
        dependencies, 231–233
        summary of key points, 233
        writing Gem::Specification, 228–231

runtime dependencies, 233

Ruport
    abstract formatting system (Fatty), Ruport 2.0, 85
    managing memory consumption issue in PDF::Writer, 82
    Table( ) feature, 31–34

Ruport::Data::Table.load( ), 33

Ruport::Data::Table.new( ), 33

S

safe_level, 281

salt, adding to password hash, 266

Sass, 216

saves, atomic, 118

Scheduler class, implementing, 257

scrutinizing code, 160–168
    finding defects in very large dataset, 166
    guidelines for, 168
    improving inspect output, 162
    using reflection, 160–162

search results, from Google web search, 276

:section: directive, rdoc, 226

secure password storage, 265

send( ) method, using with method_missing( ), 67

serialization
    human-readable (json), 275–279

yaml standard library, 164–166

SHA256 hashes, 264

shortcuts in regular expressions, 105

side effects
    avoiding in testing, 11
    reducing in Ruby code, 129–133

Sinatra application for Rock, Paper, Scissors game, 197

singleton class, 72

sjis_re function, 179, 180

sockets, network I/O via, 43–45

something( ) and something=( ) methods, 50

SortedList, adding reporting method to, 43

source encodings, setting, 183

spaceship operator (<=>), 53

spec.test_files, 230

StandardError class, 174

StandardError#report method, 174

state
    minimizing mutable state and reducing side effects, 129–133
    tracking in line-by-line text processing, 99–103

string interpolation versus ERB, 279

String iterators, 247

string literals, specifying character encoding for, 183

String#ascii_only? method, 186

String#encode method, 194

String#encode! method, 187

String#ord method, 195

String#unpack method, 195

String#valid_encoding? method, 195

StringIO class, 19

StringIO objects, returned by open-uri, 255

strings
    character-awareness, 247
    lexical parsing with regular expressions (strscan), 259–263

StringScanner class, 260

StringScanner#matched method, 263

strscan standard library, 259–263

stubbing system, building for testing, 71–74

stubs
    third party tools for, 17
    uses of, 26
    using in testing, 17

subclasses, detecting and tracking inheritance, 92

W

Wanstrath, Chris, 196
Weirich, Jim, 17, 22, 57
worst practices (see Ruby worst practices)

X

XML
    parsing in Ruby, 24
    RSS feeds, 22
XML Builder, 22, 58

Y

yaml standard library, 164–166
    file with Chinese translation for RPS game,
        198
    file with French translation for RPS game,
        198

About the Author

Gregory Brown is a New Haven, Connecticut-based Rubyist who spends most of his time on free software projects in Ruby. His main projects are Prawn and Ruport. He also is in possession of a small bamboo plant that seems to be invincible, and he is quite proud of this accomplishment.

Colophon

The animal on the cover of *Ruby Best Practices* is a green crab (*Carcinus maenas*). Also known as a European shore crab, it is native to the coasts of the North and Baltic Seas. Although relatively small—adults measure three inches across—an adult green crab can consume up to 40 clams each day and can eat other crabs as large as itself. A voracious predator, the green crab also preys on oysters, mussels, and snails, competing for food with many fish and bird species.

Despite its name, the green crab's shell color can vary from dark green to orange or red, sometimes with yellow patches on its underside. The abdomen of the male is triangular in shape, whereas the female's is broader and rounder. Males and females also react differently upon being picked up: males typically stretch out their legs, whereas females fold them in, a behavior known as the egg-protection reflex.

A natural colonizer, the green crab is potentially destructive to any ecosystem it invades. It has already invaded many coastal communities outside of its native range, including Australia, South Africa, and North America, where it is blamed for the collapse of the softshell clam industry in Maine. It is ranked number 18 on the list of the 100 world's worst invasive types of species. Numerous efforts around the world have been made to control invading populations, to varying degrees of success. One of the more effective experiments has been on Martha's Vineyard, Massachusetts, where the town of Edgartown pays bounty hunters 40 cents per pound of green crab; more than 10 tons have been caught and destroyed as a result.

The cover image is from the Dover Pictorial Archive. The cover font is Adobe ITC Garamond. The text font is Linotype Birka; the heading font is Adobe Myriad Condensed; and the code font is LucasFont's TheSansMonoCondensed.

Related Titles from O'Reilly

O'REILLY®

Our books are available at most retail and online bookstores.

To order direct: 1-800-998-9938 • *order@oreilly.com* • *www.oreilly.com*

Online editions of most O'Reilly titles are available by subscription at *safari.oreilly.com*